Self-Regulation Theory

SELF-REGULATION THEORY

How Optimal Adjustment Maximizes Gain

Dennis E. Mithaug

Westport, Connecticut
London

Library of Congress Cataloging-in-Publication Data

Mithaug, Dennis E.
   Self-regulation theory : how optimal adjustment maximizes gain /
Dennis E. Mithaug.
     p. cm.
   Includes bibliographical references and index.
   ISBN 0–275–94422–0 (alk. paper)
   1. Problem solving. I. Title.
BF449.M58 1993
155.2′4—dc20   92–17812

British Library Cataloguing in Publication Data is available.

Library of Congress Catalog Card Number: 92–17812
ISBN: 0–275–94422–0

First published in 1993

Praeger Publishers, 88 Post Road West, Westport, Connecticut, 06881
An imprint of Greenwood Publishing Group, Inc.

Printed in the United States of America

The paper used in this book complies with the
Permanent Paper Standard issued by the National
Information Standards Organization (Z39.48–1984).

10 9 8 7 6 5 4 3 2 1

Copyright Acknowledgments

The author and publisher gratefully acknowledge permission to quote from the following:

In chapters 1, 2, 3, and 4, John Dewey, *How We Think*. Boston, MA: D.C. Heath & Company, [1910], 1993. Reprinted by permission.

In chapter 7, Eugene B. Griessman, *The Achievement Factors: Candid Interviews with Some of the Most Successful People of Our Time*. New York: Dodd, Mead, 1987. Copyright © 1990 by Eugene Griessman. Reprinted by permission.

In Memory of Stanley H. Fairweather

Contents

Figures and Tables

Figures

Tables

Introduction

One explanation for how we have managed to populate our planet so extensively and dominate its environmental niches so completely is that we have evolved. Millions of years of natural selection favoring some species over others and some structures and functions over others have allowed our species to survive and, in some cases, to thrive. We have built cultural cushions to protect us from the environmental forces that decimated less flexible competitors.

Unfortunately, the downside of our cultural shield is that it too is a selective force—one step removed from the environment it defends us against. The cultures we construct for adaptive advantage turn upon us to constrain our thinking and acting when we stray from their historic underpinnings. Try as we may to throw off our cultural yokes and move to new and exciting opportunities, we plod on as before. Contrary to popular writing, the miracle of our survival is not that we always adjust, but that we ever do.

Probably the best context for understanding when and how we adjust is in the application of propositions from Darwin's theory of evolution that have some cogency when used to explain cultural change over generational time. Human beliefs and practices that pass from generation to generation contain sufficient reality-based wisdom to allow progeny to survive somewhat better than their ancestors. Once "proved effective," new practices are shared within the group and then are added to the cultural repertoire and transmitted to offspring. The process continues inexorably, and its cultural dos and don'ts grow exponentially. In the struggle for survival and competitive edge, advantage goes to the species with the best "know-how" in dealing with environmental circumstance. In the past few million years, *Homo sapiens* has transmitted enough useful information to its offspring to permit them to compete globally for domination and control over vast and varied terrains.

But not all members of our species are equally successful. Owing to the content of the beliefs and practices inherited from their ancestors, some groups are more effective at separating what works from what doesn't and then transforming those results into tools and products to aid adjustment. The explanation for how and under what conditions groups and individuals make these discriminations in the race for selective advantage is better developed for the physical and biological sciences than for the social sciences. In the former, theories of evolution explain how interactions between environmental change and species variation produce adaptive matches between organismic needs and environmental resources. But in the latter, there is little consensus among scholars about how best to explain human adaptations.

The theory of evolution describes end-state snapshots of a process that takes millions of years. All species were selected for brief moments of evolutionary time. The physical and biological sciences have advanced our understanding of how genotypic and phenotypic variation affects species survivability across environments and time. But what about comparable mechanisms affecting variation and selection of individual behavior over a lifetime? What conditions—consistent with those for species variation and natural selection—account for the direction and content of individual adjustment?

For these answers we look to the social sciences—psychology, social psychology, anthropology, and sociology—for a theory of adaptation that explains how individuals contribute to their own cognitive and behavioral variations, selections, and adjustments. In psychology, for example, three explanations describe adaptive mechanisms. *Cognitive models* describe how discrepancies between expected and actual events provoke problem solving to improve rational choosing; *behavioral models* explain how consequences of solution behaviors affect subsequent solution responding over time; and *cognitive-behavioral models* postulate that expectations for behavioral consequences determine choices between different solution responses. Although none of these models is sufficiently robust to explain the varied faces of adaptive responding across individuals, each contributes substantially to one or more of its significant features. Chapter 1, "The Problem of Adaptation," describes these contributions and explains how self-regulation theory builds upon them to expand explanatory power. The theory explains how optimal adjustment maximizes gain.

In the last 5,000 years or so, we have distanced ourselves from other species largely because of our capacity to regulate what problems we solve and how we solve them. As a consequence we have become undisputed masters of optimizing and maximizing. We have populated inclement areas of the world by finding ways of extracting essential resources that were once inaccessible. We have developed more effective tools and invented more efficient ways of using them. And now we are finding ways to maximize opportunities in space, where other earthly creatures have yet to venture and survive.

Chapter 2, "The Nature of Problem Solving," chronicles this rise to power of the human enterprise. During the first two million years of *Homo sapiens* history, when adjustment was suboptimal and gain unpredictable, discovery of better ways to adjust was infrequent. Progress depended upon *accidental problem solving*. Not until the brief period in Greek history and the later European Renaissance did *regulated problem solving* become a contending force in the human arsenal. Since then the scientific method—the logical extension of regulated problem solving—has emerged as the most effective weapon for optimizing opportunities and maximizing gain.

In the twentieth century the method became a centerpiece for reflective thinking in John Dewey's *How We Think*[1] and for successful striving in Napoleon Hill's *Law of Success*.[2] In the last forty years, research on its cognitive and behavioral foundations has yielded models and theories to explain problem defining and solution finding for individuals, groups, and institutions. Chapter 2 describes how these efforts have enhanced our understanding of self-regulation and its effects on optimal adjustment and maximum gain.

Self-regulated problem solving is problem solving to meet a goal. It includes the following phases: (1) identification of differences between a goal state and an actual state; (2) identification of events that will reduce those differences; (3) selection of actions that will produce those events; and (4) repetition of steps 1–3 until goal attainment or goal abandonment takes place. Chapter 3, "The Theory of Self-Regulation," describes the conditions that promote this process in humans. It postulates three behaviors that reflect different phases of self-regulation: expecting, choosing, and responding. The theory states that optimal adjustment maximizes gain. Its four propositions describe how the following relationship is valid: *the closer to optimal the past gains, expectations, choices, and responses, then the closer to maximum the gain.*

The *expectation proposition* states that optimal expectations depend upon past experience and the magnitude of the discrepancy between the goal state and the actual state. The closer to optimal the past gain toward goal attainment and the smaller the discrepancy between the goal state and the actual state, then the more likely the regulator will expect the maximum gain possible toward reaching the goal.

The *choice proposition* specifies conditions that affect the selection of options to produce expected gain. When regulators have made successful choices in the past and when the differences between options are salient, then they are likely to find the best option available and choose it to produce the gain they expect. In other words, they are likely to choose optimally.

The *response proposition* states that optimal past gain toward goal attainment and optimal expectations and choices lead to optimal responding. Under these conditions, regulators are likely to distribute their responses effectively and efficiently between seeking information and completing goal-directed tasks. Optimal performance occurs when regulators spend minimum time and effort seeking information about the discrepancy, options, and results and maximum time and effort completing tasks that are necessary for goal attainment.

The *gain proposition* describes the optimality effects of past gains, expectations, choices, and performances. When all four are optimal, gain toward goal attainment is maximum. The proposition describes these combined effects. Regulators maximize gain toward goal attainment when (1) past gains exactly match expectations, (2) present expectations for gain are the maximum possible, given the options available, (3) choices produce the greatest gain at the lowest cost, and (4) responses distribute efficiently between producing gain and seeking feedback.

These propositions are simple and logical. Yet they are consistent with the insightful contributions of the scholars and researchers of the past century. Their combinational effects yield uncommon empirical and explanatory power. An illustration of this is their capacity to account for self-regulated thinking and doing within a structure that postulates only three classes of behavior: choosing (expectations and options), task responding, and feedback seeking. Chapter 4, "Self-Regulated Thinking," describes how discrepancies between goal states and present states increase feedback seeking to define problems and find solutions. Chapter 5, "Self-Regulated Doing," describes the connections between self-regulated thinking and self-managed doing.

Chapter 6, "Maximum Gain," describes how learning and performance result from self-regulated thinking and doing. When self-regulated problem solvers find solutions that are effective, they repeat them. At the same time, they develop improved methods for identifying when solutions are appropriate and when they are not. As time and energy required to make these discriminations decrease, solution finding becomes more effective and solution using more efficient. This maximizes gain.

Chapters 7 and 8 demonstrate the theory's utility by explaining the extremes of self-regulation: dependence and innovation. Dependence is the lack of self-regulation; independence or self-determination is its opposite. Chapter 7, "Self-Determined Gain," shows how self-regulation theory accounts for problems of dependency in American youth. According to the theory, competence and persistence increase as a function of one's ability to discriminate between goals, options, and results. These discrimination skills are necessary for learning how to produce the persistent regulatory behavior that generates consistent gains. As these capacities increase, so do expectations for goal attainment, along with the probability of more successful self-regulated thinking and doing in the future.

Chapter 8, "Innovative Gain," shows how the same propositions that explain dependence and self-determination can also account for innovation. According to the theory, contributions in science, music, literature, and the arts are no more divinely inspired than less celebrated gains toward goal attainment. Although the basic mechanism of self-regulated thinking and doing is similar for all self-regulatory behavior, it is the systematic, passionate, and persistent application of the mechanism to solve ill-defined problems that produces profoundly wondrous and seemingly inexplicable innovative gains.

Notes

1. John Dewey, *How We Think* (Boston, MA: D. C. Heath & Company, [1910], 1933).
2. Napoleon Hill, *The Law of Success* (Evanston, IL: Success Unlimited, [1920], 1979).

Self-Regulation
Theory

Chapter 1

The Problem of Adaptation

In every culture, some individuals adapt better than others. A few even manage to optimize under conditions of continuous, unremitting change. These variations in adaptive success are also evident across groups, nations, and even civilizations. Some thrive, many maintain, and a few decline. History is replete with themes of rise and fall, suggesting that what goes up inevitably comes down. The reigning principle is that change affects adaptive responses of individuals, institutions, and cultures.

Significant progress in understanding this phenomenon began in the nineteenth century with the recognition that all life forms were products of unpredictable environmental forces. Before that, stasis—not change—was the axiomatic premise from which scholars expounded. The natural order was harmony, interrupted occasionally by divine intervention—for example, when God flooded the living world and repopulated it with help from Noah and the Ark. Even evidence about fossil discoveries came to fit the notion that divine power occasionally set aside laws of nature to re-tune existence for the sake of cosmic harmony. In 1690, John Ray's claim that newly discovered fossils were of prehistoric animals found expression in *The Wisdom of God Manifested in the Works of Creation*. In 1836, several decades before Darwin's *Origins of Species*, William Buckland explained fossil discoveries similarly:

> In the course of our enquiry, we have found abundant proofs, both of the Beginning and the End of several successive systems of animal and vegetable life; each compelling us to refer its origin to the direct agency of Creative Interference; "We conceive it undeniable that we see, in the transition from an Earth peopled by one set of animals to the same Earth swarming with entirely new forms of organic life, *a distinct manifestation of creative power transcending the operation of known laws of nature*." [italics added][1]

Gradually, alternative explanations for these anomalies surfaced. A few suggested that neither earth nor humans were epicenters of universal movement; change, not stasis, was the natural order;[2] the scientific method could explain it all. A steady erosion in the belief in universal stability followed, along with a growing sense that all existence was continuous—a view with roots in Plato and Aristotle and revived by Gottfried Wilhelm Leibniz in the "Great Chain of Being." Jean-Baptiste Robinet's volumes of *De la Nature* (On nature), published in 1761, claimed that organic species formed a linear scale of progress without gaps; scientists like Comte de Buffon and Charles Bonnet used the continuous chain idea to classify mineral and fossil discoveries. In 1809, Jean-Baptiste Lamarck's *Philosophie Zoologique* theorized that animals evolved from simpler life forms, although the mechanism for accomplishing this transformation was unclear.

By the mid–1800s evolutionary theory had attracted a significant following, and several theorists were coming to the same conclusions. Charles Darwin began his five-year voyage as a naturalist on the *HMS Beagle* in 1831, and in 1835 he discovered finches in the Galapagos Islands that were similar in ancestry to those found on the South American mainland. He reported his findings in 1839 and three years later prepared an abstract thirty-five pages long on his theory of evolution of the species. By 1858 Darwin was communicating with Alfred Russel Wallace and Asa Gray about evolution by natural selection. On November 24, 1859, Darwin published *On the Origin of Species by Means of Natural Selection or the Preservation of Favoured Races in the Struggle for Life;* and for 130-plus years that followed, evolutionary theory dominated scientific explanation throughout the natural and social sciences. In their book *The Dialectical Biologist,* Richard Levins and Richard Lewontin concluded that evolution was "a world view that encompasses the hierarchically related concepts of change, order, direction, progress, and perfectability, although not all theories of evolutionary processes include every successive step in the hierarchy of concepts."[3]

The Theory of Evolution

The theory provides a longitudinal view of evolving and devolving matches between behavior and environments on the one hand and between resources and needs on the other. Its principles account for phenotype-environment interchanges that lead to adaptive and maladaptive fits over the millennia. The theory postulates that variation and selection explain adaptive successes and failures for a multitude of species. Three propositions describe these essentials. (1) The variation proposition explains conditions under which genetic change within a species produces variation in genotypes and phenotypes. (2) The heredity proposition states that each new variant resembles its parents more than other members of its species and, as a consequence, perpetuates its own characteristics. (3) The selection proposition describes how changing environmental circumstances interact with species variation to select some variants (and their new characteristics) over others.

Environmental change initiates the process through resource availability. Species favored by their locations reproduce in greater numbers than those in less favorable habitats. Survival involves winning the competition for resources, which involves extracting essential nutrients from environments efficiently and then reproducing offspring prolifically. The following principles describe the evolutionary effects of these three mechanisms:

1. *The principle of variation*: Individuals within a species vary in physiology, morphology, and behavior.
2. *The principle of heredity*: Offspring resemble their parents on the average more than they resemble unrelated individuals.
3. *The principle of natural selection*: Different variants leave different numbers of offspring.[4]

Early proponents found these basic tenets attractive. No longer did they need to postulate unseen, mystical powers to explain existence and perseverance. Evolutionary mechanisms accounted for diverse and distant life forms cleanly, neatly. Herbert Spencer, who coined the phrase ''survival of the fittest,'' popularized Social Darwinism in the 1870s and 1880s and suggested that evolution was upwardly mobile, always improving the life forms it processed. Progress and evolution became linked in a Panglossian view of biological and social determinism. Other evolutionary theorists postulated similar notions of direction and progress—some specifying increased organ perfectability, species complexity, and organizational efficiency, even though evidence contradicted such generalizations.[5]

A consequence of these speculative applications of evolutionary theory was an over-simplification of the main principles, variation and selection. Variation occurred only within the genes and behaviors of organisms, and selection was only the instrument of unkind environments. While environments shaped, controlled, and selected, organisms reacted, thrived, or died. Determinism and reactionism summarized survival. This image of an environment inexorably moving forward with its inhabitants chasing behind emanated from Darwin's observations of the selective breeding practices described in two chapters of *Origin of Species:* ''Variation under Domestication'' and ''Variation under Nature.'' The first chapter described the effects of human selection; the second drew the parallel in nature as a consequence of scarce resources and over-populating species (an idea stimulated by Malthus's 1838 *Essay on the Principle of Population*). But an important difference distinguished the two. Natural selection was really a condition rather than an event purposefully engineered by humans. Species who found needed resources effectively and efficiently lived to reproduce, thus changing the population landscape with subsequent generations of offspring. Natural selection was a consequence of species behaviors interacting with their environments.

The anthropomorphism of natural selection—equating it with human selection—artificially separated organism from environment, pitting one against the other. The result was confusion over a species' contribution to its own survival. Organisms are both actors and reactors. Their searches for environmental support alter the nature of the environment and the nature of the support. They produce effects and are affected by effects. The relationship is bilateral, as Levins and Lewontin point out:

> The reciprocal interaction of organism and environment takes place through several pathways which link the individual and evolutionary time scales:
>
> 1. Organisms actively select those environments in which they can survive and reproduce.
> 2. For the individual this active selection determines what environmental impacts the organisms will respond to. On the evolutionary scale it determines which environments the organism adapts to, what kind of selection it experiences.
> 3. The environment acts differently on different genotypes. In some environments different genotypes may respond almost identically, while in others they may produce widely different phenotypes. . . . The environment as developmental stimulus helps turn genetic variability into available phenotypic variability, which environment as Darwinian filter selects.
> 4. The way in which the organism modifies the environment depends on its genotype. Some environmental impacts enhance survival more than others. Therefore, the environment selects the pattern of its own modification.[6]

Contemporary evolutionary theory postulates species adaptation through interactions with different environments. The idea that species adapt to fixed environmental slots implies some invariant standard of adaptation for measuring up, a predetermined niche awaiting that "correct" adjustment. This is circular. Environments do not define niches in advance of species evolution. Niches and organisms are products of mutual exchanges that specify the existence of both.

Questions of variation, correspondence, and selection are more reflective of this process. In the last twenty years, research on optimal behavior patterns illustrates this exchange for maximum gain indicative of self—regulation rather than environmental regulation. Niles Eldredge illustrates in *Macro-Evolutionary Dynamics: Species, Niches, and Adaptive Peaks:*

> Assuming that bird couples are trying to maximize their reproductive success [maximum gain] (and this is the central tenet of ultra-Darwinian theory), there would seem to be an optimum number of eggs to be laid per clutch. With too many eggs, viability falls off as the limits of nest size, sibling competition, and the ability of the parents to feed and otherwise care for their fledglings are exceeded. Too few eggs just as obviously reduces genetic representation of the parents in the

succeeding generation. Ergo, there is an ideal number of eggs—neither too few nor too many—for the average clutch for members of each species.[7]

Optimal adjustments occur when fewer investments return less but greater investments return no more. Bird couples don't waste time and energy laying more eggs than will produce viable fledglings. On the other hand, they don't lay fewer eggs than will cover their genetic bets. They lay just enough. In economic terms, their marginal costs equal their marginal gains.

Optimal adjustment requires regulation by organisms to maximize gains toward better fits with the environment. Environments may set parameters for all-or-none-survival, but within those boundaries organisms select, respond, and adjust. They define the course and substance of their own survival. They adapt by finding those variations in their own behaviors that correspond with what the environment has to offer. At the organismic level, variation means variations in both behaviors and environments, and selection means correspondence between organismic needs and environmental resources.

These distinctions resolve difficulties implied by the notion that an omnipotent environment actively selects some species over others, or its converse—that organisms actively select favorable rather than unfavorable environments. Neither account is completely accurate. Just as dramatic environmental change has selective consequences for organismic survival, so do needs of organisms have selective consequences over the types of environments to be experienced. Favorability varies within and across environments. Summer is better than winter for the conservation of energy, and nights are better than days for hiding from predators.

From the species viewpoint, adaptation involves searching, selecting, and acting on environments to fulfill needs. Environments seem passive and reactive, but adaptation appears active and directive. To satisfy food and water needs, an organism pursues one search; to meet sex and reproduction needs, it pursues another. Its behaviors are a function of the match between need and opportunity: when needs equal opportunity, behaviors satisfy need.

The theory of evolution provides few insights into these single episodes of adaptive responding. Instead, it describes end-state snapshots of processes that take millions of years to unfold. Another set of propositions is necessary to explain the mechanisms that affect variation and selection of individual behavior. What conditions—consistent with those for species variation and selection—account for the direction and content of an individual's adjustment? What behavioral and environmental mechanisms describe the variation, correspondence, and selections experienced in daily adjustment?

In psychology three models offer explanations for this adaptive mechanism: the cognitive model, the behavioral model, and the cognitive-behavioral model (which is a hybrid of the first two). In combination, the models explain how individuals optimize adjustments and maximize gains toward the satisfaction of needs. They describe self-regulated thinking, self-regulated doing, and the functional mechanisms linking them.

The Cognitive Model

William James, a contemporary of Charles Darwin, was the first to apply evolutionary propositions to psychology.[8] According to James, thinking was the means-ends mechanism that connected environment problems—or stimuli—with adaptive responses. Says John Dewey: "James sees knowledge as a phase of mental functioning. On the one hand, there is the stimulus from the environment, while on the other there is the response by the organism. Knowledge is nothing more nor less than the mediating process which occurs between the stimulus and the organism's response to it; its function is to determine the response appropriate to the stimulus. Knowledge is the *selection of a response that can adequately cope with the stimulus*" [italics added].[9] Thinking is also expecting, anticipating, and goal seeking, which lead to instrumental responses that meet the goal: "[James] notes that the functioning mind is characterized by two phenomena: first, the organism acts with reference to a future purpose; and second, it selects the methods and instruments by means of which he can hope to achieve this purpose. In the absence of these, James tells us, there is no mental function."[10]

In *How We Think*,[11] John Dewey developed pragmatic thinking further. Like James, Dewey demonstrated the means-ends function of purposeful thought called reflective thinking—"That operation in which present facts suggest other facts (or truths) in such a way as to induce belief in what is suggested on the grounds of real relation in the things themselves, a relation between what suggests and what is suggested."[12] The condition that stimulates reflective thought is a discrepancy from expectations—"a state of doubt, hesitation, perplexity, mental difficulty,"[13] and the consequence of that expectation discrepancy is feedback seeking—"an act of searching, hunting, inquiring, to find material that will resolve the doubt, settle and dispose of the perplexity."[14]

Edward Tolman used similar means-ends explanations to account for maze learning in laboratory rats. He hypothesized that learning produced cognitive connections and sequences representing environmental events and relationships. As Thomas Tighe describes:

> Specifically, repetition of an environmental sequence was assumed to develop an association whereby one element of the sequence . . . evokes an expectation of a subsequent stimulus. . . . Thus, as a consequence of the fact that traversal of each maze eventuates in food, cumulative maze training should develop the general cognition that mazes . . . afford food. Such general cognitions, applicable across a class of learning situations, were generally referred to as *beliefs* or *means-end readinesses* by Tolman, while the term *expectation* was usually reserved for situation-specific cognitions. (italics added)[15]

In the 1940s and 1950s, psychologists examined the consequences of Dewey's reflective thinking—that "state of doubt, hesitation, perplexity, mental difficulty." Leon Festinger introduced a theory of cognitive dissonance[16] that postulated that discrepancies between cognitions produce feedback seeking similar to Dewey's "act of searching, hunting, inquiring, to find material that will resolve the doubt, settle and dispose of the perplexity." Other balance theories centered on similar hypotheses about how discrepancies motivate behavior. According to Hazel Markus and R. B. Zajonc, "They [cognitive discrepancies] give the system energy and they propel the individual from one state to another in a systematic way. In other words, all these theories focus on an instability, and they all attempt to make predictions about the steady state of the organism at a subsequent time. In each case there is some form of dynamic property that can produce a change in the organism, and because the constellation of the opposing vectors is specified, there is also a possibility of predicting direction of change."[17]

By the 1970s, however, these explanations took a different turn. Instead of focusing upon tensions set up by a cognitive discrepancy, researchers examined the cognitive mechanisms responsible for finding tension-reduction solutions. The question changed from "What stimulates problem solving?" to "How does problem solving occur?" For example, research conducted by Allen Newell and Herbert Simon suggested that thinking was dependent upon the task environment and the information it yielded: "The task environment (plus the intelligence of the problem solver) determines to a large extent the behavior of the problem solver, independently of the detailed internal structure of his information processing system."[18]

In short, *problem solving depends upon information*. Problem solvers seek out information on the problem, analyze it, and then design solutions based upon that analysis. Simon described these phases of information use as (1) the *intelligence activity*, which gathers relevant information; (2) the *design activity*, which invents, develops, and analyzes options; and (3) the *choice activity*, which selects the most optimal alternative.[19] The information-processing theory emanating from this work has four propositions.

1. A few, and only a few, gross characteristics of the human IPS (information-processing system) are invariant over task and problem solving.
2. These characteristics are sufficient to determine that a task environment is represented (in the IPS) as a problem space, and that the problem solving takes place in a problem space.
3. The structure of the task environment determines the possible structures of the problem space.
4. The structure of the problem space determines the possible programs that can be used for problem solving.[20]

One of these invariant characteristics of human information-processing systems was the means-ends analysis, which reduced discrepancies between goal states and present states. Newell and Simon demonstrated that computer-generated means-ends analyses simulated expert problem solving in humans. The invariant steps of these programs were to (1) find a discrepancy between goal state and present state, (2) find an operator that will reduce that discrepancy, and (3) use that operator to reduce the discrepancy or find a condition that will allow you to use the operator. The computer programs repeated steps 1–3 until they found an operator that enabled other operators higher in the chain to eliminate the original discrepancy.

This research broke conceptual, theoretical, and experimental barriers that had plagued cognitive research for decades. It defined specific operations that connected the discrepancy condition that motivated problem solving (Dewey's ''state of uncertainty'' and Festinger's ''cognitive dissonance'') with the means-ends thinking that reduced the discrepancy.

The Behavioral Model

While cognitive researchers struggled to explain how cognitions affect behavior, behavioral researchers focused on the other side of the adaptive process— the effects of environmental consequences on behavior. The first study was Edward L. Thorndike's 1898 doctoral dissertation, *Animal Intelligence: An Experimental Study of the Associative Processes in Animals*, in which he described how having access to food after escaping a cage increased an animal's ability to escape on subsequent trials. Initial trial and error responses in which the way out was discovered gradually narrowed to only those essential for escape. Thorndike called this the law of effect.[21] In the 1930s, C. Hull, E. R. Guthrie, and B. F. Skinner added their signatures to the law or its various derivatives. Hull evoked need-reduction conditions to explain the effect: organisms learn behaviors whose consequences reduce needs. Guthrie postulated temporal contiguities between responses and consequences.[22] Skinner argued that all behavior was a function of contingencies of reinforcement—conditions that specified temporal connections between reinforcers and behaviors. In *Schedules of Reinforcement*, C. B. Ferster and B. F. Skinner demonstrated how different schedules of reinforcement produce corresponding patterns of responding.[23]

Most interesting, however, was that from the beginning there was a strong connection between behavioral explanations and evolutionary theory. For example, the English psychologist and evolutionist C. Lloyd Morgan theorized that animal behavior was a function of the hedonistic consequences it produced. This simulated Thorndike to experiment with animals and then formulate the law.[24] Nearly a century later in ''Can Psychology Be a Science of Mind?''[25] Skinner reaffirmed connections with evolutionary principles by differentiating three levels of variation and selection, each accounting for some of the variation and some of the selection.

The first was variation and natural selection, which accounted for evolution of the species. This took thousands of years and had the fault of preparing species for conditions that resembled the past. Hence it was of little use in explaining an organism's lifetime of survival. Operant conditioning via species responsiveness to contingencies of reinforcement accounted for these adjustments: "The fault [of natural selection] was corrected by the evolution of a second type of variation and selection, operant conditioning, through which variations in the behavior of the individual are selected by features of the environment that are not stable enough to play any part in evolution."[26] Individuals adjust to environmental change by matching their responses with contingencies of reinforcement (environmental opportunities for reinforcement). Operant conditioning was a second-level variation and selection mechanism. It functioned like its parent model in biology, but instead of genetic variations interacting with environmental change in geologic time, behavioral variations interacted with environmental contingencies in individual time. The mechanisms that accounted for these selections were reinforcement and discrimination. Stated propositionally, they were as follows:

1. *Reinforcement principle*: The more often a reinforcing stimulus immediately follows a response, the more likely that response will occur in the future.
2. *Discrimination principle*: The more often a reinforcing stimulus immediately follows a response in one stimulus situation but not another stimulus situation, the more likely the response will occur in the one stimulus situation but not in the other.

The first principle describes how organisms respond to the effects or consequences of interacting with the environment. When an increase in response rates follows behavior-produced events, reinforcement has occurred; when decreases follow those events, punishment has occurred.

Organisms learn which situations produce what reinforcers and punishers according to the "discrimination principle." When responding in one environment produces reinforcers and responding in another produces punishers, organisms seek out the one and avoid the other. In time, they learn to match responses with environmental signals of reinforcement opportunities, which Skinner called discriminative stimuli. The same pattern obtains for relative opportunities as well. Given several options, some producing quantitatively more reinforcers than others, organisms learn to match their behaviors according to signals indicating relatively richer reinforcement. Again, matching occurs between behavior and environmental opportunity.

Empirical support for matching is substantial. Given sufficient time to discriminate between contingencies, individuals match their responses with the relatively more reinforcing opportunities. They don't waste behaviors. They find the optimal alternative and invest in it maximally. Behavioral theorists call this the matching law, and Richard Herrnstein offers a mathematical expression to account for the resulting correspondence between responses and reinforcements—a precise description of end-state selections.

The following proposition summarizes this correspondence. Operants—behaviors that operate on environments—increase and decrease as a function of the correspondence they produce. They become "selected" to the extent that a given "match" produces more reinforcers than the alternative matches available at the time.

> OPERANT BEHAVIOR: Variation and selection of operant behaviors are a function of the correspondence between the operant variant and its reinforcement contingencies.

Skinner's explanation for behavioral selection illustrates the end-state perspective. Although he narrows time frames considerably—from eons to lifetimes—he still leaves unexplained the day-to-day variation leading to more or less optimal matches. Even if we accept explanations for end-state correspondence between behaviors and reinforcements (and there is substantial evidence for doing so), we still know little about mechanisms that get to the match. Correspondence between behaviors and environments assumes precisely what we want them to explain—that the organism knows what the correct response is. According to Herrnstein, the matching law presupposes that the subject correlates its responses with the reinforcement: "the pigeon 'knows' its pecks bring the food; the rat 'knows' the lever press avoids the shock, and so on. This usually poses no problem, for in our experiments we typically observe animals doing things they would not do except for the reinforcements we provide, and we usually make sure that the correlation between response and reinforcement is clear."[27]

Of course, this means that the matching law accounts for one-half of the adaptation phenomenon—the correspondence effects produced through changes in environmental contingencies. Consequently it has the same logical restrictions as natural selection. Skinner agrees: "Operant conditioning must solve the 'problem of the first instance.' How and why do responses occur before they have been reinforced?"[28] Like evolutionary theory, operant conditioning prepares individuals for futures that resemble the past, which leaves unanswered what happens when the future is unlike the past. According to Skinner, "The faults in variation and selection are a source of fascinating problems. We must adapt to new situations, resolve conflicts, find quick solutions."[29] But how do we match our needs and opportunities with operations that take optimal advantage of those opportunities?

The Cognitive-Behavioral Model

Cognitive-behavioral models attempt to explain both halves of the adaptive phenomenon. They describe problem solving via cognitive discrepancies on the one hand and behavioral change via reinforcement on the other. Social learning theory is an example. As pioneering theorist Julian Rotter described it, "Social learning theory in its earliest formulations was an attempt to integrate the two modern trends in American psychology—the stimulus-response or reinforcement theories on the one hand, and the cognitive or field theories on the other. Social learning theory included both behavioral constructs and internal or subject constructs; but it required the performance of objective, indirect operations to measure the subjective constructs."[30] Social learning theory postulated two self-regulating mechanisms: expectations and consequences. Self-regulators anticipate reinforcements from alternative actions and then choose those with the greatest yields. According to Rotter, "*The occurrence of a behavior of a person is determined not only by the nature or importance of goals or reinforcements, but also by the persons' anticipation or expectancy that these goals will occur. Such expectations are determined by previous experience and can be quantified.*"[31]

Another way to connect cognitions with behavioral consequences is through discrepancy reductions. During problem solving, individuals define problems by identifying differences between goal states and actual states. Then they search for operations to reduce those differences. Once they find one, they use it and then evaluate the match between its results and expectations (the goal state). They repeat the sequence—redefining the discrepancy, finding operations to reduce it, and then evaluating results—until they reach the goal or abandon the pursuit.

Frederick Kanfer and Sue Hagerman developed a model to illustrate some of these mechanisms.[32] Seven principles capture its major features.[33] Self-regulation begins when ongoing behavior produces unexpected consequences (expectation principle). This is comparable to Dewey's "felt difficulty." The discrepancy provokes feedback seeking to gather information on the subject's behavior (self-monitoring principle) and on the situation that produces and maintains the behavior (situational monitoring principle). The subject compares that feedback with expectations to determine the magnitude of the problem (self-evaluation principle). The greater the discrepancy magnitude (in the negative direction), the more likely problem solving will continue (discrepancy principle). Successful resolution of the problem increases the chances that subsequent regulatory behavior will increase (reinforcement principle).

1. *Expectation Principle*: The more unexpected the consequences of a given behavior, the more likely the occurrence of a problem.
2. *Problem Monitoring Principle*: The more often the problem occurrence, the more likely the self-monitoring.
3. *Self-Monitoring Principle*: The more often the self-monitoring, the more likely the assessment of the situation.
4. *Situational Monitoring Principle*: The more often the assessment of the

situation, the more likely the determination of its effects on long- or short-term standards.

5. *Self-Evaluation Principle*: The more often the determination of effects on long- or short-term standards, the more likely the evaluation of the magnitude of the problem.
6. *Discrepancy Principle*: The greater the magnitude of the discrepancy, the more likely the identification of the problem and the selection of behaviors that can solve it.
7. *Reinforcement Principle*: The more often a reinforcing stimulus follows the identification of a problem and the selection of behaviors to solve it, the more likely the problem solving and solution using will occur in the future.

These seven principles illustrate how self-regulation connects thinking and doing with expectations that motivate behavior and consequences that maintain and alter its occurrence. Omitted from the model, however, is how the problem-solving mechanism optimizes adjustments and maximizes gains. For example, where does means-ends mediation between expectations and behavioral consequences occur? What conditions affect the selection of operations that match consequences with expectations? Successful adaptors gather information on relevant options, make accurate discriminations to select best solutions, implement best solutions, and then compare results with expectations to adjust. These behaviors determine the correspondence between individual responding on the one hand and environmental changes on the other. Expectations and consequences alone are insufficient to explain self-regulation. Means-ends problem solving is also necessary to describe the patterns of feedback seeking and instrumental responding that match behaviors with opportunities.

Self-regulation theory includes this missing component to account for the dynamic between adjustment process and adaptive result. Rather than focusing only on process or only on result, self-regulation theory combines them to explain (1) how discrepancies between goal states and actual states lead to expectations for discrepancy reductions; (2) how expectations for discrepancy reductions lead to solution searching and solution testing; and (3) how solution searching and solution testing lead to consequences that feed back and alter subsequent discrepancies, expectations, searches, and selections.

This connection captures the essence of the self-regulating system and its interactions with changing environments. It also allows for a new accounting of how self-regulating systems oscillate between different levels of optimality on the one hand and levels of gain on the other. Finally, the new perspective leads to a fuller appreciation of the correspondence problems explained by (1) natural selection during geologic time, (2) contingencies of reinforcement during response times, and (3) conditions of optimality during systemic time.

The Correspondence Problem

Variation and selection mark the beginning and end of evolutionary epochs, respectively. Correspondence explains what happens in between. Organisms and environments interact to produce more or less optimal matches between behaviors and events. At the macro-change level, where millions of years transpire to select some species over others, random variations in genotypes, phenotypes, and events interact to form stable matches. These marriages are the "selections" resulting from natural selection. They are stable phenotypes fitting neatly and precisely into niches. These evolutionary results appear rational and purposeful— as if each species knew where it was headed and each environment knew exactly what it had selected. Teleological explanations aside, however, the selected outcome is an ultimate match.

At the micro-change level, however, where real-time interactions between species and environments suggest a different story, one can see only oscillations between matches and mismatches. From this near-random pattern emerges a *self-shaping toward increased correspondence between the needs of the organism and the resources of the environment.* As correspondence increases, so does the direction of subsequent variations and selections toward further correspondence. Variation and selection are a function of correspondence.

The Variation and Selection Explanation

Organisms create niches by selecting environmental contingencies, acting and reacting to those conditions, and then adjusting repeatedly. Given enough time, they find the best fits. In some cases, they maximize correspondence; their adjustments are optimal and gains are maximal. Problem solving ceases, and efficient and effective exchanges commence. The needs of the organism and demands of environment match perfectly. The organism "knows" what behaviors produce what gains. Laboratory research on schedules of reinforcement demonstrates this correspondence through the matching law. Subjects distribute their responses optimally across alternatives.

However, these lawful expressions of ultimate correspondence are less robust for humans, whose systems are more complex. Their greater adaptive capacities make them less stable from moment to moment but more stable from week to week. Increased flexibility over the long term requires increased sensitivity to environmental cues over the short term. This translates into more varied responding to immediate contingencies as subjects sort out what is relevant to their needs and what is not. Contrast this with operant research, which demonstrates the matching effect. There, the experimenter removes extraneous stimuli so that "the pigeon 'knows' its pecks bring the food; the rat 'knows' the level press avoids the shock, and so on. . . . [Experimenters] usually make sure that the correlation between response and reinforcement is clear. . . . It is worth noting, however, that animals (and people) in nature may often be quite confused over what causes what."[34] Only in ideal situations does correspondence maximize long enough to observe the matching law.[35] There, behavior is optimal, gain is maximum.

Variation in behavior and selection of environments depend upon correspondence. When correspondence increases, behaviors and contingencies correlate. When correspondence decreases, they vary randomly. Correspondence brings order and direction. This is the meaning of the proposition: "Variation and selection *are a function of* correspondence." The match guides what behaviors and what contingencies the organism selects.

Table 1.1 summarizes this perspective. Variation and selection are a function of correspondence between the variant and the selection. This is true for genotypes and phenotypes as well as for operant behaviors and their contingencies of reinforcement. The correspondence functions account for the large-scale variation and selection of genotypes and phenotypes (A.1.–A.3.) as well as the day-to-day interactions between operants and their environments (B.1.–B.3.). The analysis also shows propositionally what Skinner suggested conceptually in his explanation of evolutionary and behavioral change.[36]

The logic of Darwinian-Skinnerian thinking is appealing. It says that the evolution of a species depends upon matches between environments and behaviors and that these matches increase the probability of subsequent matches. This principle is indeed parsimonious. Its power is its capacity to account for the diversity of the adaptive effect—no small achievement. Still, variation and selection are only necessary conditions. They are insufficient to explain the consequences of specific variations and specific selections. What principles explain the "how" of the self-regulated match?

The Self-Regulation Explanation

All organisms regulate by connecting their needs and behaviors with environmental opportunity. Their effectiveness and efficiency in this enterprise determine their success or failure. Self-regulation is adaptation to change. In Skinner's words, organisms "must adapt to new situations, resolve conflicts, find quick solutions." But how?

For bumblebees foraging for nectar to extract from flowers, the answer is to find a safe bet. Leslie A. Real of the University of North Carolina in Chapel Hill discovered that bumblebees make decisions about the marketplace of nectar by sampling a few flowers and then choosing patches with consistent deposits. They minimize the cost of searching and risk of failing by making quick discriminations and decisions about yields. Given two patches, one mixed with large deposits interspersed with occasional duds and the other with moderate but consistent deposits and few duds, bees choose consistency. They optimize by reducing the cost of searching while increasing their nectar gains from extracting. They sample a few flowers in a patch and then decide to stay or to switch. When

Table 1.1
Variation and Selection

Variation and selection are a function of the correspondence between the variant and its selection.

1.1 The greater the correspondence between a variant and its selection, the closer to optimal the adjustment and the greater the gain.

1.2 The closer to optimal the adjustment and the greater the gain, the more likely subsequent variations and selections will maximize correspondence.

1.3 Maximum correspondence is optimal adjustment and maximum gain.

A. Genotypes and Phenotypes: Variation and selection of genotypes and phenotypes are a function of the correspondence between a genotype-phenotype variant and its selection of an environmental condition from available alternatives.

A.1. The greater the correspondence between the genotype-phenotype variant and its selection of an environmental condition, the closer to optimal the genotype-phenotype adjustment and the greater the gain from that environmental condition.

A.2. The closer to optimal the genotype-phenotype adjustment and the greater the gain in that environmental condition, the more likely subsequent genotype-phenotype variations and selections will maximize correspondence.

A.3. Maximum correspondence between a genotype-phenotype variant and its selected environmental condition is optimal adjustment and maximum gain for that condition.

B. Operant Behavior: Variation and selection of operant behaviors are a function of the correspondence between an operant variant and its selection of a reinforcement contingency from available alternatives.

B.1. The greater the correspondence between an operant and its selected reinforcement contingencies, the closer to optimal the operant rate and the greater the gain from its selection.

B.2. The closer to optimal the operant rate and the greater the gain from the selection, the more likely its subsequent variations and selections will maximize correspondence.

B.3. Maximum correspondence between operant responding and reinforcement contingencies is optimal adjustment and maximum gain.

they find consistent yields, they stay; when they find inconsistent yields—even those containing jackpots—they switch. For bees, the strategy is optimal because they must keep eating. They cannot waste time searching. Says Dr. Real: "There are lots of other bees and other pollinators in the same patch that are exploiting the same types of flowers. So what the bee needs to worry about more than anything else is the quality of this flower it's on, rather than thinking about those flowers that may be spread out around it."[37]

We humans are less pressed to apply an optimizing calculus for short-term gain (we don't need to keep eating, for example). We have time to calculate gain from foraging opportunities that produce more variable returns. We can play the odds much like track betters in order to net a greater return over the long term. We can engage a risky alternative over the short term if its gains are greater over the long term. Of course, this preference for larger, long-term payoffs is not uniquely human. Even bees can calculate the advantage of foraging in patches with variable but richer deposits. In Dr. Real's experiments, when differentials between variable-but-larger nectar gains were several times the consistent-but-smaller deposits, the bees switched. They were slow but not stupid.

Our advantage is that we don't need to wait for windfall differences before we switch. We are quicker to discover that marginal advantage over the long term. We calculate gains toward our goals that bees must routinely pass up. This increases the variety of our foraging opportunities and the number of adaptive niches those opportunities afford us. The next chapter, The Nature of Problem Solving, describes how we have developed this capacity to play the odds and calculate marginal advantage over the long term.

Notes

1. William Buckland (1836), quoted in Richard Levins and Richard Lewontin, *The Dialectical Biologist* (Cambridge, MA: Harvard University Press, 1985).

2. Levins and Lewontin, *The Dialectical Biologist*, quoted Diderot (*Le rêve de d'Alembert; Entretien entre d'Alembert et Diderot, et Suite de l'entretien*. Ed. Paul Verniere. Paris: Didier [1830], 1951, p. 56) as saying that "everything changes, all things pass, only the totality remains"; and Engels (*Dialectics of Nature*. Progress Publishers [1880], 1943, p. 69) as saying that "motion in the most general sense, conceived as the mode of existence, the inherent attribute of matter, comprehends all changes and processes occurring in the universe, from mere change of place right up to thinking."

3. Levins and Lewontin, *The Dialectical Biologist*, 9.

4. Ibid., 32.

5. Ibid., 12–27.

6. Ibid., 57–58.

7. Niles Eldredge, *Macro-evolutionary Dynamics: Species, Niches, and Adaptive Peaks* (New York: McGraw-Hill, 1989), 59.

8. John Dewey, *Types of Thinking, Including a Survey of Greek Philosophy*, translated from the Chinese and edited by Robert W. Clopton and, Tsuin-Chen Ou (New York: Philosophical Library, 1984), 134.

9. Ibid., 135.

10. Ibid., 136.

11. Dewey revised the book again in 1933: John Dewey, *How We Think* (Boston, MA: D. C. Heath and Company, 1933).

12. Ibid., 12.

13. Ibid.

14. Ibid.

15. Thomas J. Tighe, *Modern Learning Theory: Foundations and Fundamental Issues* (New York: Oxford University Press, 1982), 58–59.

16. Leon Festinger, *A Theory of Cognitive Dissonance* (Evanston, IL: Row, Peterson, 1957).

17. Hazel Markus and R. B. Zajonc, "The Cognitive Perspective in Social Psychology," in Gardner Lindzey and Elliot Aronson (Eds.), *Handbook of Social Psychology: Volume 1, Theory and Method* (New York: Random House, 1985), 207.

18. Allen Newell and Herbert H. Simon, *Human Problem Solving* (Englewood Cliffs, NJ: Prentice-Hall, 1972), 788.

19. Herbert A. Simon, *The New Science of Management Decision* (New York: Harper & Row, 1960), 2.

20. Newell and Simon, *Human Problem Solving*, 788–799.

21. Tighe, *Modern Learning Theory*, 39–40.

22. Ibid., 183–210.

23. C.B. Ferster and B.F. Skinner, *Schedules of Reinforcement* (New York: Appleton-Century-Crofts, 1957).

24. Tighe, *Modern Learning Theory*, 37–39.

25. B.F. Skinner, "Can Psychology Be a Science of Mind?" *American Psychologist* 45, no. 11 (1990): 1206–1210.

26. Ibid., 1206.

27. R.J. Herrnstein, "Formal Properties of the Matching Law," *Journal of the Experimental Analysis of Behavior* 21 (1974):160.

28. Skinner, "Can Psychology Be a Science of Mind?" 1206–1210.

29. Ibid., 1206.

30. Julian B. Rotter, *The Development and Applications of Social Learning Theory, Selected Papers* (New York: Praeger, 1982), 2.

31. Ibid., 10.

32. Frederick H. Kanfer and Sue Hagerman, "The Role of Self-Regulation," in Lynn P. Prehm (Ed.), *Behavior Therapy for Depression* (New York: Academic Press, 1981), 143–179.

33. Kanfer and Hagerman presented a model and discussion of its operations. The "principles" are a derivation of that model and discussion and are not a part of Kanfer and Hagerman's original work.

34. Herrnstein, "Formal Properties of the Matching Law," 159–164.

35. Ibid.

36. Skinner, "Can Psychology Be a Science of Mind?" 1206–1210.

37. Leslie A. Real, quoted in Natalie Angier, "Ignoring Big Chances, Bumblebees Just Seek Small, Reliable Gains," *New York Times*, 3 September 1991.

Chapter 2

The Nature of Problem Solving

For millions of years, *Homo sapiens* problem solving was probably much like that of other animals—trial and error searches to avoid harsh conditions and seek out favorable ones. But then humans learned to use language to communicate with each other about what worked and what did not. This side-stepped reinventing solutions. Successful strategies passed from generation to generation. Nevertheless the process was slow. Our earliest ancestors probably were not very effective or efficient problem solvers. The stone tools found by Louis and Mary Leaky and others in the Olduvai Gorge in Tanzania suggest that *Homo habilis* was the first to accumulate a cultural tool kit. Later, *Homo erectus* replaced *Homo habilis* and improved the use of hunting weapons.

Progress was still microscopic by current standards. *Homo erectus* used the same stone-based tools for 1.5 million years before *Homo sapiens* replaced him with metal instruments eight thousand years ago. *Homo sapiens* also domesticated animals and plants over a period of several thousands of years. These advances were probably a consequence of humans congregating in larger groups, especially following the ice age.

When increased temperatures and decreased rainfall in the north caused vegetation to dry up, herds of animals migrated south. This left the hunting nomads with a declining food supply. So they followed. Some time between 6000 and 5000 B.C. hunters from northern India, central America, Peru, Syria, and Egypt found food and water in river valleys like that of the Nile. This 750-mile, fertile stretch of land, which is now Egypt, provided ample supplies of water, plants, and animals. Nomadic hunters settling in these locations probably noticed that seeds scattered on moist riverbanks produced abundant growth. This encouraged them to scatter seeds more regularly to increase the food supply. Others imitated, and domestication of edible plants was under way. Although it took thousands of years, the new practice amounted to a revolution. As sufficiency turned into abundance, populations increased dramatically; this added pressure to produce more food to keep pace. Interest in better farming methods increased as a result.

Then around 4000 B.C. there was a great discovery. For hundreds of years farmers had watched the great river Nile rise and fall in a predictable cycle: first a flood, then a recovery, then a drought. Finally, someone discovered opportunity in that pattern. By retaining water during the flood to irrigate dry lands during the drought, farmers could increase the growing season and produce more food. This discovery was the first recorded example of optimizing the forces of nature to maximize gain.[1] Equally significant during this period was the transformation of the digging stick into an oxen-pulled scratch plough, which cut furrows in the soil. James Burke says this was "the most fundamental invention in the history of man, and the innovation that brought civilization into being, because it was the instrument of surplus."[2]

Improvements in irrigation and ploughing produced enough food to support non-food producers. By 3000 B.C. the political structure of Egyptian society was organized into water provinces connected by canals. Labor was divided between those who dug and maintained the irrigation systems and those who supervised and directed the diggers and maintainers.

Meanwhile, the need-problem-solution cycle took on a life of its own as solutions for one set of problems generated problems that required another set of solutions. For example, the need to store surplus grain led to the development of permanent containers—fire-hardened clay pots; the need to identify ownership of pots led to the development of writing on containers; and the need to coordinate an increasingly complex labor force of craftsmen (carpenters, potters, weavers, bakers, leather-workers) led to the development of a monetary system including taxation. This, in turn, required improved methods of counting, measuring, and calculating in order to build canals, record seasons, pay workers, and levy taxes.

The need-discovery cycle affected other areas of the social order as well. Agriculturally based communities with their surpluses were increasingly vulnerable to raids from outside because the producers—farmers, artisans, craftsmen, administrators, and tax collectors—were poor defenders. So they set aside a portion of their surplus to support a military force. But this created a new set of problems because warriors needed weapons, and the materials necessary for their construction came from copper deposits across the Red Sea in the Sinai. Fortunately, these neighboring communities also had unmet needs and were willing to trade minerals for foodstuffs. A barter system developed.

By 2500 B.C., just 1,500 years after the development of irrigation and ploughing, Egyptian and Mesopotamian cities had developed civil engineering to build canals, astronomical measurements to predict floods and determine when to plant and to harvest, water-lifting machinery to operate the irrigation system, writing and mathematics to coordinate the functions of the labor force, primitive metallurgy to reinforce canals and build defensive weaponry, and the wheel to transport food, materials, and supplies. These impressive accomplishments were consequences of those first two innovations 1,500 years earlier—farming and irrigation. The needs-problem-solution cycle that led to optimal matches between environmental opportunity on the one hand and human activity on the other produced an empire whose power and influence was unparalleled in the ancient world.[3] James Burke explains the significance of this transformation: "The first man-made harvest freed mankind from total and passive dependence on the vagaries of nature, and at the same time tied him forever to the very tools that set him free. The modern world in which we live is the product of that original achievement, because just as the plough served to trigger change in the community in which it appeared, each change that followed led to further change in a continuing sequence of connected events.[4]

Hellenistic Problem Solving

After nearly 2,400,000 years of passive, trial-and-error reacting to environmental circumstance, *Homo sapiens* began controlling events and producing predictable results. The rise of the Egyptian empire, the Indus culture at Harappa and Mohenjo-Daro in Punjab of India, and the early Chinese empire sharply contrasted marginal survival patterns of nomadic life that dominated other areas of the world. From 2500 B.C. to 600 B.C. these ancient civilizations set high water marks for human thought and achievement. They established calendars, sundials, water clocks, mummification procedures, medical surgeries, numeration systems, and mathematics capable of solving quadratic equations. They developed geometry, measures of area and volume, the Pythagorean theorem, smelting, the use of metals, the wheel for transportation and pottery making, papyrus and parchment, oars and sails for ships, stone and brick building technologies for large temples and palaces, technologies for quarrying and moving heavy stones for structures like the pyramids, standard weights, measures, and coins.[5]

But problem solving was still an occasional enterprise, taking many years of unsystematic observation for new methods to replace less effective ones. Improvements like those just listed occurred over a period of two thousand years, which suggests that methods of discovery were still fairly primitive. Indeed, the cultural toolbox of adaptive solutions contained much that was ineffective or counter-effective. More often than not, behaviors thought to be responsible for favorable outcomes had no relation except a coincidental association in time. Most of the cultural hand-me-downs were probably admixtures of superstition and habit.

This changed briefly from 600 B.C. to 529 A.D. with the emergence of the Greek city-states, which were originally settled around 1400 B.C. by waves of warriors who invaded Greece from the north and from the west through Asia. Although the earliest Greeks were seafarers and traders, subsequent generations became thinkers and philosophers, forerunners of our modern-day scientists. By the sixth century B.C., Ionian philosophers like Thales, Anaximander, and Anaximenes built upon the ideas and practices of the Egyptians and Babylonians by observing nature and deriving general principles to explain its workings. This was a distant departure from the practical questions motivating previous innovators. The Greeks added objective observation and reasoning to problem solving. They detached themselves, their superstitions, and their religions from the pursuit of knowledge and understanding. Several even conducted experiments to test hypotheses. Pythagoras experimented with strings to study the relation between lengths and pitches, and Empelocles immersed enclosed tubes (at one end) to prove that air had substance.

Why the Greeks took the lead in inquiry is unclear. Maybe their seafaring history, decentralized economy, and belief in personal control encouraged a freedom of expression that stimulated philosophic thinking.[6] Whatever the reason, early Greek ideas of world order were materialistic. Leucippus and Democritus saw reality in matter; the followers of Pythagoras defined reality with form and number; and Plato introduced ideal forms. By the fourth century B.C., Athens was the intellectual mecca of Greece and Aristotle was its high priest. Aristotle applied inductive and deductive reasoning to illuminate the mysteries of nature by carefully observing events and isolating and combining their common elements. Then he induced general principles to explain and deduced future events to predict. He ushered in a new era of analytic problem solving, which later became a cornerstone of the philosophy of science.[7]

Among the first to apply inductive-deductive thinking to natural phenomena were the Ionian philosophers Thales, Anaximander, and Anaximenes. Thales of Miletus, founder of the Ionian school of natural philosophy, induced geometric principles from his experiences as a land surveyor and in Mesopotamia he deduced (predicted) a solar eclipse based upon his study of astronomy. Thales also searched for unifying principles to explain all phenomena. He concluded that there were only three forms of matter: mist, water, and earth.[8]

Anaximander, a pupil of Thales, wrote one of the first scientific books and developed a theory of the origin and evolution of life. He postulated that life originated from the sea and that humans, who also came from the sea, must have resembled fish. Finally, Anaximenes, possibly a student of Anaximander, offered a naturalistic explanation for the rainbow, which at the time was considered a sign of the divine.[9]

Aristotle's contributions to rational problem solving focused on the life sciences; he classified animals and plants on a large scale (he induced general characteristics from specific instances). Supported by former student Alexander the Great, who provided sample specimens from the far reaches of his empire, Aristotle was able to develop a comprehensive classification system based upon the presence or absence of blood systems, which he then subdivided into fish, amphibians, reptiles, birds, and mammals. He concluded that there was a progressive design and connection between all life forms. In embryology he postulated that the mother was as important in procreation as the father. Most important, however, was Aristotle's method of study. He was an empiricist. He formulated principles and theories by examining 540 species and by conducting comparative dissections of 48 species.

The impact of Greek inquiry on ancient thinking was largely due to Alexander the Great, whose armies spread Greek culture to India. Alexandria became the capital of the empire, where Hellenistic thinking thrived long after Alexander's death in 323 B.C. During that era Herophilus of Chalcedon studied brain and nerve functions and distinguished arteries from veins; Greek medical teaching spread to Rome, where Galen dissected animals and developed theories of treatment that dominated medical practice for the next 1,500 years; and the Alexandrian mathematician Euclid, author of the *Elements,* used rules of logic to deduce numerous propositions from a small number of axioms—the foundation for teaching geometry through the twentieth century.

Sicilian-born Archimedes also made significant contributions in mathematics, developing formulae for the circle, ellipse, parabola, and hyperbola. Most memorable are his mathematical laws for the lever and hydrostatics formulated between 260 and 241 B.C. Legend has it that he discovered the law of hydrostatics while taking a bath and was so excited that he ran naked through the streets of Syracuse crying "Eureka," which means "I have found it."

The Hellenistic era finally came to a close around 146 B.C. when most of the Mediterranean, including Greece, was under Roman rule, which did little to encourage searching for truth. By the third century A.D. there were few new discoveries. With the decline of the Roman Empire, the rise of the Byzantine Empire in 395 A.D., and the ascendance of the Christian Church, the situation became worse. Church teachings were incompatible with empirical study and rational analysis. St. Augustine's belief that spiritual purpose was the driving force behind human conduct eliminated the need for rational thought. Knowledge of the material world was irreligious and heathenish. Thus, in 390 A.D., Bishop Theophilus had the Library of the Temple of Serapis in Alexandria destroyed and St. Cyril, Bishop of Alexandria, sponsored the murder of the mathematician Hypatia. The signs for the next millennia were ominous.

Medieval Problem Solving

By 530 A.D. the progress attained during the previous nine hundred years was disappearing quickly. First to go were the spirit of inquiry, the desire to know, and the intellectual discipline to understand. Inductive and deductive problem solving gave way to passive acceptance of Church dogma. There was no need for independent query and analysis: all answers and solutions came from centralized bureaucracies mediating between man and God.

In Europe, disintegration of the Roman Empire left large cities in decline, roads and aqueducts in disrepair, and trade suspended. Conditions conducive to communication, discourse, and cross-fertilization no longer existed. What was left was a decentralized, fragmented, feudal structure of independent manors and surrounding communities. Membership in the manorial unit became hereditary and permanent. Once born to a manor and a social position, one stayed. Neither the person nor his status could change. This minimized mobility and maximized isolation. The system was an adaptive response to the chaos created by the decline of the Roman Empire. Manors demanded loyalty in return for security from outside attack. The result was a series of self-sufficient, monolithic mini-societies that discouraged deviation from manorial ways. Originality and innovation threatened security and the status quo. Needless to say, the most notable advancements of the period were the moat and the drawbridge. In nearly all aspects, the social structure—once a fusion of Roman, Germanic, and other social mixtures—became simplified, debased:

> Agriculture was of the primitive hoe type, and little was cultivated except grains. The textile arts had all but disappeared; most garments were made from leather, usually obtained from wild game. For hand tools there was little beyond the wood hoe, a metal hand scythe, hammers, and crude knives; pots and cooking dishes were made locally of hearth-baked clay; the huts of the serfs were made of field stone, wattle, and mud; sanitation was unknown; and there seems to have been very little even of the magic with which primitive and other premodern peoples have consoled themselves for their ignorance of nature and inability to control it. The literacy of the Romans had been lost, and history was composed of local myths and legends.[10]

Medieval people were passive, unenterprising, driven by custom, and bound by superstition, with inexhaustible penchants for magic and religion. They sought whatever would ease the burdens of the material world in order to secure a better position in the spiritual world. The winner in all of this was the Church; it was strong, attracting the most energetic, ambitious, and opportunistic to fill its ranks. Meanwhile, community leadership was self-serving and incompetent. Interested more in consumption than production, it taxed trade and encouraged monopoly. Development and change came to an end. The Church, politics, or the military were the only outlets for the young and the enterprising.

While Europe languished, Islamic culture flourished, replacing Rome and the Hellenistic era with the most advanced civilization of the Western world. From 700 to 1300, trade with Indian and Chinese cultures as well as exchanges with Iranian, Turkish, Jewish, Orthodox and Nestorian Christians, and Gnostic countries stimulated intellectual activity and maintained the gains of the past. Centers of learning sprang up—like Baghdad's "House of Wisdom," which had an astronomical observatory in the eighth century and a library in Islamic Cordoba of Spain during the tenth century. The library housed 400,000 volumes, including translations of the ancients and Indians.

The Arabs also advanced scientific inquiry. They compiled information on planetary and stellar positions; combined the mathematical knowledge of the Greeks and the Indians; introduced Indian numerals with their decimal place-value system; solved equations in trigonometry; introduced the term "algebra";

conducted experiments in chemistry; refined the craft of instrument making; and developed an impressive system of health care, with one thousand government-licensed physicians practicing medicine in Baghdad. Medical science remained dormant, however, due to Islamic Law's prohibition of dissection.

By the twelfth century, Europeans began to awaken from their medieval sleep. Although the reasons for this are not clear, one possibility is that the feudal system was increasingly unable to protect its members from life's hardships—which was its only raison d'etre for existing. A series of bad crops introduced hunger in the manors and further lowered living standards. This interrupted centuries of placid, uneventful living. Also, one of the greatest mass movements in recorded history occurred when Godfrey of Bouillon led the First Crusade in 1096 to take Jerusalem and defeat the Egyptians at Ascalon in 1099. A new ideology also emerged—the spirit of asceticism—which rationalized hardship and provided outlets for its frustrations through salvation seeking.

This led to retreats into monkish life of fasting and self-abasement, and to long pilgrimages to Jerusalem. Traveling to free the Holy Land from Moslem rule promised salvation and also severed long-term bondage to the feudal manor. The Crusades continued throughout the twelfth and thirteenth centuries—time enough to crack the feudal stranglehold on economic activity and allow a rising corps of merchants to profit from the chaos and opportunity that resulted.

Constraints on individual thought and action also weakened. Geographic and social movement were incentives to explore, mingle with other peoples, and trade information and goods. As Richard La Piere described it, "The mingling of people from various manors into crusading masses and their exposure to the non-feudal culture of the Moslems fostered cultural exchanges and fusions. Thus in time the West came to borrow back from the East some of the lost cultural devices and ideas of the ancients."[11]

From 1150 to 1270 European scholars translated from Arabic to Latin the works of Ptolemy, Aristotle, Euclid, Galen, and Hippocrates. Meanwhile, Christian scholars like St. Thomas Aquinas attempted to reconcile the works of the ancients with religious precepts. Aquinas believed that the ideas of Plato and Aristotle were compatible with Christian religion. But by the fourteenth century, some scholars argued that knowledge and truth were independent of either religious dogma or Aristotle. In *Opus Maius*, written between 1267 and 1268 but not published until nearly half a century later (1733), Roger Bacon presented the unorthodox idea that the only correct route to understanding was through experimentation. He was imprisoned for heresy in 1277. In *Summa Totius Logicae*, William of Ockham introduced a basic principle of science—now known as Ockham's Razor—which stated that when competing explanations account for the same phenomenon, the simpler explanation is preferred.

Renewed inquiry also stimulated the establishment of centers of study. For nearly six centuries, intellectual activity had been at subsistence levels; then, within less than two hundred years, seven major universities appeared: the University of Toulouse in France (1229), Cambridge University in England (1231),

The Sorbonne University in Paris (1253), Heidelberg University in Germany (1386), Leipzig University in Germany (1409), St. Andrews University in Edinburgh, Scotland (1409), and Louvain University in Belgium (1426).

In sum, the Middle Ages exhibited survival problem solving. The purposeful, directive search for answers to fundamental questions that was characteristic of the Hellenistic age was gone. Even so, accidental discovery based upon physical need rather than intellectual curiosity prodded some noteworthy achievements. The absence of slavery in Europe increased the value of alternative sources of energy and motivated use of waterwheels, geared wheels, and windmills (which had also been used sporadically in ancient times). By 1086, five thousand watermills in England had harnessed water power for driving trip hammers to crush bark, tanning, and driving forge hammers and bellows. In agriculture, Europeans developed the iron plowshare and horse collar, which increased food production and stimulated commerce. During the twelfth century several cities used papermaking technologies imported from China to build paper mills, which started a printing revolution in 1440. Finally, century-long cathedral projects encouraged builders to solve problems of erecting huge structures from stone. They applied these same technologies to the building of town halls and bridges.

Enlightened Problem Solving

On May 29, 1453, the Turks captured Constantinople and its scholars fled to the West, taking with them classic Greek manuscripts. This occurred while Europe was rebounding from eighty years of Black Plague caused by flea-infested rats coming off ships from Italy. The epidemic (which killed 25 million people, a third of the population before 1351) recurred once every eight years until nearly three-fourths of the population was gone. The remaining population faced a labor shortage and searched for new ways to survive. For the first time in nearly a century, new ideas and better ways of solving problems were again welcome.

During the same period, print communication improved with the invention of moveable type in 1440. The Gutenberg 42-line Bible was available just a year after Constantinople's fall. Exploration to other parts of the world broadened interests, too. Columbus discovered America in 1492; Vasco da Gama sailed around the Cape of Good Hope to reach India in 1498. Two decades after that, the Church received the ultimate challenge: Martin Luther presented his 95 Theses in Wittenberg in 1517. This initiated the Protestant Reformation. The Renaissance had begun.

Renaissance Thought

During the fifteenth century[12] scholars absorbed the classics, adopted Arabic mathematics, changed their diets, and developed new values. Explorers brought back wealth and introduced new plants and animals from the New

World. The Reformation, which argued for a better life today as well as salvation for tomorrow, combined with world-wide markets to encourage new world views. Consider Francis Bacon's embracing view of the new age as "the opening of the world by navigation and commerce, and the further discovery of knowledge."[13]

By the middle of the sixteenth century, rational thinking again confronted religious dogma. In the 1530s Nicholas Copernicus completed *De Revolutionibus Orbium Coelestium* (On the Revolutions of Celestial Bodies) and circulated it surreptitiously among intellectuals. He argued that the earth and other planets revolve around the sun and that stars, although appearing stationary due to their great distances from earth, also moved. As he neared death, he finally consented to the publication of his work. Catholic and Protestant churches immediately opposed the theory. In 1600, the Church accused Italian philosopher Biordano Bruno of heresy for espousing the theory and had him burned at the stake.

By 1616 the Catholic Church placed *De Revolutionibus Orbium Coelestium* on the Index of prohibited books and warned Galileo to refrain from promoting its ideas. Nevertheless, he did just that in *Dialogues on Two Chief World Systems—Ptolemaic and Copernican*. In 1633 the Roman Catholic Inquisition forced him to recant his Copernican beliefs by admitting publicly that the earth did not revolve around the sun. According to accounts, he acquiesced and then quietly uttered to himself: *"E pur se muove"* (Nevertheless, it moves).

In spite of powerful pressure to buttress non-empirical, authoritative views of nature, belief in rational, experimental problem solving grew. Its success was too great to ignore. Copernicus introduced his theory of revolving celestial bodies, and Andreas Vesalius shook the pious world with *De Humani Corporis Fabrica* (On the Structure of the Human Body), which graphically depicted the true anatomy of the human body. Like Copernicus, Vesalius felt the wrath of established doctrine, which accused him of body snatching and heresy. His research came to an abrupt end.

But the challenge continued. Galileo's *De Motu* (On Motion) refuted Aristotelian physics; and Francis Bacon's *Advancement of Learning* replaced magic and superstition with objective observation and experimental inquiry. In 1604 Galileo correctly calculated that a freely falling body increases its distance with the square of time, and Johannes Kepler accurately described how the intensity of light decreases with the square of the distance from its source. Fifteen years later, Kepler explained that solar wind causes a comet's tail to point away from the sun.

In 1626 Francis Bacon completed his first scientific experiment by stuffing a chicken with snow to determine if the lowered temperature would retard its decomposition. Bacon died a month later, allegedly due to a chill caught during the experiment. A decade later, René Descartes argued for a deductive science in *Discourse on the Method of Rightly Conducting Reason and Seeking Truth in the Sciences*.

Newtonian Thought

By the close of the seventeenth century, two methods of secular truth-seeking divided discourse: those advocating rationalism based upon deductive thought, and those espousing empiricism and induction through observation and experimentation. Descartes championed the first and Bacon advocated the second. Isaac Newton settled the controversy in *Philosophiae Naturalis Principia Mathematica* (The Mathematical Principles of Natural Philosophy), which described three laws of motion and the law of universal gravitation. Newton discredited Descartes's methods of deducing propositions from unverifiable metaphysical principles by demonstrating a "method of analysis and synthesis" that coupled experimentation with both induction and deduction. He demonstrated how experimentally verified observations in nature lead to general laws (induction), which in turn explained and predicted natural phenomena (deduction). At the same time, he rejected Cartesian hypotheses—like vortices to explain gravitation—because they were empirically unverifiable.

Newton's astounding success elevated the status and acceptance of empirically based problem solving. Careful observation and experimentation through precise, accurate, and reliable measurement became a prerequisite to understanding nature. From there one could synthesize or "induce" more general statements, principles, and laws. This perspective reshaped the face of inquiry. A new breed of empirical problem solvers emerged to challenge the ancients and their methods of knowing. Science became what scientists could measure. Quantities like weight, volume, and temperature defined the universe.

The new focus infected knowledge seekers everywhere—in fields of astronomy, biology, chemistry, and mathematics. The development of reflecting telescopes and achromatic lenses extended observations far into the heavens, permitting Bernard Fontenelle to discover that the sun was one of many stars. In 1682 Edmund Halley observed the great comet that now bears his name, and in 1705 he correctly predicted its return to earth in 1758. At the other end of the spectrum of inquiry, powerful microscopes gave biologist Anton van Leeuwenhoek a close-úp view of microorganisms too small to be seen with the naked eye; Robert Boyle's chemistry experiments led him to formulate the law of gases; medical doctor Bernardino Rammazzini discovered a correlation between environmental conditions and cancer; Newton and Gottfried developed differential and integral calculus; John Graunt, Jan de Witt, John Arbuthnot, and Abraham De Moive introduced statistics; and members of the Bernoulli family developed probability theory.

Enlightened Thought

For centuries following, Newtonian thinking dominated scientific paradigms. Faith in God and unquestioning acceptance of ancient writings gradually gave way to learning and understanding through direct experience and logic. The new philosophy conjoined empiricism and rationalism. By the early eighteenth century, scientific success was evident to all. Newton had reduced complex and seemingly inexplicable mysteries of the cosmos to a few mathematical formulae, showing how disparate phenomena like falling bodies and orbiting planets were but instances of general principles.

Thinkers throughout the Western world absorbed these startling discoveries and reacted. Materialistic philosophers like Denis Diderot of France denied the existence of a spiritual god, arguing in *Pensées Philosophiques* (Philosophical Thoughts) that divinity was but a reflection of the mechanical order expressed in nature. Baron d'Holbach similarly rejected Christianity in *Le Système de la Nature*. The causality of a mechanically constructed universe implied comparable connectedness among living organisms. The Great Chain of Being (described in Chapter 1) and Jean-Baptiste Lamarck's theory of evolution reflected these principles. Eighteenth-century philosopher Immanuel Kant—who coined the term "Enlightenment" and argued for the connection between empiricism and rationalism—introduced the "nebular hypothesis," which was an evolutionary accounting of the origin of the solar system.

Meanwhile, the twin titans of enlightened thought—empiricism and rationalism—continued to win converts. Observers, classifiers, experimenters, and theory builders populated academic disciplines. Slowly, painstakingly but inexorably, they produced new discoveries and introduced alternative perspectives. Carolus Linnaeus developed the binary notation system to classify living organisms; Comte de Buffon differentiated species according to their capacities for crossbreeding; Georges Cuvier classified extinct species; and Jean-Baptiste Lamarck studied invertebrate anatomy, which furthered understanding of evolutionary theory.

In chemistry the ancient obsession with phlogiston theory finally came to a merciful end. For centuries it had erroneously postulated that fire was a combustible matter or "oily earth" (later called phlogiston), which erupted during combustion. In 1774 Antoine-Laurent Lavoisier challenged the theory in *Opuscules Physiques et Chyiques* (Small Physical and Chemical Works), which demonstrated through combustion experiments that burned substances gained weight through absorption from the air. In 1783 Henry Cavendish delivered the coup de grace by discovering that combustion of hydrogen produced water. A decade later, John Dalton formulated the law of partial pressures and the atomic theory of matter, which postulated that atoms had to exist because chemicals combined with each other only in integral proportions.

Discoveries in non-traditional pursuits moved apace as well. The study of fossils and rocks led Horace de Saussure to introduce the new science of geology. Abraham Gottlob Werner from the Mining Academy of Freiberg showed how sequences of layered rock formations reflected their age—from oldest at the bottom to the youngest at the top; and James Hutton described how erosion and volcanism produced different surface terrains on the earth.

Empiricism also affected the study of human behavior. In 1739 David Hume's

Treatise of Human Nature applied scientific methods to study problems of human nature and psychology. Twenty years later, in *De l'Esprit* (Essays on the Mind), Claude Adrien Helventius suggested that mental development was a function of sensations perceived from the environment rather than from its innate characteristics. The idea was well ahead of its time; the book was burned publicly in Paris and condemned in England by Parliament.

In *De Generis Humani Varietate* (On the Natural Varieties of Mankind), which was published in 1776, German anthropologist Johann Friederich Blumenbach classified humans according to their races—Caucasian, Mongolian, American Indian, Malayan, and Ethiopian; five years later his *Handbuch Der Verglei-chenden Anatomie* founded a new discipline, anthropology. Meanwhile, archaeologist John Frere discovered flint tools, which he claimed were the property of prehistoric humans, although few believed him. At the other end of the evolutionary time scale, in 1798 Thomas Malthus extrapolated the consequences of an expanding population in his *Essay on the Principle of Population As It Affects the Future Improvement of Society*. Later, in the second edition of *Essay on the Principles of Population,* he recommended "moral restraint" to prevent famine due to overpopulation.

As empiricism gained followers, the need to institutionalize its methods increased as well. Societies and associations on the continent and in the United States promoted new disciplines. Carolus Linnaeus and his colleagues founded a scientific society in Stockholm, Sweden, in 1739; Benjamin Franklin helped establish the American Philosophical Society in Philadelphia in 1746; and John Adams founded the American Academy of Arts and Sciences in Boston in 1780.

The new thinking also found acceptance at universities. For the first time, support for research surpassed teaching at the University of Berlin (founded in 1810) and the University of Bonn (founded eight years later). Efforts to keep abreast of the burgeoning knowledge base stimulated publication of Denis Diderot and Jean le Rond d'Alemberg's *Encyclopédie, ou Dictionnaire Raisonné des Sciences, des Arts, et des Métiers* (Encyclopedia, or Rational Dictionary of Science, Art, and Custom) in 1751. By 1768, the *Encyclopaedia Britannica* was publishing weekly issues.

Against this backdrop of enlightened inquiry emerged the industrial revolution, which added momentum to the already accelerating rate of rational-empirical problem solving. In the early eighteenth century, the handicraft industry—a holdover from production practices of the feudal order—still depended on the spinning wheel and the hand loom, which had been in existence for centuries. A need developed when the guilds that controlled textile production and sales could not keep pace with growing demands for textiles in British-controlled India. Free-lance merchants working outside the guild system solved this problem by using "cottage labor"—small farmers and their families living on the outskirts of major cities like London—to meet the demand. These entrepreneurial middlemen supplied bulk fibers (linen or wool) to cottagers who spun the yarn and dyed the fabric. The net result was a division of labor between weavers, spinners, and dyers on the one hand and their suppliers, the entrepreneurs, on the other.

The system began to break down in 1733 when John Kay invented the flying shuttle loom, which weaved yarn faster than traditional methods could produce it. This caused shortages in yarn. Then James Hargreaves invented the spinning jenny, which consisted of several spindles with fiber-feed mechanisms driven first by horsepower and later by waterpower. The jenny accelerated yarn production but could only produce one of the two types of yarn needed, so Richard Arkwright developed the water frame, which produced the other type. However, this invention created yet another problem. The water frame was too large and expensive to install in cottages, so Arkwright built a factory to house it. This solution started the modern factory system. By 1769 the industrial revolution had begun.

As factories spread over Europe, innovations in machine-based power followed. Giovanni Branca's steam-driven turbines, which had been developed a century earlier, stimulated inventors to experiment with steam power. By the end of the seventeenth century Thomas Savery introduced ''the Miner's Friend,'' a practical but inefficient steam engine for miners. Thomas Newcomen's improvements on the engine promoted its moderate use during the eighteenth century. Breakthroughs that accelerated adoption and use came with James Watts's steam condenser and Matthen Boulton's notion of rotary power, which permitted steam engines to power other machines. In 1785 the first steam-powered cotton mill opened in Papplewick, Nottinghamshire, which completed the industrial revolution in England. France completed its industrialization thirty years later, and Germany and the United States completed theirs twenty years after that.

The industrial revolution captured the accelerant nature of the need-problem-solution cycle that came to dominate human adaptation in the West by the eighteenth century. The rational-empirical method of science translated needs into a multitude of specific, doable problems, which in turn produced a multitude of possible solutions for each problem. Changes in the social structure caused by the adoption of new solutions generated another cycle of needs-problems-solutions. Science, the technology it produced, and the social conditions necessary for its adoption acted and reacted to each other to produce continuous patterns of change, adjustment, and readjustment. Adjustment to unremitting social change became the dominant characteristic of Western societies following the industrial revolution.

Also, for the first time technology as represented by unschooled, pragmatic inventors connected with knowledge-seeking scientists to further catalyze innovation and change. The eighteenth century witnessed the first direct application of science to machines. The steam engine is a prime example. The science of gases introduced in the seventeenth century allowed engineers—a new hybrid of scientist and inventor—to measure machine efficiency in accordance with emerging scientific principles. Human interactions with environments now included those of their own creation. Teaching of science and technology suddenly became important. The founding of the Ecole Polytechnique in Paris in 1794 anticipated nineteenth-century demands for talent in the new scientifically based technologies.

The Transformation of Problem Solving

Nineteenth-century empiricists expanded their spheres of influence in five qualitatively different ways. *First*, they opened new fields of inquiry in the natural sciences while probing more deeply into those already established. In anthropology and archaeology, Louis-Laurent Mortillet divided the old stone age (paleolithic) into periods (like the Achuelian and Mousterian) according to tool functions at the time; Jean-François Champollion translated the Egyptian hieroglyphics etched on the Rosetta stone discovered in Egypt by Napoleon's scholars; in 1838 German biologist Matthias Jakob Scheiden suggested that cells are fundamental building blocks of plants; in the following year Theodor Schwan laid the foundation of cell theory in biology by discovering the existence of cells in plants and animals; in 1845 Adolph Wilhelm Hermann Kolbe discovered organic chemistry by synthesizing acetic acid from simpler chemical elements; and in 1861 Friedrick August Kekule discovered that the shape of organic molecules determine their properties.

A *second* change was in the relationship between empiricism and rationalism. Since ancient times, rationalists and their metaphysical theories defined the types of questions posed and answers sought. This led to the dead-end enterprises like static Aristotelian world views, alchemy's gold making, and phlogiston theories of combustion. But by the nineteenth century, the metaphysical dominance was in decline. For the first time, data collectors outproduced data synthesizers and empiricists outnumbered rationalists. There were more empirically verified and verifiable findings than synthesizing statements to explain them.

In chemistry the concept of valence introduced in 1852 and the periodic table established in 1869 were useful—though inexplicable—tools for conducting experiments. Understanding of what they meant in a theoretical sense awaited Wolfgang Pauli's discovery of the exclusion principle in 1925. In medicine, Louis Pasteur discovered immunity through vaccination long before Ilya Ilich Mechnikov explained that white blood cells attack and ingest foreign particles in the blood. The first discovery of Neanderthal remains in 1856 made little sense until 1859, when Darwin's theory placed it in evolutionary perspective. Finally, no one fully understood Newton's gravitational force until Einstein formulated the theory of relativity nearly two and a half centuries later. The relationship between fact finding and theory building reversed positions. Top-down Aristotelian deduction of the past gave way to bottom-up inductive inquiry of the present.

The *third* transformation was the bonding between knowledge seekers and knowledge users. The most profoundly influential of these productive alliances developed from the eighteenth-century fascination with electricity, which began with Cabaeus's discovery in 1630 that electrically charged bodies attracted and then repelled each other after contact. By 1800, Alessandro Volta had invented the electric battery, which stacked alternating zinc and silver disks separated by a brine-soaked felt to produce a steady stream of current. But this was of little practical value until Hans Christian Oersted discovered a link between electricity and magnetism in 1820; this allowed Faraday to build a prototypic electric motor a year later and a prototypic electric generator ten years after that. By the beginning of the twentieth century, practical applications included electric motors to power industry, electric lights, the telegraph, telephones, and the radio.

The payoff for scientific inquiry and technological innovation was practical and profitable. It was also unsettling. Popular conceptions of a mechanically balanced and orderly universe, functioning with the precision of a gigantic time piece, came into question. Darwin's theory of evolution suggested an alternative to the Newtonian thinker's harmonic universe. "Tooth and claw" explanations for species evolution caused a *fourth* transformation in how nineteenth-century social philosophers viewed their place under the sun. Suddenly, nature was adversary and survivor-among-the-fittest was winner. Overnight, new theories of social organization applied evolutionary principles. Auguste Comte introduced sociology in 1838 and postulated that humanity was undergoing its own evolution to successively higher states of development from the theological characteristics of the ancients, to the metaphysical years of the Renaissance, and now to an era of the positivists in which "rationalism prevails over emotionalism, altruism over egoism, and knowledge over ignorance."[14] Herbert Spencer argued that societies evolve, grow, and develop like biological organisms, becoming increasingly complex and differentiated according to their needs and the operational functions that satisfy those needs. Evolution equaled progress, and human evolution was superior to that of other life forms.

The *fifth* nineteenth-century application of scientific problem solving took on the mysteries of the mind and human spirit. Consider just a few: John Stewart Mill's *Principles of Political Economy* (1848); Herbert Spencer's *Principles of Psychology* (1855); Henry Carey's *Principles of Social Science* (1858); Karl Marx's *Das Kapital* (1867); Mary Baker Eddy's *Science and Health* (1875); Leslie Stephen's *Science of Ethics* (1882); and Sigmund Freud's *Sudien über Hysterie* (1895) and *The Interpretation of Dreams* (1900).

For understanding human problem solving, the most significant was probably William James's *The Principles of Psychology* (1890), which eschewed introspection and mentalistic phenomena in favor of simpler explanations. James claimed that mental activity was as functional as its physical counterpart. And for both the purpose was the same—*to facilitate adaptation*. Ideas and their connections were means to more satisfying ends. In *Philosophical Conceptions and Practical Results* (1898), James inaugurated "Pragmatism," the movement that dominated American philosophy well into the twentieth century. Its central tenet was that an idea was only as valuable as the consequence it produced. Truth and meaning depended upon their practical effects.[15]

By the close of the nineteenth century, all human endeavor was open to empirical inquiry. Increasingly, knowledge production and knowledge application were yoked. The closer their correspondence, the more profitable their results, as illustrated in James's principles of psychology. Pragmatism's popularity in the United States was due, in part, to its capacity to unify science, technology, and capitalism on the one hand and the ethics of Protestantism and individualism on the other. No problems were beyond the grasp of that dedicated and pragmatic reacher.

The Nature of Problem Solving

By the end of the nineteenth century, American industry had fully embraced empirically based problem solving to increase productivity. In the 1880s, Frank and Lillian Gilbreth conducted motion studies to identify the types of movements and responses common to all assembly tasks. Their publication "Classifying the Elements of Work" (1924) listed seventeen fundamental hand movements called *therbligs*—"Gilbreth" spelled backwards.[16] Later, Philadelphia-born engineer Frederick Winslow Taylor added time and motion studies to improve industrial efficiency.[17] These efforts started a new brand of inquiry—industrial psychology—which was to "describe, predict, and control human behavior in order to improve human relations in industry—to improve the adjustment and satisfaction of the individual."[18]

Between 1915 and 1935 industrial psychologists assisted industry in the selection and placement of personnel; during World War I the military and industry used group-administered, paper-and-pencil intelligence and trade tests for the same purposes; during World War II empirical inquiries expanded to include studies of morale and its effect on unit behavior in the military; and in the 1940s the United States Employment Service developed procedures for classifying work through publication of *The Dictionary of Occupational Titles*.[19]

By mid-nineteenth century, empirically driven problem solving had delivered impressive results for the United States. World War II ended with allies and foes ravaged and the United States a superpower—the only one with atomic weaponry. For the second time in twenty years, U.S. entry into world conflicts made the difference—largely due to its capacity to produce and deliver needed products effectively and efficiently. Confidence soared. General MacArthur went to rebuild Japan's shattered economy, and Congress passed the Marshall Plan to reconstruct Europe.

The accumulation of technological advantage in the United States during the first half of the twentieth century was profound. By the time color television made its debut in 1951, 1.5 million homes had assigned special rooms for their TVs. Three years later, black and white viewing reached 29 million homes;

overnight, the U.S. standard of living was unmatched anywhere. Only 6 percent of the world's population drove 60 percent of all cars, communicated on 58 percent of all telephones, listened to 45 percent of all radios, and traveled on 34 percent of all railroads. No other country achieved as much, accumulated as much, or believed in itself as much.[20]

But euphoria was short-lived. In 1955, the Soviets challenged U.S. technological superiority by announcing plans to launch an earth satellite. Two years later they delivered Sputniks I and II. The United States answered with the 31-pound Explorer. The Soviets countered with the 3,000-pound Sputnik III. By the 1960s and 1970s there were assassinations, race riots, Vietnam, Watergate, and stagflation. Great society programs built upon faith in systematic application of scientific principles to social problems failed to deliver. The military-industrial complex, which had won two world wars, stalemated in Korea and failed in Vietnam. The country seemed to stumble, bungle, and fumble, and confidence in American institutions plummeted. Social critic Peter Drucker told *U.S. News & World Report* that "nobody really believes anymore that government delivers."[21]

Aside from social and cultural incongruities contributing to difficult times, there was a deeper, less noticeable problem inherent in the science-technology paradigm itself. The gap between solution finding and solution using had not narrowed significantly in centuries. Hence, expectations for gain resulting from that explosive knowledge production outstripped the technical know-how required for its optimal use. The result was no gain, let alone maximum gain. Only during the Renaissance were knowledge production and knowledge use approximately equal, with the rate of discovery approximately equaling the rate of application.

Figure 2.1 compares growth rates in scientific discovery with its application from ancient times to the present.[22] It is evident that rates of technological applications were greater than scientific discovery prior to the Renaissance. After that, rates of discovery were twice those of development and application, a ratio that has been maintained for the last 350 years. During the Newtonian era, technological development was 5 percent of scientific discovery, but since then it has been 49 percent. There has been little progress in closing the gap between how much we know and how much we use what we know. We discover twice as rapidly as we use what we discover. Relatively speaking, we are no faster at *knowledge-transfer* now than we were three and a half centuries ago.

The social sciences exhibit similar lags between knowledge production and knowledge use. In the 1950s, dissatisfaction with this discrepancy encouraged efforts to find ways for knowledge producers and knowledge users to work together to deal with the significant social problems facing modern social organizations. Amitai Etzioni explained:

> The issue is a very old one indeed. How to bring knowledge to bear on policy decisions? Plato reflected upon it in the terms of his age. His ingenious solution

Figure 2.1
The Relation between Knowledge Production (Scientific Events) and Knowledge Use (Technological Events) over Time

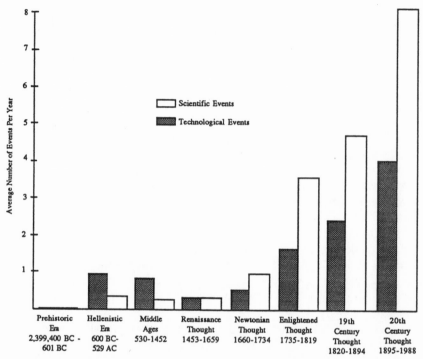

was to unify in one person both analysis and policy making by crowning him philosopher king. If this solution was practical for a city-polity, I leave it to historians. It will not serve a complex modern society, in which knowledge is mass produced—and policy makers are never knowledge makers, even if this was their specialty before they were elected or appointed to their august offices.[23]

Frustration with *knowing what* but not *knowing how* has increased exponentially during the last half of this century. Consider the impact of the microcomputer revolution on schooling—another unfulfilled promise, or as one reviewer called it, ''The Revolution That Fizzled'':

Now that America has patted itself on the back for its high-tech prowess in the Persian Gulf, the country faces an even more daunting technological challenge back home: how to make educational electronics achieve its potential. Today 2.7 million computers have been installed in the nation's 100,000 schools—roughly 1 for every 16 students—along with an avalanche of disk drives, modems, laser printers and videodisk players. Estimated cost: $4 billion a year. But experts say the impact of all this technology on the basic operation of most classrooms is practically nil. Effective and innovative uses of computers in the classroom can be found, but they are about as rare as whale sightings.[24]

This is just one of many fizzles between knowing what but not knowing how. Policy researchers and analysts claim to have answers, however. Specialized training in political science, public administration, business management, and other social science departments has produced a new breed of professionals whose aim is to provide "policy makers with pragmatic, action-oriented recommendations for alleviating the problem."[25]

The conceptual underpinnings of the approach involve scientific problem solving: defining a problem, considering solutions, selecting and implementing optimal solutions, evaluating outcomes, and then adjusting. In *Public Policy in the Eighties,* Charles Bullock, James Anderson, and David Brady identify five stages in the basic paradigm: (1) problem definition, (2) policy agenda (deciding which problems to address), (3) policy formulation and adoption (considering options and selecting the best alternative), (4) policy implementation (implementing the solution), and (5) policy evaluation (evaluating the effects of the solution and recommending adjustments).[26] In *Policy Analysis for the Real World,* Brian Hogwood and Lewis Gunn divide the same paradigm into nine parts. They *define the problem* with the first three: "deciding to decide," "deciding how to decide," and "issue forecasting"; *consider alternatives* with the next two: "setting objectives and priorities" and "options analysis"; *implement* in the seventh: "policy implementation, monitoring, and control"; and *evaluate and adjust* in the eighth and ninth: "evaluation and review" and "policy maintenance, succession, or termination."[27] Finally, in *Policy Analysis by Design,* Davis Bobrow and John Dryzek cover the same ground with five steps: (1) interpret the problem and performance goals (definition of the problem); (2) identify and collect needed information (more problem definition); (3) invent and stipulate policy alternatives (considering alternatives); (4) assess and compare policy alternatives (implementation and evaluation of solutions); and (5) construct arguments (adjusting the process).[28]

Herbert Simon's *The New Science of Management Decision* provided the disciplinary foundation for many of these formulations. Simon used three phases to explain the problem-solving enterprise: intelligence, design, and choice. Information searchers define problems, designers develop alternatives, and choosers implement actions. The process is the same one John Dewey introduced in 1910, as Simon acknowledged: "Nevertheless, the three large phases [intelligence, design, and choice] are often clearly discernible as the organizational decision process unfolds. *They are closely related to the stages in problem solving first described by John Dewey: What is the problem? What are the alternatives? Which alternative is best?*" [italics added][29]

Managers from business and industry use similar approaches. Irving Janis and Leon Mann describe seven steps for making high quality decisions: (1) thoroughly canvass a wide range of alternative courses of action; (2) survey the full range

Table 2.1
Examples of Problem-Solving Models

John Dewey (1933) Problem Solving in Thinking[1]	Newell & Simon (1972) General Problem Solving in Artificial Intelligence[2]	D'Zurilla & Goldfried (1971) Problem Solving in Behavior Modification[3]	Whitman, Burgio, & Johnston (1984) Problem Solving in Cognitive-Behavioral Interventions[4]
1. Experience a felt difficulty 2. Find its location and definition 3. Suggest possible solutions 4. Develop solution by reasoning about its effects 5. Observe and experiment with solution to conclude about its worth	1. Find discrepancy between goal state and current state 2. Find operator to reduce discrepancy 3. Apply operator and evaluate its effects on discrepancy	1. Problem definition & formulation 2. Generate alternatives 3. Decision making 4. Verification	1. Think of life as ongoing process of solving problems 2. Define completely and operationally the problem situation 3. Generate list of possible solutions 4. Decide on a particular solution 5. Implement solution and match outcomes with expectations
Haaga & Davison (1986) Social Problem Solving in Therapy[5]	Rose (1986) Problem Solving in Group Therapy[6]	Valett (1986) Problem Solving in Critical Thinking[7]	Mithaug, Martin, & Agran (1987) Problem Solving in Adaptability Instruction for Special Education[8]

1. Problem orientation
2. Problem definition & formulation
3. Generation of alternatives
4. Decision making
5. Solution implementation and verification
	1. Analyze problem
	2. Discover new approaches to solve problem
	3. Evaluate approaches
	4. Develop strategies for implementing approaches in real world
		1. Clarify goals and objectives
		2. Know where and who to obtain needed information
		3. Identify major problems
		4. Ask self questions about what's being accomplished
		5. Analyze data to answer own questions
		6. Predict consequences of alternative actions
		7. Make plan to solve problems
		8. Rehearse and model solutions for problems
		9. Evaluate effectiveness of actions
		10. Correct errors and reward progress
			1. Decision Making
			  A. Select goals
			  B. Consider options
			  C. Choose tasks
			  D. Schedule tasks
			  E. Set expectations
			2. Independent Performance
			  A. Complete new tasks
			  B. Complete task sequences
			3. Self-evaluation
			  A. Monitor performance
			  B. Compare results with expectations
			4. Adjustment
			  A. Change own behavior
			  B. Change other's behavior

1 John Dewy, *How We Think* (Boston: D. C. Heath and Company, 1933).

2 Allen Newell and Herbert A. Simon, *Human Problem Solving* (Englewood Cliffs, NJ: Prentice-Hall, 1972).

3 Thomas J. D'Zurilla & Marvin R. Goldfried, "Problem Solving and Behavior Modification," *Journal of Abnormal Psychology* 78, no.1 (1971): 107-126.

4 T. Witman, L. Burgio, & M. B. Johnston, "Cognitive Behavioral Interventions with Mentally Retarded Children," in A. W. Meyers & W. E. Craighead (Eds.), *Cognitive Behavior Therapy with Children* (New York: Plenum Press, 1984).

5 David A. Haaga & Gerald C. Davison, "Cognitive Change Methods," in Frederick H. Kanfer & Arnold P. Goldstein (Eds.), *Helping People Change* (New York: Pergamon Press, 1986), 236-282.

6 Sheldon Rose, "Group Methods," in Kanfer & Goldstein (Eds.), *Helping People Change*, 437-469.

7 Robert Valett, "Developing Thinking Skills," *Academic Therapy* 22, no. 2 (1986): 187-198.

8 Dennis E. Mithaug, James E. Martin, & Martin Agran, "Adaptability Instruction: The Goal of Transitional Programming," *Exceptional Children* 53 (1987): 500-505.

of objectives to be fulfilled and values implicated by the choice; (3) carefully weigh the positive and negative consequences of each alternative; (4) intensely search for new information and evaluate alternatives; (5) correctly assimilate new information; (6) reexamine positive and negative consequences of alternatives; and (7) detail provisions for implementing chosen alternatives.[30] Robin Hogarth recommended a similar sequence in *Judgement and Choice: The Psychology of Decision:* (1) structure the problem, (2) assess consequences, (3) assess uncertainties, (4) evaluate alternatives, (5) analyze sensitively, (6) gather information, and (7) choose.[31] All models reduce to Dewey's "What is the problem?" "What are the alternatives?" and "Which alternative is best?" Table 2.1 lists comparable applications in education.

The nature of problem solving has not changed since Newton's publication of *Principia* in 1687, nor has it changed since the first nomad of ancient times noticed unusual growth on the moist banks of the great Nile following a flood. What stimulates solution searching is still "a state of doubt, hesitation, perplexity, mental difficulty, in which thinking originates," and what generates solution finding is "an act of searching, hunting, inquiring, to find material that will resolve the doubt, settle and dispose of the perplexity."[32]

What *has* changed is the development of *systematic* searches, selections, uses, and reuses of solutions to achieve prescribed goals. This is what several centuries of trial and error problem solving have improved upon. The human species and its social organizations have learned to *regulate problem solving to optimize adjustments and maximize gains toward culturally defined goals.*

Dewey's problem solving steps describe only one-half of that regulatory process—the component that connects problem identification with solution finding. The second half involves another mechanism—one that implements and tests solutions for their contribution toward goal attainment. The next chapter describes this mechanism and how it interacts with problem solving to explain self-regulated problem solving to meet a goal.

Notes

1. James Burke, *Connections* (Boston: Little, Brown and Company, 1978), 9.
2. Ibid.
3. Ibid., 12.
4. Ibid.
5. Alexander Hellemans and Bryan Bunch, *The Timetables of Science: A Chronology of the Most Important People and Events in the History of Science* (New York: Simon and Schuster, 1988), 3.
6. Ibid., 20.
7. Ibid., 21.
8. Ibid.
9. Ibid.
10. Richard T. La Piere, *Social Change* (New York: McGraw-Hill, 1965), 334.
11. Ibid.

12. According to Hellemans and Bunch, *Timetables of Science*, 90.

13. Ibid., 90.

14. Szymon Chodak, *Societal Development* (New York: Oxford University Press, 1973), 26.

15. Adam Kuper and Jessica Kuper (Eds.), *The Social Science Encyclopedia* (New York: Routledge, 1985), 418.

16. Frank B. Gilbreth and Lillian M. Gilbreth, "Classifying the Elements of Work," *Management and Administration* 8, no.2 (1924): 151.

17. Frederick W. Taylor, *Common Sense Applied to Motion and Time Study* (New York: Harper, 1911), cited in Edwin E. Ghiselli and Clarence W. Brown, *Personnel and Industrial Psychology* (New York: McGraw-Hill, 1955), 58.

18. Thomas W. Harrell, *Industrial Psychology* (New York: Rinehart & Company, 1949), 3–4.

19. Ibid., 12–13.

20. Dennis E. Mithaug, *Self-Determined Kids* (New York: Lexington Books, Macmillan, 1991).

21. Cited in John Naisbitt, *Megatrends: Ten New Directions Transforming Our Lives* (New York: Warner Books, 1982), 150.

22. This chart comes from a count of event entries for the physical sciences—chemistry, earth science, and physics—and for technology in Hellemans and Bunch, *The Timetables of Science*, for the time periods indicated in the chart.

23. Amitai Etzioni, "Introduction," in Ann Majchrazak, *Methods for Policy Research* (Beverly Hills: Sage Publications, 1984), 7.

24. Philip Elmer-Dewitt, "The Revolution That Fizzled," *Time*, May 20 (1991): 48.

25. Majchrazak, *Methods for Policy Research*, 12.

26. Charles S. Bullock III, James E. Anderson, and David W. Brady, *Public Policy in the Eighties* (Monterey, CA: Brooks/Cole Publishing, 1983), 6–9.

27. Brian W. Hogwood and Lewis A. Gunn, *Policy Analysis for the Real World* (London: Oxford University Press, 1984).

28. Davis B. Bobrow and John S. Dryzek, *Policy Analysis by Design* (Pittsburgh: University of Pittsburgh Press, 1987), 208–211.

29. Herbert A. Simon, *The New Science of Management Decision* (New York: Harper & Row, 1960), 3.

30. Irving L. Janis and Leon Mann, *Decision Making: A Psychological Analysis of Conflict, Choice, and Commitment* (New York: The Free Press, 1977), 11.

31. Robin M. Hogarth, *Judgement and Choice: The Psychology of Decision* (New York: John Wiley & Sons, 1980), 130.

32. John Dewey, *How We Think* (Boston: D. C. Heath and Company, 1933), 12.

Chapter 3

The Theory of Self-Regulation

All living organisms self-regulate, even the smallest. Consider the *E. coli* bacterium swimming in search of food. It too solves problems to meet goals, as molecular biologist Max Perutz explained:

> Organisms are problem-solvers seeking better conditions—even the lowest organism performs trial and error measurements with a distinct aim. This image brought to mind Howard Berg's striking film of chemotaxic bacteria. He showed how a bacterium's flagellar motor makes it run and tumble randomly until the bacterium senses a gradient of nutrient. The bacterium then reduces the frequency of tumbling and lengthens the runs towards a greater concentration of nutrient.[1]

Cell movement, from random tumbling to homing in, reveals the same purposeful, self-regulating behavior found in other species, including humans. In *The Cerebral Symphony*, neurobiologist William Calvin described routes taken by single-cell organisms moving successively closer to food. Their approaches appear as purposeful as any we might follow, given similar information about food proximity. According to Calvin, "most philosophers looking through a magnifying glass at that food-finding path would have ascribed intelligence to that purposeful performance of the little bacterium. At such a marginal magnification, it would seem to 'home in' on the morsel. But the bacterium has no brain: it's just a single cell with some inherited simple abilities such as swimming, tumbling, and sensing increasing yield."[2]

Indeed, intelligence may not be necessary for self-regulation. But self-regulation is necessary for intelligence. In fact, the more complex the organism's central nervous system, the more adaptive is its self-regulatory capacity.

Homeostasis

Self-regulation begins when organisms detect conditions that are discrepant from internal control standards. The greater the discrepancy, the more likely that regulatory action will attempt to return the system to tolerable values. Claude Bernard described these functions in 1851 when he discovered that nerves control blood vessel dilation, which then controls body temperature. In *Les Leçons de physiologie experimentale* (Lessons in Experimental Physiology) he introduced the theory that internal bodily conditions remain constant while external environmental conditions change:

> The organism is merely a living machine so constructed that, on the one hand, the outer environment is in free communication with the inner organic environment, and, on the other hand, the organic units have protective functions, to place in reserve the materials of life and uninterruptedly to maintain the humidity, the warmth and the conditions essential to vital activity. Sickness and death are merely a dislocation or disturbance of the mechanism which regulates the contact of vital stimulants with organic units.[3]

In 1933, American physiologist Walter Bradford Cannon introduced "homeostasis" to describe mechanisms that maintain critical physiological variables within tolerable limits.[4] Body temperature and blood pressure cannot be too high or too low; and blood cannot be too alkaline or acidic, contain too much carbon dioxide, or have too much or too little sugar. When these critical variables exceed tolerable limits, organisms sicken and die.

Homeostasis is physiological self-regulation. When internal temperatures fall below 98.6 degrees Fahrenheit, the body shivers to generate heat; when temperatures rise above 98.6 degrees, it perspires to evaporate liquids from the skin's surface. Comparable mechanisms influence behavioral interactions with the environment. When internal states are depleted of vital nutrients, the organism explores for food much as the *E. coli* bacterium does.

Research on homeostatic functions in animals accounts for a wide range of regulatory patterns, including hunger, thirst, interactions between hunger and thirst, temperature control, sex, aggression, fear, exploration, and sleep.[5] Behaviors once thought to be simple functions of drive reduction through immediate reinforcement now are better understood in terms of self-regulation. Even complex behavior patterns like aggression and fear may depend upon the self-regulatory mechanisms as explained in Frederick Toates's *Animal Behaviour— A Systems Approach*:

> Animals subject to predation have evolved mechanisms whereby the sight, sound, or smell of a predator (or even an innocuous intrusion) evokes avoidance behaviour. In the evolutionary development of such behavioural traits it has, for obvious reasons, proven useful for the species to inherit such anticipatory mechanisms. It

would not reflect good evolutionary design for an animal only to take avoidance action in response to direct contact with a predatory or conspecific attacker.

Archer . . . argues that, with more sophisticated sensory equipment, animals would monitor the environment for specific dangers. In Archer's terms what constitutes danger is " . . . *any large discrepancy between observed and expected stimuli . . .* ". In other words, in the course of its activities the animal acquires a model or hypothesis of the expected state of certain features of the environment, and fear is evoked when the actual state of these environmental features differs significantly from the expected state. [italics added][6]

This description sounds remarkably similar to John Dewey's "state of doubt, hesitation, perplexity, mental difficulty,"[7] which motivates "an act of searching, hunting, inquiring, to find material that will resolve the doubt, settle and dispose of the perplexity."[8]

Cybernetics

Homeostatic principles help explain brain functions and thinking.[9] For example, Norbert Wiener's *Cybernetics* presented a comprehensive mathematical analysis of feedback functions in self-regulated systems,[10] and W. Ross Ashby's *Design for a Brain* provided a physiologically based accounting of how the brain (not the "mind," mind you) produces adaptive behavior. Ashby explained that by employing negative feedback mechanisms, the organism recognizes deviations from critical values that trigger behaviors to return conditions to tolerable levels. Ashby also described how adaptive behavior becomes efficient: "When the rat in a maze has changed its behaviour so that it goes directly to the food at the other end, the new behaviour is better [more adaptive] than the old because it leads more quickly to the animal's hunger being satisfied."[11]

According to the homeostatic explanation, neuro-physiological structures monitor incoming signals (feedback), compare them with required values, and then produce behaviors that operate on the environment to increase or decrease signals. Once incoming signals are within acceptable ranges, regulatory behavior ceases. The system has adjusted.

Ashby eschews teleological explanations that organisms behave because "they want to receive a positive consequence." Instead, he argues that behavior depends upon the physical and chemical nature of the organism, which permits no other action at the moment. Even trial and error responding such as that described for the single-cell bacteria provides information about what works and what doesn't. All trials are important, even those yielding negative results. They indicate where not to proceed:

The process of trial and error can thus be viewed from two very different points of view. On the one hand it can be regarded as simply an attempt at success; so that when it fails we give zero marks for success. From this point of view it is merely a second-rate way of getting to success. There is, however, the other point of view that gives it an altogether higher status, for the process may be playing the invaluable part of *gathering information*, information that is absolutely necessary if adaptation is to be successfully achieved.[12]

Ashby's self-regulating system operates on a simple principle: behavior changes if the trial is unsuccessful; it maintains if the trial is successful.[13]

Self-Regulating Systems

The mechanisms responsible for self-regulation are (1) the existence of test variables that define preferred states, (2) internal feedback that compares system conditions with those standards, and (3) response systems that change internal (system) and external (environmental) events. Interactions between these mechanisms match systems with their environments. When comparisons with internal standards indicate discrepancies beyond tolerable limits, the system adjusts itself internally or alters events externally until conditions match the standard. This is the cybernetic explanation for reinforcement, extinction, and punishment: when the trial is successful, similar behaviors occur again (they are reinforced); when the trial is unsuccessful, different behaviors occur (original behaviors are extinguished).

In *Plans and the Structure of Behavior*, George Miller, Eugene Galanter, and Karl Pribram postulated a similar mechanism—the Test-Operate-Test-Exit (TOTE) unit—to explain reflex behavior: "The general pattern of reflex action, therefore, is to test the input energies against some criteria established in the organism, to respond if the result of the test is to show an incongruity, and to continue to respond until the incongruity vanishes, at which time the reflex is terminated. Thus, there is 'feedback' from the result of the action to the testing phase and we are confronted by a recursive loop."[14] They differentiate the TOTE mechanism from reinforcement as follows:

> That is to say: (1) a reinforcing feedback must strengthen something, whereas feedback in a TOTE is for the purpose of comparison and testing; (2) a reinforcing feedback is considered to be a stimulus (e.g., pellet of food), whereas feedback in a TOTE may be a stimulus, or information (e.g., knowledge of results), or control (e.g., instructions); and (3) a reinforcing feedback is frequently considered to be valuable, or "drive reducing," to the organism, whereas feedback in a TOTE has no such value.[15]

Like homeostasis and cybernetics, TOTEs reduce discrepancies between expected and observed states. Discrepancies occur between expected and actual *events*—for example, when discrepancies between nutrient needs and food intake generate consummatory behavior—or between expected and actual *information about events*—for example, when previous information is different from recent information about food locations and *feedback seeking* occurs to resolve the discrepancy. In other words, *discrepancies between events generate instrumental behavior, and discrepancies between different information about events generate feedback seeking.* In tandem, the two behavior types produce purposeful, adaptive behavior.

The two behavior classes also produce different consequences, as explained by J. Annett in *Feedback and Human Behavior*. Annett distinguishes between *kinesthetic feedback* produced by instrumental responding and *results feedback* generated by feedback seeking.[16] Kinesthetic feedback guides performance smoothly and purposefully. Consider the coordination required to hit a home run. The batter watches the ball leave the pitcher's hand and approach the strike zone. He decides to swing at the very last moment and then adjusts his body and arm movements precisely as the ball passes over the outside corner of the plate. The process takes seconds, but the decision, the timing, and the swing take less. Kinesthetic feedback—information about the relation between bat and ball in time and space—is responsible. Only after the swing, ball contact, and crack of the bat does the batter know he's hit the ball. And only when he sees the ball's trajectory out of the stadium does he know he's hit a home run. This is results feedback.

Both feedback types obey the control principles described by William Powers in *Behavior: The Control of Perception*. In the nervous system, perceptual control begins with comparisons between *reference* and *perceptual* conditions. Reference conditions are always at zero values. Perceptual conditions deviate from zero when signals from external stimuli deviate too far from acceptable values. Sense organs transform stimuli into neural impulses, which define perceptual conditions. Comparison between reference and perceptual conditions produces *matches* and *discrepancies*. Discrepancies trigger regulatory responses. According to Powers, all behavior is a function of the control of certain quantities with respect to specific reference conditions. "The only reason for which way any higher organism acts is to counteract the effects of disturbances (constant or varying) on controlled quantities it senses. When the nature of these controlled quantities is known together with the corresponding reference conditions, variability all but disappears from behavior."[17]

The controlling condition is the discrepancy between a neural standard (reference condition) and feedback from the environment (perceptual condition). Powers says that the "controlled quantity does not directly cause behavior: *only the difference (if any) between that quantity and its reference condition calls for a 'response.'* Furthermore, it is not the actual environmental situation that leads to responses, but that situation as perceived by the organism."[18]

Only when a discrepancy exists does self-regulation occur. Otherwise, ongoing behaviors maintain. Discrepancies interrupt routines and stimulate alternative responses. Living systems are in a continuous state of dynamic equilibrium or homeostasis with respect to these reference values. They return to these activity levels when "perceived" environmental inputs fail to match reference values. "If there are no effects in the environment tending to drive the controlled quantity away from its reference condition, there will be no change in the organism's pattern of behavior. Any disturbance, however, will call for an action which opposes the effects of the disturbance on the controlled quantity.''[19]

This explanation also accounts for reinforcement and punishment. Incoming neural signals from the environment may increase, decrease, or have no effect on discrepancies. When they reduce discrepancies, behaviors associated with those signals occur again. This is positive reinforcement. And when incoming signals increase discrepancies, behaviors responsible for those signals decrease. This is punishment. Behaviorists describe these effects as strengthening or weakening of behaviors, but Powers says the system is simply regulating behavior to reduce intrinsic error.

Powers uses this control principle to explain complex behavior as well. He provides a neurological basis for a hierarchy of control units in nested loops leading to successively more complex levels of organization to guide and direct behavior. The hierarchic activities that differentiate some of these levels include the following: (1) conversion of environmental energy inputs to neural signals, (2) conversion of neural signals into perceptual sensations, (3) conversion of perceptual sensations into patterns of objects, (4) control of relationships between experiences, (5) control through use of programs and routines for adaptive responding, (6) control through principles defining general conditions for different classes of regulatory behavior, and (7) control through system concepts that classify all input according to values.

This explanation shows how physiological mechanisms can account for purposeful, goal-directed behavior, while at the same time avoiding the teleological explanation that behavior occurs in order to fulfill a purpose. Behaviors are a function of system regulation. They are effective and efficient to the extent that they reduce discrepancies between expected and observed goal states defined by the system.

The same mechanisms that explain system maintenance can also account for system evolution. While zero-sum discrepancy reductions impose internal controls necessary for self-regulation, the driving force for *system evolution* is the gradual, near-imperceptible *resetting of reference states* over time. Within the absolute limits of condition settings that are essential for survival—like food, water, temperature—all system conditions are subject to a ''standards drift.''

Weight watchers reset reference states for food consumption each time they eat more or less than their diets recommend. The more they eat, the more they ''feel'' like eating. And the less they eat, the less they ''feel'' like eating. The hunger pains associated with these new eating levels stimulate consummatory behavior to return the system to this new baseline. Evolving reference conditions also affect cognitions. Consider what happens when standards for solving important problems become more demanding, methods of finding solutions more effective, and success in meeting goals more frequent. The standard for satisfactory problem solving causes feedback seeking, choosing, and performing to improve, also. The result is more effective and efficient solutions. The probability of optimal adjustment and maximum gain increases as well.

This accounts for the paradox between homeostasis and evolution. Systems *adjust* by reducing discrepancies, but they *evolve* by gradually resetting reference conditions. The short-term effects maintain the system more or less within base-line values regardless of environmental encouragement to the contrary. But the long-term effect of persistent environmental encouragement is a systemic evo-lution of reference values in the direction of the new environmental condition. This dynamic interplay between maintenance and evolution resolves the apparent contradiction between surviving today and preparing for tomorrow.

In *Uncommon Wisdom*, former theoretical physics researcher Fritjof Capra interviewed some of the world's foremost thinkers in the physical, medical, and social sciences and discovered similar systems perspectives at work. One of those models—Prigogine's theory of self-organizing systems—also explained the paradox of balance between maintenance and change. Capra described it as follows:

> Now everything fell into place. I had learned from Prigogine and Jantsch that living, self-organizing systems not only have the tendency to maintain themselves in their state of dynamic balance but also show the opposite, yet complementary tendency to transcend themselves, to reach out creatively beyond their boundaries and generate new structures and new forms of organization. The application of this view to the phenomenon of healing showed me that the healing forces inherent in every living organism can work in two different directions. After a disturbance the organism may return, *more or less*, to its previous state through various pro-cesses of self-maintenance. Examples of this phenomenon would be the minor illnesses that are part of our everyday life and usually cure themselves. On the other hand, the organism may also undergo a process of self-transformation and self-transcendence, involving stages of crisis and transition *and resulting in an entirely new state of balance*. [italics added][20]

Self-organizing systems "more or less" return to preset conditions, which permits incremental movement toward "new states of balance." They can also change abruptly, for example, when discrepancies from preferred levels resist self-regulatory behavior to restore balance. Given that the organism can tolerate (survive) the new level, discrepancies disappear when the condition becomes the new standard. If a prolonged illness causes sudden weight loss and the new weight maintains long enough, it becomes the new homeostatic reference for food seeking and consumption.

The Self-Regulated Problem Solver

The following principles describe common features of homeostatic-cybernetic mechanisms:

1. The more frequent the discrepancy between an expected and observed condition, the more frequent the self-regulatory behavior.

2. The greater the match between expected and current states as a consequence of regulatory behavior, the more likely that regulatory behavior will occur in the future.
3. The more persistent the discrepancy between expected and current condition, the more likely the expected condition will become the current condition.

The first principle describes the consequence of discrepancies between expectations (reference states) and observations (perceptual states). Discrepancies increase the probability of engaging in behaviors that will reduce or eliminate them. The second principle describes the reinforcement effect of discrepancy reduction. When regulatory behavior reduces a discrepancy, it will occur again to reduce a similar discrepancy. The third principle describes the consequences of a persistent discrepancy—one that is unresponsive to regulation. When this occurs, the system accommodates the discrepancy by adjusting other variables to match the outlier value. Such system reorganization may be beneficial or detrimental, leading to new levels of learning, growth, optimization, and maximization, or producing deterioration, decline, and dissolution.

Although these principles define when regulation occurs and what happens when it succeeds or fails, they do not specify how regulation leads to different adjustments and various gains. For example, what conditions of psychological discrepancy motivate humans to solve problems and achieve goals? What patterns of feedback seeking, choosing, and responding generate persistent problem searching and solution finding? In other words, what behavioral mechanisms— consistent with those just described—are necessary and sufficient for optimal adjustment and maximum gain?

Self-Regulation Models

Figure 3.1 presents several self-regulation models of human adjustment. Jackson and Boag postulate a "standards" box against which subjects monitor and compare behaviors to detect discrepancies. The Kanfer and Hagerman model describes discrepancy conditions in greater detail—from the detection of "unexpected consequences" to the assessment of their effects on long- and short-term standards. Jeffrey and Berger postulate a phase in which subjects self-monitor to detect discrepancies, as do Carver and Scheier with their "Self-Focus." Finally, Corno and Mandinach describe person-conditions that affect one's capacity to seek appropriate feedback during "Alertness," which detects discrepancies.

Although the discrepancy mechanism is evident across models, the problem-solving mechanism is not. The Jackson-Boag and Kanfer-Hagerman models rely upon subjects' self-evaluations and self-assessments to find and select behaviors to reduce discrepancies. The Jeffrey-Berger approach arranges antecedent events to solve problems; Corno and Mandinach propose "Planning" to select strategies

Figure 3.1
Models of Self-Regulation

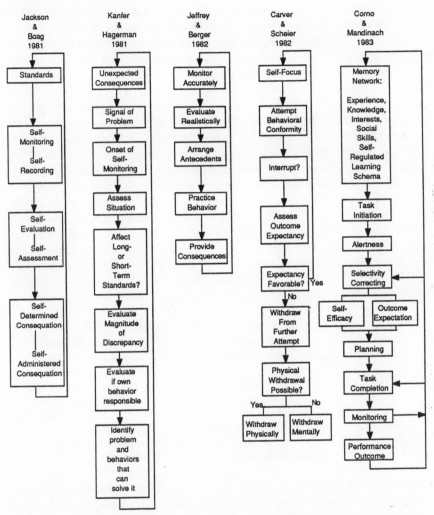

that will improve learning. The Carver-Scheier model does not address problem solving aside from the regulatory option of "Behavioral Conformity."

All models use one or more feedback loops to illustrate the locus of regulatory effect. Four of the models locate regulation at the end of the process, for example, when behavioral consequences feed back to initial phases. Carver and Scheier postulate that regulation follows an evaluation of results. The terminology for regulatory effects also varies. Carver-Scheier and Corno-Mandinach use feedback loops to describe systemic change, and the others use reinforcement.

The Corno-Mandinach model has several interactive components in the regulatory mechanism. The return arrows indicate feedback for "Task Completion," "Selectivity Correcting," and the "Memory Network." That model also features different feedback sources—one from task completion and one from results. These connections illustrate the interdependent nature of system components.

In spite of differences in detail, similarities between models are significant. All include discrepancies, choices, actions, and feedback—the essentials of self-regulation. At the same time, the models explain different phenomena. The Jackson and Boag model accounts for the efficacy of self-control for persons with mental retardation;[21] the Kanfer and Hagerman model is for persons suffering from depression;[22] the Jeffrey and Berger model explains the management of obesity;[23] Corno and Mandinach's model explains self-regulated learning;[24] and Carver and Scheier explain self-regulation in general.[25]

These differences notwithstanding, the models presume a common characteristic of self-regulation—that individuals strive for consistent and predictable relationships with environments. They want expectations to match observations. When there's a match, individuals maintain what they're doing. But when there's a discrepancy, they check to see if the deviation affects important needs and interests. If it does, then they regulate to adjust to the new circumstance. The results of these adjustments feed back to affect subsequent expectations. This process is similar to the homeostatic functions of the bio-physical system Judith Rodin described:

> To extend the homeostasis metaphor to a general principle of self-regulation, all such processes begin with motivation and commitment toward self-maintenance, which includes the establishment of essential goals. There must also be specific skills for monitoring and modifying relevant events on the basis of cues from multiple levels of information, including the internal and external environment. Also necessary is reinforcement for making these responses and a feedback process that actively checks for progress toward the goals. Whether we are talking about a visceral organ or the individual as a whole, self-regulation involves carrying out specific plans of action and using specific skills. In this way, the individual copes effectively with environmental and internally produced events.[26]

The object of regulation is to thrive as well as survive. Homeostatic functions define physiological surviving; self-regulatory functions describe *biopsychosocial* thriving—optimizing adjustments and maximizing gains. According to Rodin, self-regulation is a general "process [that] provides a theoretical continuity among all processes that involve the maintenance of the individual at the most optimal level possible."[27]

Self-Regulation Theory

The theory presented in this book provides that "theoretical continuity among all processes" to account for how individuals strive for and then maintain this "most optimal level of adjustment possible."[28] It combines problem solving with self-regulation to explain *self-regulated problem solving to meet a goal.* Self-regulation explains how problem solving starts and why solution following begins, maintains, and changes over time; problem solving explains how problems transform into options, and how options transform into solutions. In tandem, the two processes account for problem solving to meet a goal.

Another way of describing the relationship is through nested problem-solving loops. A given problem-solving episode is a single loop within the main problem-solving loop called self-regulation. The main problem for self-regulation is discrepancy reduction. Subsidiary problems nested within that problem require solutions to reduce that discrepancy. Three classes of behavior connect subsidiary problems within the structure of the self-regulating system: feedback seeking, choosing, and instrumental responding. *Feedback seeking* includes all behaviors whose frequencies are a function of the information they produce. *Choices* are responses that signal the behaviors that will follow. *Instrumental activity* comprises behaviors whose frequencies are a function of the task consequences they produce. These three behaviors occur continuously and concomitantly throughout self-regulation.

The Conceptual Model. Research on problem solving in humans is structurally similar to the self-regulation processes just described. According to Allen Newell and Herbert Simon, problem solving has three steps: (1) find the discrepancy between goal state and current state, (2) find an operator to reduce discrepancy, and (3) apply an operator and evaluate its effects on the discrepancy. Newell and Simon and their colleagues used these operations to program computers to find solutions to complex problems involved in chess,[29] memory, learning, physics, engineering, education, rule induction, concept formation, perception, and understanding.[30]

Although a given problem-solving sequence may appear complex, involving branched sequences of nested problem analyses as well as multitudes of loops within loops along main routes, only three operations accounted for solution finding. Simon described these operations for a computer program called the General Problem Solver (GPS):

A problem is defined for GPS by giving it a starting situation and a goal situation (or a test for determining whether the goal has been reached), together with a set of operators that may be used, separately or severally, to transform the starting situation into the goal situation by a sequence of successive applications. Means-ends analysis is the technique used by GPS to decide which operator to apply next:

1. It compares current situation with goal situation to detect one or more differences between them.
2. It retrieves from memory an operator that is associated with a difference it has found (i.e., an operator that has the usual effect of reducing differences of this kind).
3. It applies the operator or, if it is not applicable in the current situation, sets up the new goal of creating the conditions that will make it applicable.[31]

The GPS translated goal states into subunit problems recursively *until it found an operation it could perform*. Then it worked backwards until the final problem solution satisfied the goal. Newell and Simon illustrated this means-ends analysis with an everyday problem:

> I want to take my son to nursery school. What's the difference between what I have and what I want? One of distance. What changes distance? My automobile. My automobile won't work. What is needed to make it work? A new battery. What has new batteries? An auto repair shop. I want the repair shop to put in a new battery but the shop doesn't know I need one. What is the difficulty? One of communication. What allows communication? Telephone. . . . and so on.[32]

The outline that follows shows the connections between recursive means-ends problem solving and self-regulation. The goal is to get the child to nursery school. The operations regulated by Parent are means-ends analyses that end with an operation Parent can do now—telephone the repair shop. Although problem solving ends here, self-regulation continues. Instead of regulating problem analyses, Parent regulates actions to implement the solution: he calls the repair shop, explains the problem, and arranges for the repairman to deliver the battery and install it in the car. Actions, in turn, produce consequences requiring evaluations and adjustments. Steps 5 and 6 illustrate: the repairman shows up on time, installs the battery, and the car starts. As a consequence Parent drives his son to nursery school and meets the goal.

My Goal: Get my son to nursery school.
  1. *Problem*: How to reduce distance from home to nursery school.
     Solution: Use car to take son to nursery school.
  2. *Problem*: Car won't start, battery is dead.
     Solution: Get new battery to start car.
  3. *Problem*: Don't have new battery at home.
     Solution: Get new battery at repair shop.
  4. *Problem*: Repair shop doesn't know I need a new battery.
     Solution: Telephone repair shop to bring out new battery and
                 install it.
  5. *Action*: Telephoned repair shop.
     Consequence: Auto repairman came and installed new battery.
     Evaluation: Car will start now.
  6. *Action*: Drive son to nursery school.
     Consequence: Son is at nursery school.
     Evaluation: I have met my goal.

Like Simon and Newell's General Problem Solver, the human self-regulator (1) identifies discrepancies between goal states and current states, (2) finds a solution-behavior (operator) that reduces or eliminates the discrepancy, (3) implements the operator to reduce the discrepancy, (4) evaluates its effects, and

Figure 3.2
Self-Regulated Problem Solving to Meet a Goal

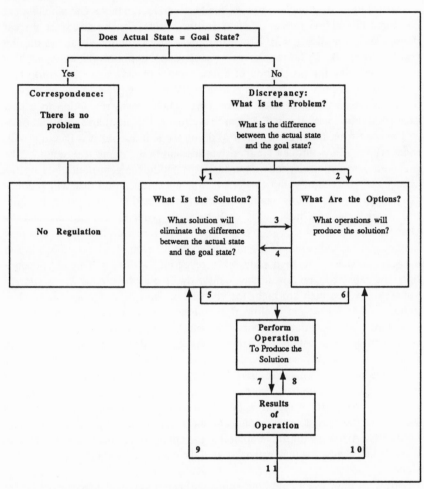

(5) repeats steps 2–4 until the goal is met. Steps 1–3 are identical to Simon's "find a discrepancy," "find an operator," and "apply the operator." Step 4 is another "find a discrepancy," and Step 5 is "find the operator" and "apply the operator."

Figure 3.2 illustrates self-regulated problem solving. The process begins when there is a discrepancy—the actual state does not equal the goal state. This precipitates the question: "What is the problem?" which is equivalent to Newell and Simon's "Find the discrepancy between goal state and current state." This affects the search for solutions by determining the requirements for goal attainment (causal arrow 1) and the discriminations necessary to identify operations that will meet those requirements (causal arrow 2).

One solution to getting son to preschool is to drive him there. But when Parent considers this option further ("What are the options?"), he discovers the car doesn't start (causal arrow 3). Now Parent must find a solution to car-not-starting (causal arrow 4). So he repeats the process and examines options again, this time considering the installation of a new battery (causal arrow 3 again). This option looks like it will work and is also one Parent can perform. So he decides to call a repairman to replace the battery, which moves regulation to a new phase—solution use. But will Parent make that call (causal arrows 5 and 6)?

The shift from finding a solution to doing the solution reflects Parent's willingness to "follow through" rather than his ability to "think it through." The probability of acting depends upon the expectation for gain multiplied by the chances of succeeding—the chances of finding an operation that will produce the expected gain. In this example, Parent's expectations for getting the child to nursery school are high because all he needs is for the car to start; and the chances of getting the car started are good, too, because all it needs is a new battery. This combination of high expectations for gain plus high probability of success translates into high probability of acting. *Willingness to act* depends upon the expected gain toward the goal (arrow 5) plus the *probability of success* (arrow 6). When both are high, the chances of follow-through are high; when either or both is low, the likelihood of follow-through is correspondingly low.

A third type of regulation occurs after solution implementation (arrow 7). The repairman arrives, installs the battery, and parent drives the child to nursery school. These are the consequences of doing the solution. They feed back to affect the next performance, choice, and expectation (arrows 8–11). Arrow 8 informs Parent that he has performed the operations necessary for the solution. He called the repairman and arranged for the battery installation. Arrow 9 informs Parent that he was able to implement the solution operation effectively and efficiently. Arrow 10 informs Parent that the choice of replacing the battery was a good one because the new battery started the car and the car has started reliably since.

Arrow 11 informs Parent of the ultimate effect of the regulatory episode. With battery installed and the car ready to go, Parent drove son to preschool, which made the actual state (child at preschool) equal the goal state (child at preschool). Now Parent "knows" what to expect when the problem arises again. This is his new baseline for deciding when and how to pursue similar goals in the future.

The Self-Instructional Model. The model in Figure 3.2 connected problem definitions and solution searches with choices, actions, and adjustments. In order to meet a goal, Parent coordinated thoughts and actions. The self-instructional model in Figure 3.3 illustrates ten questions that assist this coordination: (1) "Do I want or need something?" (2) "What's the difference between what I need or want and what I have?" (3) "What gain will reduce the difference between what I have and what I need or want?" (4) "What options will produce

Figure 3.3
Self-Instructions for Self-Regulation

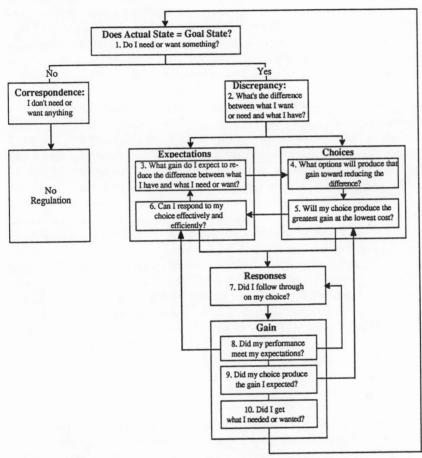

that gain toward reducing the difference?'' (5) ''Will my choice produce the greatest gain at the lowest cost?'' (6) ''Can I respond to my choice effectively and efficiently?'' (7) ''Did I follow through on my choice?'' (8) ''Did my performance meet my expectations?'' (9) ''Did my choice produce the gain I expected?'' and (10) ''Did I get what I needed or wanted?''

Note that self-regulated thinking *precedes* and *succeeds* self-regulated doing. The first two questions alert the regulator about discrepancy conditions and the need for regulatory responses. Questions 3–6 direct the regulator toward identifying actions that will produce results to decrease or eliminate the discrepancy. The seventh question reminds the regulator to take actions necessary to implement selection options. Questions 8–10 inform the regulator of the efficacy of the enterprise, which permits improved regulatory efforts next time.

Also evident in the figure is the *means-ends analysis* or recursive loop that occurs when the regulator searches for a solution and an operation that will produce it. Questions 3–6 illustrate the sequence: "What gain (solution) do I expect to reduce the difference between what I have and what I need or want?" which leads to "What options will produce that gain (solution) toward reducing the difference?" which leads to "Will my choice produce that gain toward reducing the difference?" which finally leads to "Can I respond to my choice effectively and efficiently?" Note that positive answers to the first three questions and a "No" on the fourth forces the regulator to repeat the process with a revised expectation for gain.

The Theoretical Model. Self-regulation theory postulates that the closer to optimal the self-regulation, the closer to maximum the gain toward goal attainment. It builds upon principles derived from models of homeostasis and cybernetics, which indicated that (1) goal-directed behavior occurs during conditions of discrepancy, (2) self-regulatory responses attempt to reduce discrepancies, and (3) persistent discrepancies establish new baselines. The theory postulates four propositions that describe how adjustments produce gains. Table 3.1 presents these assumptions and propositions.

The expectation proposition states that previous success (gain) and magnitude of the discrepancy will affect the optimality of expectations. The more success Person has experienced toward goal attainment (the closer to optimal the past gain) and the smaller the discrepancy between present state and goal state, then the more likely Person will expect the maximum gain possible from the options available.

Experience in producing gain toward goal attainment increases Person's capacity to judge what is possible under the circumstances (options). The size of the discrepancy affects Person's judgements, too. For example, the smaller the discrepancy, the more likely Person will find a gain (solution) that will either eliminate the difference or maximize its reduction. Conversely, as discrepancies between goal states and actual states increase, the probability of finding completely effective solutions decreases. Large discrepancy reductions frequently require multiple solutions with varying reduction effects. This makes it difficult to identify the option that produces the greatest incremental gain toward goal attainment. Arrows 1 and 9 in Figure 3.4 illustrate these effects on expectations for gain. Arrow 1 represents the effects of discrepancy size, and arrow 9 reflects the influence of past gain toward goal attainment.

The choice proposition specifies conditions under which Person chooses the operation that produces the greatest gain at the lowest cost. Again, there are two factors that influence optimal choosing. The first is experience or past gain toward the goal: the closer to optimal the past gain, the more likely Person will select the best operation to produce expected gain. The second factor is the difficulty of identifying important differences between options. The proposition states that the more salient the differences between options, then the more likely Person will choose optimally. During less than ideal choice circumstances where dif-

Table 3.1
The Theory of Self-Regulation

The closer to optimal the adjustment, the closer to maximum the gain toward goal attainment.

Assumptions

A. Goal-directed behavior is a function of the discrepancy between the goal state and the current state: the more frequent the discrepancy between expected and current states, the more frequent the self-regulatory behavior.

B. The closer the match between expected and current states as a consequence of self-regulatory behavior, the more likely similar self-regulatory behaviors will occur for discrepancies between similar expected and current states.

C. The more persistent the discrepancy between the expected and current state, the more likely the current state will become the expected state.

Propositions

I. The Expectation Proposition: The closer to optimal the past gain toward goal attainment and the smaller the discrepancy between the actual state and goal state, the closer to optimal the expectation for gain.

II. The Choice Proposition: The closer to optimal the past gain toward goal attainment and the more salient the differences between options, the closer to optimal the choice.

III. The Response Proposition: The closer to optimal the past gain, expectations, and choices, then the closer to optimal the distribution of responses between task completion to meet the goal and feedback about goal state-actual state discrepancies, options, task performance, and gain.

IV. The Gain Proposition: The closer to optimal the past gain, expectations, choices, and responses, then the closer to maximum the gain toward goal attainment.

ferences are subtle and options are many, discriminations are difficult and time consuming (costly). They reduce the likelihood of choosing optimally.

Arrows 2 and 10 in Figure 3.4 illustrate these effects. Arrow 2 reflects the effects of the choice contingency during a discrepancy condition. The contingency is the number and type of discriminations Person must make in order to identify the most profitable option. Arrow 10 reflects the effects of past gain toward goal attainment. When both factors are in favorable directions—easy discriminations and significant past gains—optimal choosing is likely.

The response proposition specifies the conditions under which Person maximizes responses to produce gain and minimizes responses that seek feedback. Arrows 5, 6, and 8 in Figure 3.4 illustrate these causal connections. Arrow 5 reflects the effects of expectation optimalities, arrow 6 reflects the effects of choice optimalities, and arrow 8 reflects the effects of past gain optimalities. Improvements in any of these conditions indicate the regulator's greater experience and understanding of what causes what. This leads to more effective and efficient distribution of responses. Person spends less time and effort monitoring performance accuracy, goal state-actual state discrepancies, options, and results

Figure 3.4
Model of Self-Regulation Theory

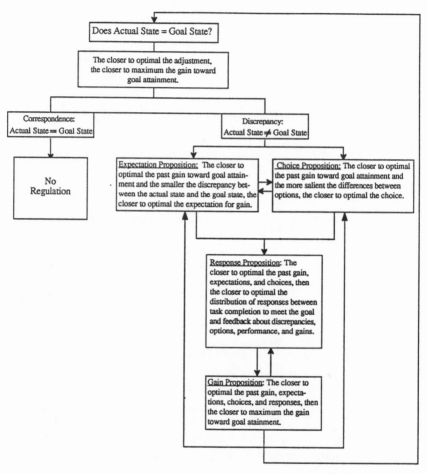

and more time and effort performing the operations necessary to produce gain toward goal attainment.

The gain proposition describes the effects of adjustment optimalities on gain toward the goal. The proposition states that as past gains, expectations, choices, and responses approach maximum optimalities, gain toward reducing the discrepancy between the actual state and goal state maximizes, too. The upper limit—maximum gain—occurs when (1) past gain equals expected gain, (2) expectations for gain equal the maximum possible from the options available, (3) choices produce the greatest gain at the lowest cost, and (4) resource allocations maximize responding to produce gain and minimize feedback seeking on goal states, choices, performances, and gains.

Arrows 7 and 11 illustrate these effects. Arrow 7 reflects the cumulative optimality effects of past gain, expectations, choices, and performances, and arrow 11 reflects the effects of these optimality adjustments on gain toward goal attainment.

In summary, self-regulation theory states that we maximize progress toward goals when (1) past gains match expectations, (2) present expectations are the maximum possible, (3) choices are the best possible, and (4) follow-through on choice is as effective and efficient as possible. Under these conditions, regulation is optimal and return from the environment is maximal.

The next three chapters describe the meaning and significance of optimal adjustments and maximum gain. Chapter 4 describes how the expectation and choice propositions explain self-regulatory thinking; Chapter 5 describes how the choice and response propositions explain self-regulated doing; and Chapter 6 demonstrates how the gain proposition explains adaptive fits with environmental contingencies. The last two chapters use self-regulation theory to explain two variants of self-regulated behavior: self-determination and innovation.

Notes

1. Max Perutz (1986), quoted in William H. Calvin, *The Cerebral Symphony: Seashore Reflections on the Structure of Consciousness* (New York: Bantam Books, 1990), 31.

2. Calvin, *The Cerebral Symphony*, 32.

3. Claude Bernard, quoted in Richard W. Jones, *Principles of Biological Regulation* (New York: Academic Press, 1973), 4.

4. Walter Bradford Cannon, *The Wisdom of the Body* (New York: Norton, 1932).

5. Frederick M. Toates, *Animal Behaviour—A Systems Approach* (New York: John Wiley & Sons, 1980).

6. Ibid., 194–195.

7. John Dewey, *How We Think* (Boston, MA: D. C. Health and Company, 1933), 12.

8. Ibid.

9. Leonard Kristal, *The ABC of Psychology* (New York: Facts on File Publications, 1982), 111.

10. Norbert Wiener, *Cybernetics* (New York: John Wiley, 1948).

11. W. Ross Ashby, *Design for a Brain: The Origin of Adaptive Behaviour* (New York: John Wiley & Sons, 1960).

12. Ibid., 83.

13. Ibid., 84.

14. George A. Miller, Eugene Galanter, and Karl H. Pribram, *Plans and the Structure of Behavior* (New York: Holt, Rinehart and Winston, 1960), 25–26.

15. Ibid., 30.

16. J. Annett, *Feedback and Human Behavior* (Baltimore: Penguin Books, 1969).

17. William T. Powers, *Behavior: The Control of Perception* (Chicago: Aldine Publishing, 1973), 47–48.

18. Ibid., 48.

19. Ibid.

20. Fritjof Capra, *Uncommon Wisdom: Conversations with Remarkable People* (New York: Bantam Books, 1989), 203–204.

21. Henry J. Jackson and Paul G. Boag, "The Efficacy of Self-Control Procedures as Motivational Strategies with Mentally Retarded Persons: A Review of the Literature and Guidelines for Future Research," *Australian Journal of Developmental Disabilities* 7 (1981): 65–79.

22. Frederick H. Kanfer and Susan Hagerman, "The Role of Self-Regulation," in L. P. Rehm (Ed.), *Behavior Therapy for Depression: Present Status and Future Directions* (New York: Academic Press, 1981), 143–179.

23. D. Balfour Jeffrey and Laurence H. Berger, "A Self-Environmental Systems Model and Its Implications for Behavior Change," in Kirk R. Blankstein and Janet Polivy (Eds.), *Advances in the Study of Communication and Affect, Volume 7: Self-Control and Self-Modification of Emotional Behavior* (New York: Plenum Press, 1982), 29–69.

24. Lyn Corno and E. B. Mandinach, "The Role of Cognitive Engagement in Classroom Learning and Motivation," *Educational Psychologist* 18 (1983): 88–108.

25. Charles S. Carver and Michael F. Scheier, "An Information Processing Perspective on Self-Management," in P. Karoly and F. H. Kanfer (Eds.), *Self-Management and Behavior Change: From Theory to Practice* (New York: Pergamon Press, 1983), 93–128.

26. Judith Rodin, "Biopsychosocial Aspects of Self-Management," in Karoly and Kanfer (Eds.), *Self-Management and Behavior Change,* 65.

27. Ibid.

28. Ibid.

29. Allen Newell and Herbert A. Simon, *Human Problem Solving* (Englewood Cliffs, NJ: Prentice-Hall, 1972), 661–784.

30. Herbert A. Simon, *Models of Thought* (New Haven: Yale University Press, 1989).

31. Ibid., 36.

32. Newell and Simon, *Human Problem Solving*, 416.

Chapter 4

Self-Regulated Thinking

For centuries philosophers had us believe the raison d'être for thinking was to induce the ideal and deduce the real. From Plato's ideal forms in 350 B.C. and Immanuel Kant's 1781 *Critique of Pure Reason* to Alfred North Whitehead's *The Concept of Nature* in 1920, searches for fundamental order and logic in knowledge and truth characterized contemporary thinking about thinking. Plato developed the doctrine of archetypal ideals, the keystone of true reality. Individual experiences were fleeting, evanescent, and transitory rather than true and ideal. Ideas were real and eternal, unchangeable entities that escaped constraints of time and space. Plato's deification of idea and ideal influenced Greek thinkers like Aristotle, Roman philosophers, fathers of the Christian Church, scholastics of the Middle Ages and Renaissance, and even some nineteenth-century German philosophers.

By the eighteenth century, Immanuel Kant had classified thought into the analytic and the synthetic. Analytic thinking was propositional, expressing truth through statements like "Cold water is water," which depended upon equivalence between subject and predicate (both contained "water"). Synthetic thinking, by contrast, was not self-evident. Verification that "The water is cold" required touching it or taking its temperature. Kant subdivided analytic and synthetic into empirical and a priori. Empirical knowing required direct contact with environments through sense perception (checking water to see if it was cold); a priori knowledge was possible through pure thought ("two plus two equals four"). The resulting four-fold epistemological system—empirical-analytical, empirical-synthetic, analytical–a priori, and synthetic–a priori—led Kant in *Critique of Pure Reason* to discover synthetic–a priori judgements, which were later to provide the philosophical foundation for transcendentalism. According to this view, all objects in the material world are unknowable, nonexistent entities perceived through sensations in the form of intuitions. A priori concepts organize thinking about these intuitions into categories of quantity, quality, relation, and modality.

Pursuit of the ideal continued into the twentieth century. In *The Concept of Nature*, Alfred North Whitehead resurrected Platonic idealism and infused it with scientific thinking. Whitehead was a British mathematician and philosopher who made lasting contributions to theoretical mathematics in his three-volume *Principia Mathematica* (co-authored with his student and fellow mathematician-philosopher Bertrand Russell). By postulating that the living processes that constitute our experience were eternities in God's cosmic order, Whitehead reconciled Plato's theory of ideas with mechanistic descriptions of nature.

Why We Think

For more than two thousand years, rationalism and idealism defined thinking about thinking. It is not surprising that a renaissance, an industrial revolution, and an emergence of the scientific method were necessary for new modes to emerge. Darwin's theory of evolution was one of several triggers that encouraged alternative philosophic views. In the same year that Darwin published *On the Origin of Species by Natural Selection*, Karl Marx published *Critique of Political Economy* before teaming with Friedrich Engels to transform Hegel's dialectical logic into dialectical materialism—the revolutionary ideology of communism. At about the same time, Herbert Spencer formulated a "survival of the fittest" philosophy of social progress, and German philosopher Friedrich Wilhelm Nietzsche returned to the primal and natural with his will to power, which he claimed was an expression of cosmic will.

Amidst this exploding array of challenges to sacred world views, Charles Sanders Pierce introduced pragmatism in *How to Make Our Ideas Clear*, which was published in 1878. He argued that the value of a concept depended upon its capacity to predict events verifiable through experience. Twenty years later, William James discovered Pierce's new philosophy and used it in his address before Professor Howison's Philosophical Union at the University of California in 1898. James described his discovery as follows: "Mr Pierce, after pointing out that our beliefs are really rules for action, said that, to develop a thought's meaning, we need only determine what conduct it is fitted to produce: that conduct is for us its sole significance. . . . To attain perfect clearness in our thoughts of an object, then, we need only consider what conceivable effects of a practical kind the object may involve—what sensations we are to expect from it, and what reactions we must prepare."[1]

Pragmatism became a dominant force in philosophical thinking through the twentieth century, probably because of its efficacious dispensing of ancient philosophical disputes that were too esoteric for average thinking and too distant for daily living. Shrouded in layers of idealism and transcendent purity, philosophers of past ages freely justified everything but verified nothing. Truth and meaning were cosmic; life and living were cosmetic.

The pragmatist's principle reversed all this, stating that there was no difference that didn't make a difference. Rather than searching for first causes, supreme principles, and divine ideals, pragmatists verified logical conclusions by examining tangible consequences. Philosophic purpose was to connect thinking with what it produced in the material world, not what it abstracted in an ideal one. This operational imperative asked what difference an idea made. If it made none, then we were to abandon it. The principle demanded we seek answers only to questions that counted.

The idea was not entirely new. As James pointed out, Socrates and Aristotle used it occasionally, as did John Locke (1632–1704), George Berkeley, Jr. (1685–1753), and David Hume (1711–1776). But James used it universally. Pragmatism was no add-on to a battery of intellectual tricks. It was replacement thinking for philosophic obscurantism: "The pragmatist turns his back resolutely and once and for all upon a lot of inveterate habits dear to professional philosophers. He turns away from abstraction and insufficiency, from verbal solutions, from bad a priori reasons, from fixed principles, closed systems, and pretended absolutes and origins. He turns towards concreteness and adequacy, towards facts, towards action and towards power."[2]

Pragmatism demanded commitment to a method of thought rather than allegiance to a theory of cause. All ideals, metaphysical beliefs, and postulated cosmic structures bowed to the common test—the cash-in value of differences discovered. Pragmatic thinking was hard and unremitting work, however. After all, the shelf-life of new ideas was their capacity to deliver verifiable differences in the material world.

Finally, after 2.5 million years of trial-and-error thinking and nearly two thousand years of thinking about that trial-and-error thinking, a handful of philosophers concluded that the closer the match between thinking and observing, the more valid the thought and the more useful the observation. Pragmatics combined empiricism and rationalism in thought-operations that clarified rather than mystified and concretized rather than idealized. Intellectual barriers separating philosopher kings and artisan subjects disappeared. The reason for thinking was the same for all—to verify what's known and to know what's verified. Hypotheses, principles, and theories were true only if they predicted that observable, verifiable difference.

Types of Thinking

The theory of knowledge buttressing pragmatism was the notion that thinking on purpose meant connecting environmental events (stimuli) with adaptive reactions (responses). Experience with previous environmental events—which James called knowledge—improved these connections. As John Dewey explained, "Knowledge is nothing more nor less than the mediating process which

66

occurs between the stimulus and the organism's response to it; its function is to determine the response appropriate to the stimulus. Knowledge is the selection of a response that can adequately cope with the stimulus. It is not independent of, but is intimately involved with both stimulus and response."[3]

Dewey said that this simple truth gets lost the more knowledge we accumulate:

> Man has garnered so much knowledge from the innumerable stimulus-response activities in his experience that he has fallen into the trap of assuming that knowledge has value in and of itself. But as a matter of actual fact, *we can gain knowledge only by controlling the stimulus on the one hand and by selecting our response on the other*. The importance of knowledge conceived thus as a mediating process lies in the fact that it "slows down" both the stimulus and the response, *so the organism can take time to plan*. [italics added][4]

Unfortunately, slowing down the effects of stimuli is difficult. It is easier to respond impulsively to incoming information than it is to pause, reflect, and choose optimally. Dewey identified four types of thinking—thought streaming, scenario thinking, belief thinking, and reflective thinking—to explain different levels of regulated thought. Thought streaming was unregulated thinking—a function of brain mechanisms that produce unordered, purposeless idea sequences. It was the mind's natural condition, a baseline of mental activity that occurred in the absence of regulation. Dewey explained:

> All the time we are awake and sometimes when we are asleep, something is, as we say, going through our heads. When we are asleep we call that kind of sequence "dreaming." We also have daydreams, reveries, castles built in the air, and mental streams that are even more idle and chaotic. To this uncontrolled coursing of ideas through our heads the name of "thinking" is sometimes given. *It is automatic and unregulated*. Many a child has attempted to see whether he could not "stop thinking"—that is, stop this procession of mental states through his mind—and in vain. More of our waking life than most of us would care to admit is whiled away in this inconsequential trifling with mental pictures, random recollections, pleasant but unfounded hopes, flitting, half-developed impressions. [italics added][5]

Everyone thinks, at least in this sense. But Dewey worried: "he who offers 'a penny for your thoughts' does not expect to drive any great bargain if his offer is taken."[6] What a penny buys may be that most recent random thought.

Reflective thinking, by contrast, is regulated, ordered, and purposeful. Its only similarity with thought streaming is that it too comes in sequences of connected thoughts. Unlike streaming, reflective thinking follows rules that determine order. The first thought signals the second, the second makes way for the third, and so on in an inexorable progression toward an end or conclusion: "Reflection involves not simply a sequence of ideas, but *con*-sequence—a consecutive ordering in such a way that each determines the next as its proper outcome, while each outcome in turn leans back on, or refers to, its predecessors. The successive portions of a reflective thought grow out of one another and support one another; they do not come and go in a medley.''[7]

Between these two extremes—thought streaming and reflective thinking—lie the less disciplined modes of regulated thought Dewey called scenario thinking and belief thinking. Scenario thinking includes fantasies, stories, and imagined sequences of logically connected events that make sense but have no purpose or direction. They are, in Dewey's words, ''successions of imaginative incidents and episodes that have a certain coherence, hang together on a continuous thread, and thus lie between kaleidoscopic flights of fancy [as in thought streaming] and considerations deliberately employed to establish a conclusion.''[8] Children pour forth internally coherent and logical stories and fantasies that have no purpose other than self-amusement.

Reflective thinking is more than a scenario. It is logically sequenced with direction and purpose. Like a train, it goes somewhere—to a conclusion not evident from any single idea considered alone. The purpose determines the selection and ordering within the sequence. Change the purpose and you change the selecting and the ordering. Scenario thinking has no such constraints. It may start from any point and end at any other point. Its only rule is to make sense during the progression from one idea to another within the sequence. Idea scenarios evolve according to their own antecedents and their own consequences, while reflective ideas fit within the parameters defined by the purpose. Reflective thinking has ''a goal to be reached, and this end sets a task that controls the sequence of ideas.''[9]

Belief thinking—Dewey's third type—also has order and purpose. It answers questions, satisfies curiosity, and assuages worry. Aristotle used it in the syllogism to postulate a static, ordered universe. Through logically sequenced statements deduced from their antecedents, the syllogism produces conclusions not evident from individual statements. Examples 1 and 2 illustrate. The first argues for the existence of God based upon logic from the first premise and definition of God from the second. In the second example we conclude that Socrates is mortal, given the premises that all humans are mortal and that Socrates is human.

Both syllogisms are logical and they both have purpose and a conclusion. But only one fulfills the third criterion of reflective thinking—verifiability. Aristotle's claim that Socrates is mortal is verifiable, which validates the sequence. Not so for Example 1. The conclusion that God exists is not verifiable independent of its premise. Accepting the premise compels acceptance of the conclusion.

Example 1: Characteristics of God
        1. All things contained in the concept of X can be truly affirmed of X.
        2. Necessary existence is contained in the concept of God.
        3. Therefore, God exists.
Example 2: Characteristics of Humans
        1. All humans are mortal.

        2. Socrates is human.

        3. Therefore, Socrates is mortal.

Example 3: Pre-Columbian Theory of Earth's Shape

        1. The earth is flat.

        2. Flat surfaces have edges.

        3. Therefore, if you travel in one direction far enough, you will fall
           off the edge of the earth.

Example 3 has a verifiable conclusion. It is also more interesting than Examples 1 or 2. During pre-Columbian years, sailors looked across the sea, saw nothing, and concluded the earth was flat. Consequently, they believed that if you traveled too far in one direction you would come to the edge and fall off. The premise that the world was flat implied a verifiable conclusion. When Columbus returned from his journey, he reported new lands rather than the earth's edge.

Columbus's starting premise was that the world was round (Example 4). Therefore, by sailing west he would eventually reach China (east of his starting point). Twenty years after Columbus discovered the Americas, Ferdinand Magellan verified the premise by circumnavigating the world.

Example 4: Columbian Theory of Earth's Shape

        1. The earth is round.

        2. Round surfaces have circumferences.

        3. Therefore, if you follow the circumference,
           you will end where you started.

People who engaged in Example 3 thinking were not reflective thinkers because they never tested their conclusions. Columbus was different, as Dewey explained:

> Because Columbus did not accept unhesitatingly the current traditional theory, because he doubted and inquired, he arrived at his thought. Skeptical of what, from long habit, seemed most certain, and credulous of what seemed impossible, he went on thinking until he could produce evidence for both his confidence and his disbelief. Even if his conclusion had finally turned out wrong, it would have been a different sort of belief from those it antagonized, because it was reached by different method. *Active, persistent, and careful consideration of any belief or supposed form of knowledge in the light of the groups that support it and the further conclusion to which it tends* constitutes reflective thought. Any one of the first three kinds of thought may elicit this type; but once begun, it concludes a conscious and voluntary effort to establish belief upon a firm basis of evidence and rationality.[10]

Reasons for Thinking

Dewey gave us several explanations for why we think. First, thinking is what brains do. Ideas and images course through our heads whether we want them to or not. Left to their own, unfocused and unregulated, they take action. James and Dewey called this the stream of consciousness, and William Faulkner (1897–1962), one of America's greatest novelists, wrote page-long convoluted sentences depicting its nature. Recently, neuroscientists have described it, too. In *The Cerebral Symphony,* William Calvin posited a neurological basis for the stream. He said that the natural state of cerebral affairs is spontaneous neural firing. But sometimes these firings occur in patterns or chains that—through a self-selective mechanism Calvin called the Darwin Machine—shape themselves into coherent sequences, logical patterns, and plans for action.[11]

A second reason for thinking is because it is reinforcing. Stories, fantasies, imaginings are enjoyable. The number of hours spent watching television, going to movies, and reading fiction attests to their value. Although there may be moral principles or lessons that accompany reverie, its purpose is entertainment. It provides temporary relief from reflective thought, which refreshes the thinker for concentrated reflection later.

A third reason for thinking is to deduce from experience those conclusions that optimize choosing and doing next time. For years, conventional wisdom dubbed sailing the Atlantic hazardous and westward landings via sea impossible. Given a flat earth and westward edge, prudent seamen sailed east. Logic recommended it. Such is the nature of analysis from givens.

Reflective thinking breaks through internally consistent logic systems by assessing the validity of premises in light of alternative hypotheses and evidence. Reflection demands demonstrations and tests to verify premises and conclusions. The regulated thinker contrasts expectations for a hypothesized course of events with observations of an actual course of events and then checks for accuracy. Analysis defines expectations and inquiry tests them. Dewey explained:

> The earlier thought, belief in the flatness of the earth, had some foundation in evidence; it rested upon what men could see easily within the limits of their vision. But this evidence was not further looked into; it was not checked by considering other evidence; *there was no search for new evidence.* Ultimately the belief rested on laziness, inertia, custom, absence of courage and energy in investigation. The later belief rests upon careful and extensive study, upon purposeful widening of the area of observation, upon reasoning out the conclusions of alternative conceptions to see what would follow in case one or the other were adopted for belief. As distinct from the first kind of thinking [thought streaming], there was an orderly chain of ideas; as distinct from the second [scenario thinking], there was a controlling purpose and end; as distinct from the third [belief thinking], there was personal examination, scrutiny, inquiry.[italics added][12]

Regulated thinking optimizes adjustment and maximizes gain through "active, persistent, and careful" search for new evidence. It positions inquiry outside the parameters defined by existing analytic structures and belief systems. It permits development of new understanding about what works and what doesn't, what optimizes and what doesn't. While other thought forms contribute to the

Table 4.1
Summary of Dewey's Four Types of Thinking

Types of Thinking	Sequence of Ideas	Sequence of Ordered Ideas	Purposeful Sequence of Ordered Ideas	Verified, Purposeful Sequence of Ordered Ideas
Thought Streaming	Yes	No	No	No
Scenario Thinking	Yes	Yes	No	No
Belief Thinking	Yes	Yes	Yes	No
Reflective Thinking	Yes	Yes	Yes	Yes

development of reflective thinking, they fail to deliver optimal choice for maximized gain. Table 4.1 summarizes their relation to self-regulated thought.

Why We Regulate Thinking

Left undisturbed by physiological need and environmental stimuli, we spend much of our time thought streaming, scenario thinking, and belief thinking. With our minds on automatic pilot, we routinely process information effectively and efficiently, which frees us to dream aimlessly, spin tales freely, and develop beliefs independently of consequences. But immunity from real-world events is short-lived. Intruding messages contradict expectations and alert us to difficulties. They command our attention and channel our thinking. We must consider them, albeit reluctantly.

Consider Mary's experience with intrusion. Every morning, she drives to work following the same route at the same hour in the same traffic. The routine is automatic. She enjoys the opportunity to let her mind wander. Suddenly there's a horn blast, screeching tires, and a crash. She looks ahead and sees the lane blocked with some cars rear-ending others. Mary steps on the brake and stops in time. All traffic comes to a halt. She looks at her watch and realizes she'll be late to an important meeting. So she checks side streets, sees one, and takes an alternative route. The episode lasts forty-five seconds but seems longer. Mary just took charge of her thinking.

We take charge when environmental signals alert us to the unexpected. In Mary's situation, unexpected events signaled an impending problem. The first signal indicated the possibility of hitting another car, which prompted her to step on the brake. The second indicated a possible delay in getting to work, which motivated her to find an alternative route. Both signals focused attention on an event, stimulated assessment of its significance, and then generated searches for alternative responses.

Mary's experience illustrates the cause and purpose of self-regulated thinking: detecting the unexpected and searching for solutions to deal with it. Dewey said that "*reflective thinking* . . . involves (1) a state of doubt, hesitation, perplexity, mental difficulty, in which thinking originates, and (2) an act of searching, hunting, inquiring, to find material that will resolve the doubt, settle and dispose of the perplexity."[13] His traveler illustrates:

> A man traveling in an unfamiliar region comes to a branching of the road. Having no sure knowledge to fall back upon, he is brought to a standstill of hesitation and suspense. Which road is right? And how shall his perplexity be resolved? There are but two alternatives: he must either blindly and arbitrarily take his course, trusting to luck for the outcome, or he must discover grounds for the conclusion that a given road is right. Any attempt to decide the matter by thinking will involve inquiring into other facts, whether brought to mind by memory, or by further observation, or by both. The perplexed wayfarer must carefully scrutinize what is before him and he must cudgel his memory. He looks for evidence that will support belief in favor of either of the roads—for evidence that will weigh down one suggestion. He may climb a tree; he may go first in this direction, then in that, looking, in either case, for signs, clues, indications. He wants something in the nature of a signboard or a map, and *his reflection is aimed at the discovery of facts that will serve this purpose.*[14]

Discrepancies between expectations (a sign indicating what road to take) and observations (two roads leading to unknown destinations) generated feedback seeking (memory searches, climbing a tree for a better view, short trips down one road and then the other). The man searched for clues indicating which road leads to his destination. The discrepancy motivated reflective thinking, which in turn stimulated feedback seeking. According to Dewey, "*Demand for the solution of a perplexity is the steadying and guiding factor in the entire process of reflection.* Where there is no question of a problem to be solved or a difficulty to be surmounted, the course of suggestions flows on at random; we have the first type of thought described."[15]

Discrepancies

Dewey's analysis of reflective thought uncovered cognitive phenomena psychologists have tried to explain for decades: humans strive for consistency between expectations and observations. In 1932 Edward Chase Tolman, a contemporary of Dewey's, published *Purposive Behavior in Animals and Men*; the book attempted to explain how expectations account for learning and performance in animals and humans. Tolman's stimulus-response learning theory accounted for the behavior of laboratory animals by examining relationships between goals and expectations. When need for food was great and expectations to satisfy it were consistent with environmental conditions, adjustments were optimal and gains maximal. However, when experimental changes required alternative routes to goals, rats searched for more efficient routes. In time, they again optimized their adjustments and maximized their gains, as Thomas Tighe explains:

> For example, when a hungry rat is placed in a maze, it engages in trial-and-error path selection . . . until the goal and food are finally reached. . . . Should the true maze path be altered at the point or should obstacles be inserted on the true path, the path taking will be observed to persist while the particulars of behavior change to meet the new situational demands.
>
> *The purposive character of behavior is further attested to by the fact that acts conform to the most direct route to a goal.* [italics added][16]

Even when altered routes were slightly longer or more difficult, the rats discerned those differences and optimized by finding the shortest route. Tolman's explanations for optimal adjustment included the notions of *purpose* and *expectation*. When optimal routes suddenly became less so—when they didn't meet the animal's expectations—behaviors changed. The animal explored alternatives until it found the optimal approach to its food goal.

Purpose is an anticipated goal state that stimulates feedback seeking for conditions that will produce that state. When it is hungry, the laboratory rat searches for information that points to food; when it is thirsty, information about water controls the search. When there is no physiological need, unusual environmental cues prompt exploratory searches. Tighe illustrates with this description of a moderately hungry rat in a novel environment: "During this phase the rat may pay little or no attention to relatively familiar features of the environment; it is not uncommon to observe a hungry subject totally ignore the food in the goal box while continuing investigation of the surround. As the rat becomes familiar with the maze . . . there is a corresponding shift in attention. . . . Task-extraneous features of the maze are not totally ignored and 'food-searching' behavior emerges."[17] Expectations and results interact to determine feedback seeking, choosing, and instrumental responding. When expectations equal results, no change in these behaviors is likely. Everything works as planned and the system functions as before. However, when expectations and results don't match— when there is a discrepancy—feedback seeking increases. The organism searches for that optimal choice to reduce the discrepancy through instrumental responding.

In the 1940s Fritz Heider introduced balance theory to explain the effects of these cognitive discrepancies.[18] His underlying premise was that cognitions, like homeostatic physiological states, tend toward stability and balance. For example, when you perceive person X as positive and evaluate her actions as positive, cognitions are balanced and there is no strain. Imbalance occurs when person X engages in negative actions. You can reduce the strain-induced imbalance by changing your evaluation of person X or your evaluation of her actions. Heider applied this analysis to dyads and triads in various combinations of persons, objects, and events by positing the following relationships:

- If no balanced state exists, then forces toward this state will arise.
- A dyad is balanced if the relations between the two entities are all positive or all negative.
- Disharmony results when relations of different sign character exist.
- A triad is balanced when all three of the relations are positive or when two of the relations are negative and one is positive.[19]

Leon Festinger's theory of cognitive dissonance also postulated balance: "Two elements are in dissonant relation if, considering these two alone, the obverse of one element would follow from the other. To state it a bit more formally, x and y are dissonant if not-x follows from not-y."[20] Propositions describing the effects of cognitive discrepancies include the following:

1. Cognitive dissonance (discrepancy) is a noxious state.
2. Individuals strive to reduce dissonance and to avoid events that increase it.
3. Individuals strive to maintain consonance (consistency) and to avoid events that decrease consonance.
4. Dissonance increases with the importance of the cognitions involved and with the number of cognitions creating the dissonance.
5. As dissonance increases, individuals engage in behaviors described in propositions 2 and 3.
6. Individuals reduce or eliminate dissonance by adding new cognitions or changing existing ones.
7. Adding new cognitions reduces dissonance when the new cognitions decrease the proportion of dissonant cognitive elements or when they alter the importance of those dissonant elements.
8. Changing existing cognitions reduces dissonance when new content increases their match with other cognitive elements or when new content reduces the importance of dissonant cognitions.
9. If internal cognitive change is not possible—by altering existing cognitions or adding new ones—information seeking behaviors that change dissonant cognitions to consonant cognitions will increase.[21]

In summary, discrepancies between observations and expectations generate cognitive dissonance; dissonance motivates action for its reduction. Individuals change cognitions internally by altering expectations to match observations or by devaluing the importance of the discrepancy. They also change cognitions externally by seeking out information that supports their expectations or that suggests ideas consonant with ones causing the dissonance. According to Hazel Markus and R. B. Zajonc, "It follows from the basic assumptions of dissonance theory that the individual will seek information that reduces dissonance and avoid information that increases or maintains it."[22] Robert Wicklund and Jack Brehm agree: "Festinger's original argument assumed the operation of a selective exposure process whereby information that increased consonant elements or decreased dissonant elements would be sought out. It was also assumed that dissonance-increasing information would be shunned. He divided the selective processes into approach and avoidance elements, and the accumulated evidence makes a case primarily for the approach segment of selectivity."[23]

Individuals search for information that increases consonance and reduces dissonance. In other words, *discrepancies between expectations and observations motivate feedback seeking*.

Feedback

During solution searches, problem solvers scan environments for signs indicating what behaviors will produce desired consequences. They also look for cues that their search is getting "warmer"—that the distance between the present state and the solution state is getting shorter. In the game "Twenty Questions," players ask a series of successively limiting questions—is it animal, vegetable, or mineral? If it's animal, is it human? If it's human, is it old, living, or dead? Each question generates information about where to search next. Feedback responses are a function of the information sought. Questions about humans increase; questions about animals decrease. The information trail of the feedback seeker documents the thinking of the problem solver. What information does she ask to see? What effort does she exert to get it? How long does she spend examining it? Similarly, with "Twenty Questions" the answer-giver follows the progress and thinking of players by noting the type and sequence of questions asked.

Information-processing research uses a similar procedure. It tracks the thinking of the problem solvers by monitoring the types of feedback seeking exhibited. Allen Newell and Herbert Simon, who pioneered this approach, postulated that problem-solving behaviors (which include feedback seeking, choosing, and task responding) are a function of the "task environment (plus the intelligence of the problem solver)," which determines "to a large extent the behavior of the problem solver, independently of the detailed internal structure of his information processing system."[24]

This research has yielded innovative measurement methodologies, including verbal protocols—written records collected as subjects "thought aloud" during problem solving—and recorded eye movements to detect types of information subjects examine when making decisions.[25] The most promising has been the *process-tracing method*, which structures information that subjects physically seek out in order to use. J. Kevin Ford and his colleagues reviewed forty-five studies using this method and found that as task complexity increases (increasing the number of alternatives, dimensions, or both alternatives and dimensions), the rules governing the search become less complex.[26] Task complexity also affects the depth, variability, and speed of the search. As task options increase, single-dimension searches for information decrease, searches across alternatives increase, and time spent searching increases. In other words, the more costly the search, the more likely the solver will choose suboptimally (which is consistent with the Choice Proposition).

Researchers have even tried to classify different types of feedback seeking. H. Mintzberg and colleagues contrasted internal and external feedback seeking with passive searches (waiting for information to come in) at one end and active searches at the other. These latter included the trap search (sending out signals to attract the needed information) and the active search (directly seeking alternatives).[27] For all searches, however, *problem solvers use the least expensive method to gain the minimal information necessary to decide*.

Irving Janis and Leon Mann identified seven criteria to evaluate vigilant decision making: (1) thoroughly canvassing a wide range of alternatives; (2) surveying the full range of objectives to be fulfilled and values to be implicated by the choice; (3) carefully weighing the positive and negative consequences of each alternative; (4) intensely searching for new information and evaluating alternatives; (5) correctly assimilating new information; (6) reexamining positive and negative consequences of alternatives; and (7) carefully planning the implementation of chosen alternatives.[28] Criteria 1, 2, an 4 involve feedback seeking; criteria 3, 5, and 6 require analysis of the information it produces. According to the theory, decisionmakers adhering to all seven criteria choose optimally.

Many, of course, do not choose optimally. Some fail because they are impulsive. They choose before they have obtained information on all options. Research on impulsive and reflective children indicates that in uncertain situations, reflective children take more time to respond than impulsive children. Reflective children also gather more information on alternatives. Consequently, they make fewer errors.[29] Rational choosing is teachable and learnable, however. When impulsive children observe reflective children who use scanning strategies before choosing, they too become reflective.[30] Similar training improves the feedback seeking and reflective thinking in emotionally disturbed children[31] and impulsive, inner-city children.[32]

Children with emotional or behavioral problems are not the only ones needing assistance, however. Raymond Nickerson[33] reported studies demonstrating that when high school, college, and graduate school students try to explain situations or generate plans of action, they fail to explore possibilities adequately.[34] One explanation given for their inadequate reasoning is *insufficient feedback seeking*.[35]

This has led to the development of teaching materials and strategies that prompt students to conduct internal and external searches more effectively and efficiently. For example, Robert Vallet's program teaches students with learning disabilities "constructive critical thinking" by requiring them to (1) clarify goals and objectives before beginning important tasks, (2) know where and how to obtain information (external feedback seeking), (3) identify major problems, (4) ask key questions concerning what they are trying to accomplish (internal feedback seeking), (5) carefully analyze data, (6) predict consequences of alternative courses of action, (7) develop a plan for solving the problem, (8) rehearse and practice solutions, (9) evaluate effectiveness of actions (external feedback seeking), and (10) correct errors and reward themselves for progress.[36]

This is probably a good strategy, because Barry Zimmerman and Manuel Pons found that feedback seeking was central to self-regulated learning.[37] Following a comprehensive review of research on metacognition, the authors identified fifteen of the most important self-directed learning strategies. These strategies comprised items in a questionnaire given to high- and low-achieving high school sophomores in a middle-class suburban community. The authors wanted to know which self-directed behaviors discriminated between the two groups. They found that the most discriminating behavior was "seeking information," with a standardized discriminant function coefficient of .58. The next closest was "keeping records and monitoring" at .43, followed by "organizing and transforming [information]" at .42, "goal-setting and planning" at .41, and "rehearsing and memorizing" also at .41.

Differential feedback seeking also explains unexpected findings in operant research on matching. R. J. Herrnstein's matching law states that in choice situations, responses and their reinforcing consequences move toward equivalence over time.[38] When subjects have sufficient opportunities to choose and respond, they eventually optimize. Unfortunately, the law does not completely account for human choice. Researchers reporting this discrepancy call it a problem of sensitivity to reinforcement schedules.[39] George King and A. W. Logue's research concluded that "Humans' sensitivity to reinforcer amount may vary as a function of the degree of *feedback* that the subjects receive concerning the consequences of responding" [italics added].[40] In other words, the greater the information on the profitability of one choice over another, the more likely subjects choose and respond optimally.

Reasons for Regulated Thinking

Self-regulated thinking and Dewey's reflective thinking occur when the gain toward goal attainment justifies the costs incurred to produce it. The motivating factor is *gain*. Reflective thinking takes time, effort, and concentration. Before committing to a pursuit, we ask: "Is it worth it?" "Do the gains produced by solving a problem justify the costs of finding a solution?" The expectation proposition explains:

> The greater the past gain toward goal attainment and the smaller the discrepancy between the actual state and the goal state, the closer to optimal the expectation for gain.

Figure 4.1
Expected Gains and Estimated Costs

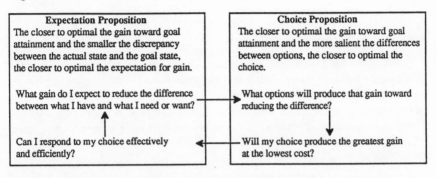

In order to determine gain, we seek out information on the potential of a given option. We gather information on the gain toward goal attainment that is likely from a given option. We also gather data on the behaviors that option will require us to perform. Then we decide if the gain is worth its cost. Costs increase when we don't know what operations will produce the gain and when we are uncertain if we can perform those operations. Costs also increase when the effort required to gather information increases. Both conditions make discrimination more difficult, decrease the chances of choosing optimally, and increase costs. The choice proposition explains:

> The greater the past gain toward goal attainment and the more salient the differences between options, the closer to optimal the choice.

The decision to pursue a goal is not easy. It involves making comparisons between advantages of goal attainment versus the costs incurred to produce the necessary gain. Figure 4.1 illustrates the interactions between expected gain and estimated cost.

Our ability to solve problems and choose optimally affects our estimations of the cost of producing gain. In general, cost estimations for familiar goal pursuits (the greater the *past gain*) are lower than for new ones because we "know" what to do and what outcomes to expect. We are competent and experienced. We have learned the discriminations that are most important and know how to make them effectively and efficiently. We don't waste time and effort.

Self-regulated thinking occurs when the gains from thinking it through outweigh the costs of making critical discriminations. We determine expected gains by seeking information on the consequences of different options to reduce discrepancies. This requires making discriminations between response requirements (costs) and gain consequences of all possible operations. Past experience and competence improve these discriminations. The more capable we are in a given pursuit, the more likely we will discriminate sufficiently well to choose optimally. This reduces costs and increases gains.

How We Regulate Thinking

Once committed to a goal pursuit, we must decide what will reduce the discrepancy between the goal state and the present state. Problem solving begins by identifying effective and efficient options. The goal can be as ambitious as getting nominated for public office en route to becoming president of the United States or as mundane as getting to an appointment on time. The preschool scenario illustrates the problem.

The Problem: Getting John to Preschool

Your goal is to get your son John to preschool by 1:00 P.M. It's now 8 A.M. You consider driving him yourself or calling a taxi. You decide to drive. But then you remember that you left the car lights on last night and the battery, which is four years old, is dead. So the car won't start. You consider buying a new battery or jumpstarting the car. Then you remember that you loaned your jumpstart cables to a friend. You decide it would be faster to call the local auto shop and have someone deliver and install a new battery. Then you'll be certain to get John to preschool on time. You make the call.

Achieving the goal of getting John to preschool requires solutions to several problems, which you solve using a means-ends analysis similar to the one illustrated in Figure 4.2.

Your first expectation for gain toward that end is for John to be driven to preschool, the starting point of the analysis. To produce this result (gain), you consider two options: calling a taxi or driving yourself. You rule out the taxi because you don't want to stay at school waiting for John and you aren't comfortable sending John in a cab alone. So you decide to drive. This option satisfies your gain-cost ratio.

But when you think about driving John, you recall that the battery is dead. Consequently you are unable to enact that choice. So you set a second expectation: to start the car. To produce this gain you consider two options—jumpstarting the car or getting a new battery. The jumpstart option is appealing because it's fast and inexpensive. But then you realize you can't jumpstart without cables.

This leads to the third expectation, to get a new battery. Again you consider options: having a friend pick one up at the store and deliver it for you to install or calling the auto shop and requesting someone to deliver and install the battery for you. After considering the costs of requesting your friend to help (she will expect to stay for lunch, which will take additional time you don't have), you decide it is faster and more effective in the long term to call the auto shop. The

Figure 4.2
Self-Regulated Thinking

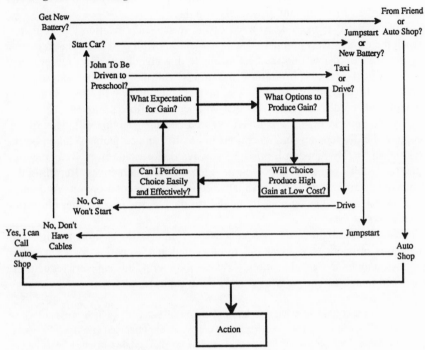

battery is old and needs replacing, anyway. The analysis ends with the decision to call the auto shop, a response you *can* perform. Furthermore, it's likely to be successful. Auto shops know how to install batteries and start cars.

This episode demonstrates the combined effects of (1) *identifying an expectation* for gain (getting a new battery) toward goal attainment (John at preschool), (2) *choosing an operation* that will produce the gain at a reasonable cost (delivery and installation of the battery), and (3) *having confidence* in your ability to perform the behavior necessary to enact that choice (calling the auto shop). With all three conditions present, you are likely to call the auto shop; this will start a chain of events leading to goal attainment—the car will start and then you can drive John to preschool.

This succession of choices also illustrates foresightful thinking. You considered the possibilities before engaging them. This permitted the selection of a reasonably good choice with a cost you could afford.

Self-regulated thinking involves finding cause and effect sequences that transform actual states into goal states. It requires that you remember the discrepancy while searching for operations that will reduce it. Although the present example is simple enough, there is room for deviation. You could become so involved in getting the car started—finding the best battery for the lowest cost, finding a shop with the lowest service fee, and so on—that you forget to get John to preschool on time. In fact, the car-not-starting problem may become a greater problem than John missing preschool for a day.

Self-regulated thinkers keep track of the means-ends relationship until they reach their goal. They compare discrepancy states with possible gain-producing operations in order to find the best means to that end. They don't forget where they are in the process or confuse the means with the end. They stay focused and goal-directed. Like Dewey's lost traveler, they engage in "reflection [that] is aimed at the discovery of facts that will serve . . . [their] purpose."[41]

The example in Figure 4.2 turned out well because you had sufficient knowledge of the discrepancy and its options to identify an acceptable solution before taking action. By thinking it through, you avoided wasted effort. Remembering that the battery was dead gave you time to consider alternatives. Recalling that your jumpstart cables were unavailable eliminated a second option. And anticipating the cost of having your friend deliver the battery reduced your obligation to reciprocate later.

This capacity to think of consequences of different options before taking action increases efficiency. We can run through multiple scenarios for each option before conducting a single action. Over the long term, this capacity reduces our cost and increases our gain, as Arnold Rose explains:

> Thinking is a kind of substitute for trial-and-error behavior (which most animal species engage in) in that possible future behaviors are imagined (as "trials") and are accepted or rejected (as "successes" or "errors"). Thought can lead to learning, not through hedonistic rejection of errors or reinforcement of successful trials, but through drawing out deductively the implications of empirical data already known. *Thinking is generally more efficient than actual trial-and-error behavior in that (a) imaginative trials usually occur more rapidly than behavioral trials, (b) the individual can select the best solution (or future course of action) known to him rather than merely the first successful solution, and (c) he takes less risk in experimenting with trials that are likely to be dangerous.* Through thinking, man brings the imagined or expected future into the present, so that present behavior can be a response to future expected stimulus, and courses of action can be laid out for quite some time into the future. [italics added][42]

Experience with similar goal pursuits and their options improves the efficiency of our goal pursuits. It is the data base for searching memory banks to identify likely options. The expectation proposition identifies this influence as past gain: "The greater the past gain . . . the more likely the optimal expectation for gain." In Figure 4.2, you had solved similar "dead battery" problems before by using jumpstart cables and you also knew that your friend would expect a favor in return for her help. This information was available through memory recall. No need to search for new facts. Remembering and thinking reflectively were sufficient.

Dewey's traveler was not as fortunate: "Any attempt to decide the matter by thinking will involve inquiring into other facts, *whether brought to mind by memory, or by further observation, or by both*. The perplexed wayfarer must carefully scrutinize what is before him and he must cudgel his memory'' (italics added). Inquiring into new facts increased the traveler's costs. It required more effort than just memory recall. As Dewey suggested, the traveler may have to climb a tree, go first in one direction, then in another, "looking, in either case, for signs, clues, indications."[43]

Searching for new solutions requires *self-regulated doing*. When present experiences fail to yield answers, new experiences are necessary. We must identify a solution, test it, and then determine if it produces the gain we expect. If it does, that gain affects subsequent expectations and choices. It adds to our knowledge base about what works and what doesn't. The next time we face a similar problem, "past gain" helps identify the "correct" solution via a memory search rather than an empirical test. This is how learning—remembering what works and what doesn't—increases efficiency. It eliminates the need for conducting a test. Chapter 5 describes how self-regulated doing serves us when our memories and our experiences fail us.

Notes

1. William James, *Essays in Pragmatism*, edited by Alburey Castell (New York: Hafner Publishing, 1948), 142–143.

2. Ibid., 144.

3. John Dewey, *Types of Thinking, including a Survey of Greek Philosophy* (New York: Philosophical Library, 1984), 135.

4. Ibid.

5. John Dewey, *How We Think: A Restatement of the Relation of Reflective Thinking to the Educative Process* (Boston: D. C. Heath and Company, 1933), 3–4.

6. Ibid., 4.

7. Ibid.

8. Ibid., 5.

9. Ibid., 6.

10. Ibid., 8–9.

11. William H. Calvin, *The Cerebral Symphony: Seashore Reflections on the Structure of Consciousness* (New York: Bantam Books, 1990).

12. Dewey, *How We Think*, 8.

13. Ibid., 12.

14. Ibid., 14.

15. Ibid.

16. Thomas J. Tighe, *Modern Learning Theory* (New York: Oxford University Press, 1982), 53.

17. Ibid., 57.

18. Fritz Heider, "Attitude and Cognitive Organization," *Journal of Psychology* 21 (1946): 107–112.

19. Fritz Heider, *The Psychology of Interpersonal Relations* (New York: John Wiley, 1958), 202.

20. Leon Festinger, *A Theory of Cognitive Dissonance* (Evanston, IL: Row, Peterson, 1957), 13.

21. Hazel Markus and R. B. Zajonc, "The Cognitive Perspective in Social Psychology," in Gardner Lindzey and Elliot Aronson (Eds.), *The Handbook of Social Psychology* (New York: Random House, 1985), 202.

22. Ibid., 206.

23. Robert Wicklund and Jack W. Brehm, *Perspectives on Cognitive Dissonance* (Hillsdale, NJ: Lawrence Erlbaum Associates, 1976), 189–190.

24. Allen Newell and Herbert A. Simon, *Human Problem Solving* (Englewood Cliffs, NJ: Prentice-Hall, 1972), 788.

25. J. W. Payne, M. L. Braunstein, and J. S. Carrol, "Exploring Pre-Decisional Behavior: An Alternative Approach to Decision Research," *Organizational Behavior and Human Performance* 22 (1978): 17–44.

26. J. Kevin Ford, Neal Schmitt, Susan L. Schechtman, Brian M. Hults, and Mary L. Doherty, "Process Tracing Methods: Contributions, Problems, and Neglected Research Questions," *Organizational Behavior and Human Performance* 43 (1989): 75–117.

27. H. Mintzberg, D. Raisinghani, and A. Thoret, "The Structure of Unstructured Decisions," *Administrative Science Quarterly* 21 (1976): 246–275.

28. Irving L. Janis and Leon Mann, *Decision Making: A Psychological Analysis of Conflict, Choice, and Commitment* (New York: The Free Press, 1977), 11.

29. Jerome Kagan, L. Pearson, and L. Welch, "The Modifiability of an Impulsive Tempo," *Journal of Educational Psychology* 57 (1966): 359–365.

30. Eugene H. Ridberg, Ross D. Parke, and E. Mavis Hetherington, "Modification of Impulsive and Reflective Cognitive Styles through Observation of Film-Mediated Models," *Developmental Psychology* 5, no. 3 (1971): 369–377.

31. A. J. Finch, Jr., and L. E. Montgomery, "Reflection-Impulsivity and Information Seeking in Emotionally Disturbed Children," *Journal of Abnormal Social Psychology* 1 (1973): 358–362.

32. Byron Egeland, "Training Impulsive Children in the Use of More Efficient Scanning Techniques," *Child Development* 45 (1974): 165–171.

33. Raymond S. Nickerson, "On Improving Thinking through Instruction," in Ernst Z. Rothkopf (Ed.), *Review of Research in Education: 15* (Washington, DC: American Educational Research Association, 1988), 3–57.

34. Studies reported in Nickerson's "On Improving Thinking through Instruction," were as follows: C. F. Gettys, *Research and Theory on Predecision Processes* (Norman: Decision Processes Laboratory, University of Oklahoma, 1983), and C. F. Gettys and P. D. Englemann, *Ability and Expertise in Act Generation* (Norman: Decision Processes Laboratory, University of Oklahoma, 1983).

35. Nikerson, "On Improving," cites J. Baron, *Rationality and Intelligence* (New York: Cambridge University Press, 1985).

36. Robert E. Valett, "Developing Thinking Skills," *Academic Therapy* 22, no. 2 (1986): 187–198.

37. Barry J. Zimmerman and Manuel Martinez Pons, "Development of a Structured Interview for Assessing Student Use of Self-Regulated Learning Strategies," *American Educational Research Journal* 23, no. 4 (1986): 614–628.

38. R. J. Herrnstein, "On the Law of Effect," *Journal of the Experimental Analysis of Behavior* 13 (1970): 243–266.

39. For a review of this research, see George R. King and A. W. Logue, "Humans'

Sensitivity to Variation in Reinforcer Amount: Effects of the Method of Reinforcer Delivery,'' *Journal of the Experimental Analysis of Behavior* 53 (1990): 33–45.

40. King and Logue, ''Humans' Sensitivity to Variation in Reinforcer Amount,'' 45.

41. Dewey, *How We Think*, 8.

42. Arnold M. Rose, ''A Summary of Symbolic Interaction Theory,'' in R. Serge Denisoff, Orel Callahan, and Mark H. Levine (Eds.), *Theories and Paradigms in Contemporary Sociology* (Itasca, IL: F. E. Peacock Publishers, 1974), 144–145.

43. Dewey, *How We Think*, 8.

Chapter 5

Self-Regulated Doing

All living organisms regulate their behaviors when it is in their best interests to do so. Humans are no different. History is replete with stories of rationally directed achievement. Unfortunately, it also has much to remind us of the irrational and the erratic. Moreover, there are substantial differences in rationally directed pursuits even across cultures. For some, self-regulated adjustment is a habit, a philosophy. For others, independent thinking and acting are intermittent and foreign. Why? How do we explain why some cultures inculcate the spirit of inquiry and the desire for control while others perpetuate belief in tradition and its right to control?

Some social scientists have postulated that the value placed on self-regulated responding in pursuit of goals can explain the widespread adoption of empiricism and its spirit of capitalism in the sixteenth and seventeenth centuries. This is why only a handful of nations now lead the world in the technological age. The value placed on practical, continuous work for tangible, personal goals increased innovation, accelerated industry, and created wealth. The spirit of enterprise generated by moral imperatives translated into commandments to perform work for beneficial result here and now. Supporting this creed was religious doctrine, which placed rationalism in worldly affairs on a par with idealism in divine affairs. The new ethic was pragmatic and utilitarian. It demanded connections between effort expended and results obtained.

In time, rationally controlled pursuit became both cause and consequence of the social transformations that characterized Western Europe during the seventeenth century. As the feudal order dissolved and Catholic monopoly on divine access crumbled, individuals assumed greater responsibility for their destinies. Increasingly, personal achievement divorced itself from the Church and the feudal manor. At the same time rationalism and empiricism gained followers, and science and technology charted their notable accomplishments. The ethic and the industrial revolution ushered in an entrepreneurial class of strivers who set new standards for hard work and persistent, pragmatic action. By the nineteenth century, the gap between Western countries and others of the world was widening.

The ethic also opened the door for personal success. The same philosophies that motivated the rise of industrialism in the eighteenth and nineteenth centuries contributed to the rise of "personal ambitionism" in the twentieth century. By mid-century, social scientists were examining the nature of the self-regulatory ethic along with the mechanisms that connected its vital parts—rational thinking and regulated doing. Early studies on the effects of verbal behavior suggested lawful relations between thinking and doing. Research on their correspondence suggested mechanisms responsible for how self-regulated doing affects and is affected by self-regulated thinking.

The Ethics of Self-Regulated Doing

All this began on October 31, 1517, when Martin Luther protested the Catholic Church's selling of indulgences—absolutions to wealthy sinners for relief from suffering for their sins—by posting ninety-five theses on the door of Palace Church in Wittenberg, Germany. A year later, the Cardinal Cajetan to Diet of Augsbury ordered Luther to recant. But Luther challenged the infallibility of papal decisions instead. By 1520 Pope Leo X had excommunicated Luther as a heretic. The following year, Luther was banned from the Holy Roman Empire and imprisoned in Wartburg, where he began his German translation of the Bible. In 1522 Wittenberg printer Hans Lufft began printing the new Bible (100,000 copies over the next forty years). The Protestant Reformation had begun.

By 1543 it spread to Sweden, Scotland, France, Denmark, and Norway; French theologian and religious reformer John Calvin opened another assault on the Church with *Christiane Religionis Institution*; and the Spanish Inquisition burned the first Protestants at the stake. But the movement continued. According to historian R. R. Palmer, "by 1560 the chief Protestant doctrines had been affirmed, and geographically Protestantism had made many conquests. The spiritual unity of Latin Christendom had been broken. . . . whatever spiritual or administrative unity might still have been derived from the Roman supremacy was now lost by the Protestant revolt. Christendom was disintegrating into a purely intangible ideal."[1]

Protestantism broke sharply from the past. Its followers rejected papal authority, eschewed international organizations, repudiated supernatural status for priests, and replaced Latin with the vernacular in religious services. Protestant clergy married; the number of sacraments was reduced to two or three; and the miracle of the Mass was discarded. Gone also were obligatory confessionals, priestly absolutions, ideas of purgatory, and cults of saints and of the Virgin

Mary. The only source for Christian belief was Holy Scripture.[2] And although Protestant churches demanded absolute conformity to their replacement doctrines, rights of private judgement in matters of conscience prevailed.[3] The door was ajar for opportunistic enterprise. According to historian R. R. Palmer, "it has often been maintained that one of the motivations in Protestantism was economic—that a new acquisitive, aggressive, dynamic, progressive, capitalistic impulse shook off the restrictions imposed by medieval religion. . . . It is possible that Protestantism, by casting a glow of religious righteousness over a man's daily business and material prosperity, later contributed to the economic success of Protestant peoples."[4]

The Protestant answer for salvation was personal responsibility—*self-regulated doing* in pursuit of the "calling." Luther's dismantling of Catholic monopoly on heavenly access encouraged pursuit of alternative routes. For the masses, this was a mixed blessing. Freedom is fine, but what happens when one chooses the wrong path to salvation? According to sociologist Robert Merton, this issue deeply concerned scientists like Robert Boyle, John Ray, Thomas Sprat, and John Wilkins. Their answer was to use *scientific enterprise to satisfy God's will*: "The justification efforts of Sprat, Wilkins, Boyle, or Ray do not simply represent opportunistic obsequiousness, but rather an earnest attempt to justify the ways of science to God. The Reformation had transferred the burden of individual salvation from the Church to the individual, and it is this 'overwhelming and crushing sense of the responsibility for his own soul' which explains the acute religious interest."[5]

The Protestant Ethic and Capitalism

In *The Protestant Ethic and the Spirit of Capitalism*,[6] German sociologist Max Weber (1864–1920) explained the development of industrial society by noting that prior to and during the Middle Ages, social conditions in Western and non-Western societies were stable. But this changed in the seventeenth and eighteenth centuries when the industrial revolution occurred. While social and economic change accelerated in Europe, there was little change in India and China. Weber concluded that religion explained the difference. Eastern religions prevented change and Protestantism encouraged it. The Protestant emphasis on individual responsibility increased initiative and innovation.

In Confucian China, the ideal man was filially devoted to the welfare of ascendents both living and dead. He was a social conformist who worked at "fitting in" in hopes of gaining heavenly rewards on his way "out." In Buddhist India, the ideal man was the ascetic, solely concerned with spiritual matters and the attainment of divine grace. Living was a means to achieving that end. Mundane affairs evoked passive resignation. In China the ideal achiever was the Confucian scholar; in India it was the Buddhist beggar. Neither system encouraged enterprise.[7]

The same was true in Western Europe during the Middle Ages. Christian dogma placed man on trial because he had failed his Maker. Penance was punishment in this world followed by grace and salvation in the next. Life was a series of tests to be passively and patiently endured. The ideal man was the cloistered monk living in poverty and isolation and devoted to prayer. Resignation and acquiescence to life's troubles were optimal adjustments. As a consequence, manor life was unenterprising, fatalistic, and conformist—much like that in China and India.[8]

The Reformation injected a new ethic into sixteenth-century life. For the first time, individuals had reason to act purposefully, rationally, and productively. The emergent values included self-reliance, individual enterprise, personal responsibility for achievement, and aggressive domination of worldly affairs. According to Weber, this new "spirit" that spread throughout Europe during the centuries following the Middle Ages emanated from Protestant sects and churches and Calvinistic doctrines of predestination. The Reformation separated individuals from their guarantees of salvation via the Church.

The resultant withdrawal symptoms were severe, however, as Stephen Kalberg describes:

> The deep anxiety introduced by this religion's predestination doctrine in respect to the overriding question of one's personal salvation proved more than believers could reasonably bear. Gradually, worldly success came to be viewed as a sign that God had bestowed his favour and thus, as evidence of membership among the predestined elect. In this way, since it allowed the devout to believe they belonged among the chosen few and thereby alleviated intense anxiety, worldly success itself became endowed with religious—indeed, a salvation—incentive, or "psychological premium." Methodical labour in calling (*Beruf*) proved the surest pathway toward worldly success, as did the continuous reinvestment of one's wealth—an unintended consequence of this attitude—rather than its squandering on worldly pleasures.[9]

Weber's thesis was that the development of capitalism—the prime stimulus for economic and social change from the sixteenth century on—was due to the increased rationalism of practical pursuit: "that development of the spirit of capitalism is best understood as part of the development of rationalism as a whole, and could be deduced from the fundamental position of rationalism on the basic problems of life."[10] The spirit of capitalism was the motivational condition that "spirited" unremitting pursuit of money and acquisition. The journey was the goal, as Szymon Chodak explained:

> The spirit of capitalism is evident where man is dominated by the making of money, where acquisition and action in pursuit of more acquisition become the ultimate purpose of life. Those under its spell cannot stand waste of time in idle ramble or even in the spontaneous enjoyment of life. Life is to be spent in achieving. The pursuer of acquisition is hence restlessly and constantly in action to achieve the maximum in the shortest time possible. He advocates greater efficiency, since

this leads to more results in his incessant fervent striving. He acts systematically generating and building systems of action in calculation and anticipation of others' actions. He is under a constant urge to rationalize his enterprise, the organization under his control, and the capitalist organization in general. Credibility, punctuality, honesty, inventiveness, adaptability to new circumstances are prized by him, since such qualities are instrumental in efforts of achieving.[11]

For capitalists, tradition impeded progress and the ethic facilitated it: "the God of Calvinism demanded of his believers not single good works, but a life of good works combined into a unified system."[12] The ethic sanctified work and repudiated idle thought. It rejected irrational ascetic practices in contemplative affairs but encouraged it in everyday affairs—especially in family life and in the vocational calling.[13]

Puritans and Calvins were articulate advocates of the ethic. Richard Baxter, a Presbyterian and an apologist of the Westminster Synod, wrote *Christian Directory*, a compendium of Puritan ethics in which he discussed the moral dangers of acquisition. These dangers did not involve accumulation per se, but rather the relaxation and idleness it might produce. Life's purpose on earth was continuous work: "For the saints' everlasting rest is in the next world; on earth many must, to be certain of his state of grace, 'do the works of him who sent him, as long as it is yet day.' "[14] Time wasted was sinful. Life was too short. "Loss of time through sociability, idle talk, luxury, even more sleep than is necessary for health, six to at most eight hours, is worthy of absolute moral condemnation. . . . It [time] is infinitely valuable because every hour lost is lost to labour for the glory of God."[15] In effect, the ethic encouraged production and discouraged consumption, which promoted saving and reinvestment—an ideal formula for economic development. Weber summarized the effects: "This worldly Protestant asceticism . . . acted powerfully against the spontaneous enjoyment of possessions; it restricted consumption, especially of luxuries. On the other hand, it had the psychological effect of freeing the acquisition of goods from the inhibitions of traditionalistic ethics. It broke the bonds of the impulse of acquisition in that it not only legalized it, but . . . looked upon it as directly willed by God."[16]

The ethic viewed wealth pragmatically. The luxurious and extravagant were out, but the conservative and practical were in. Expenditures for reasonable needs were okay; practical middle-class living was ideal.[17]

The Protestant Ethic and Science

Weber's research suggested co-variations between the ethic on the one hand and scientific and industrial progress of the seventeenth and eighteenth centuries on the other.[18] The causal inference rested with the predisposing power of the new value structure, which encouraged its followers in their acquisitive pursuits. Weber cited the scientific and technological leads of Protestant over non-

Protestant countries as evidence that Protestants were more likely than Catholics to pursue entrepreneurial and professional jobs. In predominantly Catholic France, where Protestants were a minority, their influence in business was disproportionately large; in Germany, which had equal proportions of Protestants and Catholics, Protestants again dominated economic activity. The pattern was also evident in American business, in Canada, and in Holland. Stanislav Andreski's review of Weber's theory concluded:

> We can adduce another argument from co-variation in support of Weber's thesis, using as our units of comparison states, instead of sections of populations located within the boundaries of one state, and pointing out that capitalism developed furthest and fastest in predominantly Protestant countries. In the world of today only the first part of this statement is true: the economies of the English-speaking countries, dominated by the Protestants, continue to represent the furthest stage in the evolution of capitalism, but their rates of growth are exceeded by those of France, Italy, and Western Germany. The latter fact, however, does not invalidate the thesis of Weber, but only demands that we make explicit what is implicit: namely, that this thesis applies in full only to the situation where accumulation by private individuals constitutes the driving force of economic development.[19]

During the early development of entrepreneurship and industrialization of the seventeenth and eighteenth centuries, individual initiative was the only means of development. No corporations, think tanks, or research centers existed—only individuals acting optimally and gaining maximally *on their own*.

Robert Merton found support for Weber's thesis in *Puritanism, Pietism and Science*,[20] where he showed how Protestantism of the seventeenth century compelled systematic, rational, and empirical approaches to dealing with nature and obeying God. By analyzing the values of prominent scientists of the day, Merton connected religious motive and scientific interest. The works and attitudes of chemist Robert Boyle, mathematician John Wilkins, botanist John Ray, zoologist Francis Willughby, and others suggested that "certain elements of the Protestant ethic had pervaded the realm of scientific endeavor and had left their indelible stamp upon the attitudes of scientists toward their work."[21]

Merton found near point-to-point correspondence between Protestant belief and science. His review of Thomas Sprat's *History of the Royal-Society of London*—which included authentic accounts of the views, motives, and aims of association members—showed that Puritanic demands for systematic, methodic labor in the pursuit of one's calling matched perfectly the credo of the experiment, which "can never be finish'd by the perpetual labours of any one man, nay, scarce by the successive force of the greatest Assembly."[22] The Protestant ethic sanctioned aggressive, systematic pursuit of knowledge for the will of God. Rationalism was servant to empiricism and its laboratory of inductive reasoning. The scientific method and interest in its pursuit developed together. Merton concluded that "with Protestantism, religion provided this interest: it actually imposed obligations of intense concentration upon secular activity with an emphasis upon experience and reason as bases for action and belief.''[23]

Business and industry were also dominated by Protestants. Merton found that nine of the ten founding members of the ''invisible college'' (later to become the Royal Society) were Puritan. And forty-two of the sixty-eight original members of the Royal Society of 1663 were Puritan. Dorothy Stimson's studies also showed how the spread of experimental science in seventeenth-century England was due to encouragement from moderate Puritans.[24]

The new emphasis upon utilitarianism and empiricism manifested itself in other ways, too. Protestant educators founded universities that emphasized rigorous studies in scientific disciplines; Catholics founded institutions that pursued the classics.[25] As a result, those schools graduated students with distinctively different careers. Protestant schools produced proportionately more scientists, and Catholic schools graduated proportionately more Latin and Greek scholars. Merton's review of Alphonse de Candolle's study *Histoire des Sciences et des Savants* showed that in Europe, where Catholics outnumbered Protestants by 61 to 39 percent, Protestant scientists named foreign associates by the Academy of Paris from 1666 to 1883 outrepresented Catholic scientists by 82 to 18 percent. Comparable differences were evident in secondary schools. While Protestants and Catholics were distributed in the general population by 37 to 61.5 percent, respectively, they were enrolled in science and mathematics programs at 69 to 31 percent. Merton also found that in every instance contrasting Protestant and Catholic associations with science, Protestants dominated.

The Protestant Ethic and American Achievement

The Protestant belief system established cultural expectations for rational inquisition and prudent acquisition. It translated ambition into achievement, innovation into entrepreneurship, and industry into production. The contemplative life idealized by the Greeks and practiced by the feudal monks gave way to rational, purposeful, productive action. Control, domination, and regulation of the present life was the best preparation for the afterlife. The ethic popularized and rationalized optimal action for maximum gain. By mid-nineteenth century, the ethic had grown from its sixteenth-century European roots to become the cultural cornerstone of rugged individualism in America. In *The Culture of Narcissism: American Life in an Age of Diminishing Expectations*, American historian Christopher Lasch wrote that:

> the Protestant work ethic stood as one of the most important underpinnings of American culture. According to the myth of capitalist enterprise, thrift and industry held the key to material success and spiritual fulfillment. America's reputation as a land of opportunity rested on its claim that the destruction of hereditary obstacles to advancement had created conditions in which *social mobility depended on individual initiative alone*. The self-made man, archetypical embodiment of the

American dream, owed his advancement to habits of industry, sobriety, moderation, self-discipline, and avoidance of debt. He lived for the future, shunning self-indulgence in favor of patient, painstaking accumulation; and as long as the collective prospect looked on the whole so bright, he found in the deferral of gratification not only his principle gratification but an abundant source of profits. [Italics added][26]

In the United States, other sources of inspiration perpetuated the myth, making it independent of its religious moorings. American youth read Horatio Alger's (1834–1899) *Ragged Dick, Luck and Pluck,* and *Tattered Tom.* Though underprivileged, Alger's characters were still able to win fame and fortune through honesty, diligence, and perseverance. Alger wrote more than one hundred such works to demonstrate the power of the ethic.

Andrew Carnegie, American philanthropist, industrialist, and founder of the Carnegie Steel Company, was contemporary proof of the myth. Born in Dunfermline, Scotland, in 1835, Carnegie came to the United States at age thirteen to work as a bobbin boy in a cotton mill in Allegheny, Pennsylvania, earning $1.20 a week. From there he worked up to messenger boy in a Pittsburgh telegraph office, then to private secretary and telegrapher to a railroad official, and finally to superintendent of the Pittsburgh division of the railroad. After the Civil War, he formed his own company and built iron railroad bridges. By 1899, Carnegie controlled 25 percent of all U.S. iron and steel production, and in 1901 he retired after selling his company to the United States Steel Corporation for $250 million. He never received a formal education.[27]

In the 1920s, Carnegie helped translate the myth into a workable philosophy by challenging Napoleon Hill to study successful people and identify factors that explained their success. Carnegie asked, ''What is there in the climate of this great nation that I, a foreigner, can build a business and acquire wealth? How is it that anyone here can achieve success? I challenge you to devote twenty years of your life to the study of American achievement and come up with an answer. Will you accept?''[28] Hill did. For the next twenty years he studied over five hundred of the most famous and successful men in American industry, including Henry Ford, Theodore Roosevelt, James J. Hill, Wilbur Wright, William Jennings Bryan, George Eastman, Woodrow Wilson, William Howard Taft, Luther Burbank, Clarence Darrow, Alexander Graham Bell, John D. Rockefeller, Thomas A. Edison, and F. W. Woolworth. In 1928, Hill reported his findings in *Law of Success.* He concluded from his study and analysis of 16,000 men and women that

ninety-five percent of all who were analyzed were failures and but five percent were successes. (By the term ''failure'' is meant that they had failed to find happiness and the ordinary necessities of life without struggle that was almost unbearable.) . . . One of the most startling facts brought to light by those 16,000 analyses was the discovery that the ninety-five percent who were classed as failures were in that class because they had no definite chief aim in life, while the five percent constituting the successful ones not only had purposes that were definite, but they had also, definite plans for the attainment of their purposes."[29]

A decade later, Hill published *Think and Grow Rich*, the most influential self-help book ever written. Two decades after that, he collaborated with W. Clement Stone in *Success Through a Positive Mental Attitude*. In both works, Hill articulated his success strategy which included: (1) choice of a definite goal to be obtained, (2) development of sufficient power to attain one's goal, (3) perfection of a practical plan for attaining one's goal, (4) accumulation of specialized knowledge necessary for the attainment of one's goal, and (5) persistence in carrying out the plan.[30]

Stone captured the essence of this gutsy rags-to-riches philosophy of success by describing his own start as a six-year-old boy earning his way on the streets of Chicago in the 1900s:

> I was six years old and scared. Selling newspapers on Chicago's South Side wasn't easy, especially with older kids taking over the busy corners, yelling louder, and threatening me with clenched fists. . . .
>
> Heolle's Restaurant was near the corner where I tried to work, and it gave me an idea. It was a busy and prosperous place that presented a frightening aspect to a child of six. I was nervous, but I walked in hurriedly and made a luck sale at the first table. Then diners at the second and third tables bought papers. When I started for the fourth, however, Mr. Hoelle pushed me out the front door.
>
> But I had sold three papers. So when Mr. Hoelle wasn't looking, I walked back in and called at the fourth table. . . . About five minutes later, I had sold all my papers.[31]

Hill and Stone became philosophical godparents for success philosophies expressed in such popular works as Og Mandino's *The Greatest Salesman in the World;* Norman Vincent Peale's *Power of Positive Thinking;* Denis Waitley's *Seeds of Greatness;* and Robert H. Schuller's *Discover Your Possibilities*.

The 1980s tested these claims of success through positive attitude and productive striving. In *The Great American Success Story: Factors That Affect Achievement,*[32] George Gallup and Alec Gallup reported on a survey sample of the nation's most successful men and women to identify behavior patterns and characteristics that explained their achievements. Interviews with a random sample of 1,500 people listed in the eighty-third edition of Marquis's *Who's Who in America* identified five characteristics: common sense, special knowledge of one's field, self-reliance, general intelligence, and, of course, the ability to get things done.

B. Eugene Griessman reported similar results in *The Achievement Factors: Candid Interviews with Some of the Most Successful People of Our Time.*[33] Here he described his personal interviews with people like Hank Aaron, Mario Andretti, Julie Andrews, Mary Kay Ash, Arthur Ashe, Jr., Isaac Asimov, Helen Gurley Brown, Paul "Bear" Bryant, Art Buchwald, Robert Byrd, Erskine Caldwell, Ray Charles, Aaron Copland, Jacques-Yves Cousteau, Malcolm Forbes, Eric Hoffer, John Houston, Kris Kristofferson, Jack Lemmon, Arthur Murray, Jack Nicklaus, Sandra Day O'Connor, Linus Pauling, Norman Vincent Peale, Richard Petty, William Proxmire, Ronald Reagan, David Rockefeller, Andy Rooney, Charles Schulz, Herbert Simon, Burrhus Frederic Skinner, Gloria Steinem, Ted Turner, and Tennessee Williams.

The most commonly cited success factors were (1) being *competent* in the field of choice, (2) *enjoying* one's work, and (3) *persisting* at that work through difficult times. Charles Garfield studied peak performers in business, science, sports, and the arts over a period of twenty years and found five factors. Peak performers achieved remarkable results because they

1. Defined and pursued missions that motivated;
2. Developed plans and engaged in purposeful activities directed toward achieving goals that contributed to the mission;
3. Engaged in self-observation and effective thinking that assured maximum performance;
4. Corrected and adjusted activities to remain on the critical path to the goal; and
5. Anticipated and adapted to major change while maintaining momentum within an overall game plan.[34]

They were self-regulated doers. They planned thoughtfully, followed through effectively, and adjusted to results continuously. They engaged in that same power-packed sequence of focused, utilitarian thinking, action follow-through, and opportunistic flexibility found in the Protestant ethic. Anthony Robbins described a similar action package in *Unlimited Power*:

> People who have attained excellence follow a consistent path to success. . . . The first step . . . is to know your outcome. . . . The second step is to take action . . . the third step is to develop the sensory acuity to recognize the kinds of responses and results you're getting from your actions and to note as quickly as possible if they are taking you closer to your goals or farther away . . . the fourth step . . . is to develop the flexibility to change your behavior until you get what you want. . . . If you look at successful people, you'll find they followed these steps. They started with a target, because you can't hit one if you don't have one. They took action, because just knowing isn't enough. They have the ability to read others, to know what responses they were getting. *And they kept adapting, kept adjusting, kept changing their behavior until they found what worked.* [italics added][35]

The Science of Self-Regulated Doing

In "Origins of American Scientists," Robert Knapp and Hubert Goodrich studied the impact of the Protestant ethic on scientific careers. Data on the number of male graduates from American colleges and universities between 1924 and

1934 who earned doctorates and were later listed in the 1944 edition of *American Men of Science* indicated that agricultural colleges produced the highest number of notable scientists and Catholic institutions the lowest:

> Our data have shown the marked inferiority of Catholic institutions in the production of scientists and, on the other hand, the fact that some of our most productive smaller institutions are closely connected with Protestant denominations and serve a preponderantly Protestant clientele. Moreover, the data presented by [other studies][36] on American "starred scientists," although limited, indicate very clearly that the proportion of Catholics in this group is excessively low—that, indeed, some Protestant denominations are proportionally several hundred times more strongly represented. These statistics, taken together with other evidence, leave little doubt that scientists have been drawn disproportionately from American Protestant stock.[37]

Knapp and Goodrich suggested that "Protestants have more readily abandoned their fundamentalist religious outlook and thus have been freer to accept the tenets of scientific philosophy."[38]

In another study, David C. McClelland and his colleagues traced the origins of achievement to parental attitudes about early independence training. Theorizing that children who become independent early are more likely to achieve later, McClelland postulated a connection between Protestant parenting and economic development in Protestant countries. His propositions were as follows:

1. Protestant families are more likely to initiate early independence training than Catholic families;
2. Early independence training leads to higher levels of achievement motivation;
3. Therefore, Protestants, who experience this training, are likely to have higher levels of achievement motivation than Catholics;
4. When coupled with values espoused in the Protestant ethic, high achievement motivation leads to more vigorous economic activities;
5. Therefore, economic development is likely to be greater in Protestant countries.[39]

McClelland tested the first two propositions by giving questionnaires about parenting practices to Protestant, Jewish, Irish-Catholic, and Italian-Catholic mothers and fathers. The respondents indicated the ages at which they expected their children to be independent at different tasks. As expected, Protestant and Jewish parents expected independence at significantly earlier ages than did Irish-Catholic and Italian-Catholic parents. This confirmed the first proposition.

In a second study,[40] M. Winterbottom obtained n-achievement scores from stories told by twenty-nine normal eight- to ten-year-old boys who responded to protocol questions on an achievement instrument.[41] Then she interviewed mothers to assess their emphasis on independence training. Boys who scored high on achievement usually had mothers who emphasized independence, which supported the second proposition.

Although scholars have argued the merits of Weber's theory for decades, the theory still offers a credible accounting for the technological gains of Western countries during the last four hundred years. The ethic was probably one of several factors that transformed submissive, superstitious, and conforming individuals of the feudal culture into utilitarian-minded opportunists of the industrial culture.

Nevertheless, the theory has limitations, its chief one being that it says very little about very much. The theory gives a crude accounting of the *consequences of utilitarian values* across culturally distinct populations. At the same time it leaves the "how" of this transformation unexplained. For example, how do *utilitarian values* translate into *utilitarian actions* for individuals within the same culture? Clearly, persons within a given culture do not act uniformly according to any ethical code or value. What mechanisms account for these variations?

Even Winterbottom's parenting study lacks cogency. Parenting practices that emphasize independence training are certainly consistent with utilitarian behavior, but not predictive. Independence training alone does not explain achievement. Other factors like self-control and persistence may be equally important.

Consider James Michener, who apparently learned persistence and self-control outside the traditional family structure. A foundling at age two, adopted and raised with foster children by Mabel Michener and occasionally sent to the local poorhouse for support, Michener recalls his humble origins: "I never had skates, I never had a bicycle, I never had a wagon—nothing that the other kids had. Nothing. A guy said he could never figure out how I tied my shoelaces because they were all just knots. That was my background. . . . At 14, I left home with 35 cents in my pocket and hitched to Florida. It never occurred to me that I wouldn't make it. I think that before I was 15, I had been from Canada to Key West." By age 82 James Michener had completed 37 books translated into 52 languages, 9 movies, 4 television shows, and a musical. He received a Pulitzer Prize and the Presidential Medal of Freedom.

Why did Michener succeed? Probably because of behaviors learned early and practiced late: "[His] life epitomizes . . . common sense, frugality, hard work and good old-fashioned American virtue, [he] writes every morning from 7:30 to 12:30. 'I sit right here at this typewriter,' he says, demonstrating with two fingers. 'When I'm done with my draft, John reads it. See, everything here in pencil is his. Then I give it to my secretary and she puts it on the word processor. Can't work without it these days.' "[42] Louis L'Amour practiced these behaviors, too. Author of 101 of the world's most popular westerns, L'Amour wrote five pages a day, including Sundays and holidays. Science fiction writer Isaac Asimov says his success is due to *persistence* and *industry*. What causes this persistence and industry?

Social Control

Prior to the industrial revolution, conformity to cultural norms was the penultimate value guiding human activity. Control of individual behavior came through sanctions imposed by guardians of sacred statutes passed down from generation to generation since the beginning. Even as our primitive ancestors learned to divide their labors to increase food production, they regulated their actions according to custom. Deviation from norms meant punishment, ostracism, even death. Conformity earned praise, rewards, even deification. Independent thinking was unthinkable and individual initiative was suicidal. Change was gradual and imperceptible.

Nevertheless, labor divided and subdivided again and again as human groups learned better organizations for the common good. The rise of human civilization thousands of years before the birth of Christ illustrates the range of complex organizational structures made possible through continuous application of this simple principle. In the Western world, pre-industrial civilization reached its zenith with the Roman Empire, which stretched from Egypt to Europe. By then social control depended upon compliance with Roman law as well as conformity to local custom. When the Empire crumbled, the Catholic Church and local authorities took control and the feudal system developed. Its purpose was to restore security for the common good. The Church cast a constraining spell by punishing deviation. Accept the will of God or suffer damnation. Passive acquiescence was the modal response. External social control obviated the need for internal self-control.

The production systems of the times mirrored these constraining prescriptions. Extended families in rural areas were self-sufficient, and landownership during feudal times was monopolistic. Consequently there were few innovations in agricultural methods. In towns where the guild system controlled production, skill ladders of apprentice, journeyman, and master determined entry into the profession and progress through its ranks. This too was constraining. The main purpose was to restrict the supply of skilled workers in order to maintain control and support prices.[43] Although the system should have increased the supply of skilled labor through its seven-year apprenticeship sequence, incentive to do so was absent. When demand for products increased, the guilds were unresponsive because their goal was to produce less for more. William Form explained:

> To apply the current terminology, the guild system was the very embodiment of overcertification. Its main purpose was to monopolize the local market for the masters, to limit the supply of skilled workers, to exploit journeymen and apprentices by extending their training and delaying their certification. Journeying removed trained workers from the local labor market and provided cheap skilled labor to masters in other markets. The years spent in journeying far exceeded the time needed to perfect skills. By the end of the seventeenth century, examinations for attaining the master's status were so expensive that only a small minority could afford them.[44]

By the eighteenth century, the system had a virtual stranglehold on young talent. Parents paid masters to accept their children into an apprenticeship program that would not deliver, because only children of other masters made it

98

through the system. Birth, not competence, determined who was in and who was out. The system encouraged incompetence: "Most of the hand-produced articles of the nineteenth century that survive today (antique furniture, tinware, glass, dishes) is of poor quality and not the product of skilled workers. And products manufactured by farm families were of even poorer quality."[45]

For most of human history social control was communal, not contractual, and particularistic, not universalistic. One's status in the social order depended upon conformity to accepted codes of behavior rather than invention of new modes of production. Advancing through the social structure depended upon ascription via birthright rather than achievement through performance. Independent thinking and acting were candidates for serious sanction. The clergy and the police reinforced one message: *conform.*

The industrial revolution changed that. Authorities could no longer define ideal behavior for each occasion. Change occurred too rapidly. Even religion offered choice. Within the Protestant movement different sects offered different ideologies and practices. Within these alternatives, individuals could choose their own paths to salvation. Population concentrations at industrial sites meant that strangers mingled with each other in the workplace, extended families broke apart, and communal control dissolved. Individuals became responsible for themselves. Rules for controlling behavior became rational, practical, and utilitarian. Achievement replaced ascription and innovation undermined conformity. The new message was *self-control.*

As Pope Leo XIII commented in *Rerum Novarum,* "The elements of conflict are unmistakable. We perceive them in the growth of industry and the marvelous discoveries of science; in the changed relations of employers and workingmen; in the enormous fortunes of individuals and the poverty of the masses; in the *increased self-reliance* and the closer mutual combination of the labor population; and, finally, in the general moral deterioration" (italics added).[46] In "Industrial Man," Paul Meadows wrote about this new age of self-control:

> Industrial technology . . . calls for a new kind of human discipline. It calls for a regimentation of the human spirit, a regimentation which must be austere, in order to command respect. The discipline must be this-worldly, so the daily task will not be neglected. It must be empirical, so that obedient self-sacrificing will be generously forthcoming. This pattern of motivation rests—at least in the industrial West—on the self-interested and omniscient individual who has status and is legitimate because he has been "called" to the job—the sacredness of industrial work.[47]

As communal groups exerted less external control, individuals needed to exert more self-control. Nations on the leading edge of technological change depended upon new waves of self-directed individualists who were more eager to produce and less willing to conform. Where would they come from? Could reconstituted urban families raise children for self-determined futures? Could schools teach students rational-empirical problem solving and flexible adjusting? Could the twentieth-century industrial giants sustain the entrepreneurial innovation that empowered their technological achievements through two hundred years of economic development?

Just twenty-five years ago, Wilbert Moore stated that success of commercial-industrial economies depended upon the capacity of schools to teach problem solving and to inculcate positive attitudes for a self-determining citizenry:

> [In school the] child is expected to adjust to orderly change, by the hour, day, week, and year. The child is also expected to compete and is given fairly immediate information and sanctions according to his relative success or failure. At some point . . . he is asked to take a *"constructive," problem-solving orientation to tasks and not simply a mechanical apprehension and memorization process of accumulating information and skills.*
>
> Now these characteristics imply habits and even attitudes of mind that are highly appropriate to a social order that is not only very competitive and changeful but also provides opportunities for rational innovation. *For an industrial society the most valuable product of the school is . . . a population accustomed to uncertainty and positively oriented to continuous learning and creative problem-solving. No society . . . is going to achieve much economic (or any other) modernization without effective education in the attitudinal sense among fairly broad sectors of the population.*[italics added][48]

This analysis still applies. Public schools must teach students to think and act rationally and empirically. Unfortunately, they have yet to accomplish that goal. In a review of research on the teaching of thinking, Raymond Nickerson concluded:

> In the aggregate, the findings from these studies force the conclusion that it is possible to finish 12 or 13 years of public education in the United States without developing much competence as a thinker. Many students are unable to give evidence of a more than superficial understanding of concepts and relationships that are fundamental to the subjects they have studied, or of an ability to apply the content knowledge they have acquired to real-world problems. The general picture of the thinking ability of U.S. students that is painted by these reports is a disturbing one.[49]

John Dewey addressed similar problems fifty years ago when he challenged schools to discontinue monotonous hand-me-down knowledge transfers through teacher-controlled instruction in an educational system that was "one of imposition from above and from outside. It imposes adult standards, subject-matter, and methods upon those who are only growing slowly toward maturity. The gap is so great that the required subject-matter, the methods of learning and of behaving are foreign to the existing capacities of the young."[50]

Dewey's solution was learning through experience. *Teach students to think in order to act in order to learn from results.* Conduct premeditated experiments with life: "systematic utilization of scientific method as the pattern and ideal of intelligent exploration and exploitation of the potentialities inherent in experience."[51] The precondition necessary to learn these systematic explorations and exploitations was self-control. Progressive education substituted external teacher-control with internal self-control. Students who control their impulses have time to think and act rationally, systematically, and empirically. Therefore, *the first goal of education should be to establish self-control.* According to Dewey:

Thinking is thus a postponement of immediate action, while it affects internal control of impulse through a union of observation and memory, this union being the heart of reflection. What has been said explains the meaning of the well-worn phrase "self-control." *The ideal aim of education is creation of power of self-control. But the mere removal of external control is no guarantee for the production of self-control. . . . Impulses and desires that are not ordered by intelligence are under the control of accidental circumstances.*[italics added][52]

Self-Control

Dewey believed that students develop self-control through immersion in empirical problem solving that meets their own needs according to their own interests and abilities. Rather than receiving teacher-imposed problems, drill sheets, and memorization tasks, students need opportunities to apply systematic, rational problem defining and solution searching with meaningful situations. He believed interaction with nature nurtures self-control by connecting rational thought and action with opportunity for gain. Unfortunately, the timing of this "new" philosophy was premature. Dewey published *Democracy and Education* in 1916,[53] but research applications exploring its implications were not available for decades after that.[54]

Finally in the 1950s, with Russian psychologist Vygotsky's discovery of causal links between verbalization and behavior in young children,[55] researchers began to understand Dewey's insights. Alexander Luria built upon Vygotsky's work by proposing a three-stage theory of verbal regulation. In the first stage the child's behavior is independent of verbalizations. In the second, there is some verbal regulation. In the third stage, the child no longer talks aloud to control behavior "because at the moment when semantic control is developed, the child can use his internal subvocal speech. As a result of this interiorized process, the child can obey instructions without speaking loudly and without using the reinforcement of his own externally heard speech."[56]

In the 1960s Jerome Kagan studied cognitive tempo and found that some children report solutions before they have taken time to determine the accuracy of their answers.[57] Later, Walter Mischel proposed an expectancy-value model that postulated that children delay seeking rewards by estimating the probability of consequences;[58] and S. L. Bem and K. Daniel O'Leary demonstrated the effects of self-talk on the ability to direct and initiate action.[59] Since then[60] there

Table 5.1

Outcomes Targeted by a Sample of 250 Self-Regulation Studies

Academic Behaviors	Study Skills	Behaviors	Social & Vocational Behaviors	Self-Help & Leisure
Problem Solving	Study habits	Attendance	Affectionate	Shopping behaviors
Object	Neat papers	Disruptive behavior	behaviors	Community
Discrimination	Paying attention	Persistence	Voice volume	behaviors
Memorization	Test anxiety	Locus of control	Persuasive behaviors	Self-help skills
Comprehension	Academic	Perception of pain	Social behaviors	Taking medication
Thinking on own	performance	Delay of reward	Parenting	Quitting smoking
Ascription of failure	Student's methods of	Classroom	Interactions	Exercise
Self-directed learning	learning	misbehaviors	Interpersonal	Weight loss
Achievement	Underlining	Self-injury	problem	Domestic tasks
Summarizing	Paraphrasing	Hair-pulling	solving	Room cleaning
Matching to sample	Work sheet tasks	Lever pressing	Social deficits	Bowling game
Abstracting	Seat work	Headache	Social isolation	Marble game
Improved	Success/failure	Impulsivity	Sequencing	Life enhancement
remembering	Note-taking	Assertiveness	vocational	skills
via sequencing	Making inferences	Depression	tasks	Control in betting
Verbal mediation	Test-taking	Staying on task	Assembly tasks	game
Learning from	Performance on	Hallucinations	Vocational tasks	
movies	assignments	Hyperactivity	Production rate	
Arithmetic	Planning and	Aggression	Following	
Estimating circles	implementing own	Anxiety	instructions	
Addition	projects	Maladaptive behavior	Work performance	
Math study	Self-scoring	Personal problems	Career decisions	
Goal setting for	Information seeking	Thumbsucking	Workshop production	
math	Study strategies	Success behaviors	Writing newspaper	
Counting	Attending	Task sequencing	headlines	
Early math	Homework tasks	Fantasies	Processing job	
operations	Plans for action	Anger	applications	
Work attack	Comprehensive	Self-mutilation		
Comprehension	monitoring	Talk-outs in class		
Scanning				
Imagining pronouns				
Technical reading				
Decoding				
Spelling				
Sight words				

has been veritable explosion in research on self-regulation. From 1957 to 1986 there were over 800 reports on some component of the process, one-third focusing on persons with handicaps, two-thirds on persons without handicaps, one-half studying the process in children, and nearly one-third studying it in adults.[61] This research canvassed a full range of behaviors, as Table 5.1 illustrates.

Dewey's goal that "[the] ideal aim of education is creation of power of self-control"[62] became feasible. Research caught up with theory sixty years later. Carl Thoresen and Michael Mahoney finally captured Dewey's message about scientific thinking in their prologue to *Behavioral Self-Control:*

To exercise self-control the individual must understand what factors influence his actions and how he can alter those factors to bring about the changes he desires. *This understanding requires that the individual in effect become a sort of personal scientist. . . .* The person begins by observing what goes on, recording and analyzing personal "data," using certain techniques to change specific things (e.g., thought patterns or the physical environment), and, finally, deciding if the desired change has occurred. Again, in making such a decision, the person looks to the data about himself.[italics added][63]

An Explanation For Self-Regulated Doing

This chapter began with an explanation of why some people and some cultures self-regulate better than others. In Europe during the Middle Ages, social and religious values encouraged conformity. But during the Reformation and Enlightenment that followed, innovation and industry found a place in an ethical pragmatism. The result was a rise in personal responsibility and an increase in innovation and industry. Although this explanation is sociologically cogent, it fails to explain individual differences. Do all self-determined individuals come from families that inculcate the spirit of striving? Or are other factors necessary for goal-directed pursuit?

One explanation for the efficacy revolution at the *individual* level is the reward effect. Individuals adopted more effective solutions when it was in their interests to do so. During the Reformation, Enlightenment, and the industrial revolution, adoption and innovation were more rewarding than maintenance and conformity. According to the reward principle, when new practices produce better results than old ones, those practices are more likely to continue in the future.

George C. Homans used this explanation in *Social Behavior: Its Elemental Forms*. He said that we engage in activities because of their *value* and *success*. His value proposition states: "The more valuable to a person is the result of his action, the more likely he is to perform the action."[64] His success proposition states: "For all actions taken by persons, the more often a particular action of a person is rewarded, the more likely the person is to perform that action."[65] Homans used these propositions to explain innovation in the British cotton industry between 1770 and 1840 as follows:

I. Men are more likely to perform an activity, the more valuable they perceive the reward of that activity to be. (Value proposition)
II. Men are more likely to perform an activity, the more successful they perceive the activity is likely to be in getting that reward. (Success proposition)
   A. The high demand for cotton textiles and the low productivity of labor led men concerned with cotton manufacturing to perceive the development of labor-saving machinery as rewarding in increased profits. (Value proposition)
   B. The existing state of technology led them to perceive the effort to develop labor-saving machinery as likely to be successful. (Success proposition)
      1. Therefore, by both (I) and (II) such men were highly likely to try to develop labor-saving machinery.
      2. Since their perceptions of the technology were accurate, their efforts were likely to meet with success, and some of them did meet with success.[66]

The decision to develop labor-saving machinery was risky because it deviated from established practice. Nevertheless, a few expected rewarding consequences from its use because the demand for cotton was so great and existing production so low (value proposition). The incentives were sufficient to motivate investigating this option further, which they did and found that its prospects for success were good (success proposition). According to Homans, the expected *value of the consequences* of adopting labor-saving equipment and the *perceived success* of developing equipment that would save labor and money explained the adoption: "Such men were highly likely to try to develop labor-saving machinery."

The Self-Regulation Explanation

Self-regulation theory specifies the *value* of engaging in adoptive behavior according to the "optimality" of expected gain toward goal attainment: "The closer to optimal the past gain and the smaller the discrepancy between the actual state and the goal state, the closer to optimal the expected gain" (*expectation proposition*).

Using Homans's example, would-be innovators perceived a discrepancy between the productivity of labor-intensive methods and the productivity of machine-driven methods. The availability of labor-saving equipment made eliminating this discrepancy feasible. So when they gathered information on the net gain in profits using labor-saving machinery, they expected greater financial gain with the machinery.

Next, they considered their chances of success. Could they find operations that would actually produce this gain? Could they develop and install labor-saving equipment needed to produce low-cost textiles? The *choice proposition* describes how these factors affected their choice of operations to produce expected gain: "The closer to optimal the past gain and the more salient the differences between options, the closer to optimal the choice."

The innovators gathered more information, this time identifying specific tasks necessary to build machinery, install it in factories, and train workers to operate it. What investments would this require? How long would it take? When could production resume? They developed alternative plans for completing tasks, compared costs, and then selected the option that would produce the greatest gain at the lowest cost.

According to the choice proposition, the optimality of their choice depended upon their ability to identify important differences between old and new methods. In this case, the difference between using labor-intensive methods and labor-saving equipment was too obvious to ignore. The potential gains from the latter approach were so many times greater that choosing to innovate was easy.

Homans's explanation stops here, suggesting that: "Since their perceptions of the technology were accurate, their efforts were likely to meet with success, and some of them did meet with success." Self-regulation theory goes further, predicting that because the optimality of expectations for gain and choices of operations to produce that gain were so high, the innovators wasted little time

Figure 5.1
The Effects of Thinking on Doing

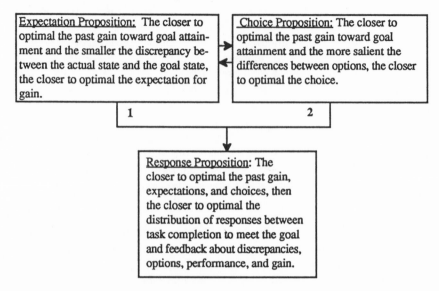

and effort researching further. They immediately set about completing the tasks necessary for goal attainment—they built machinery, installed it in plants, and then trained workers to operate it. They completed the necessary work as quickly and as effectively as possible. According to the *response proposition*, they maximized their task responses and minimized feedback seeking: "The closer to optimal the past gain, expectations, and choices, then the closer to optimal the distribution of responses between task completion to meet the goal and feedback seeking about goal state-actual state discrepancies, options, task performance, and results."

As optimality of expectations for gain (value) and choice (success) increased, follow-through on choice became more likely. Innovators committed themselves fully to adopting the new technology. In mathematical terms, the value of an activity multiplied by the probability of its success equaled the probability of solution adoption—or follow-through.[67]

Figure 5.1 illustrates how value and success affect adoption, or in terms of the theory, how optimal expectations and choices affect performance. As past gains, expectations, and choices approach their optimalities, responding also approaches its optimality. Causal arrows 1 and 2 reflect these thought-to-action influences. According to the response proposition, feedback seeking is inversely proportional to optimality. As regulators become more certain of gain and success, they become less likely to seek out information on discrepancies, expectations, choices, and results. Only during conditions of uncertainty—suboptimal expectations and choices—do they monitor progress closely.

Self-regulation theory states that the closer to optimal the adjustments, then the closer to maximum the gain toward goal attainment. The *gain proposition* deduces this prediction from the first three propositions by stating that as the optimalities of past gains, expectations, choices, and performances increase, gain toward goal attainment maximizes: "The closer to optimal the past gain, expectations, choices, and responses, then the closer to optimal the gain toward goal attainment."

Although adjustments are not always optimal nor gains always maximal, any gain will affect subsequent expectations, choices, and performances. Propositions 1–3 specify how this occurs. As gain increases, subsequent expectations, choices, and performances become more optimal, and these increased optimalities further increase gain. When the cycle persists, optimal adjustment and maximum gain are likely.

Prior to initial gain, however, the opposite condition is present: gain awaits increases in the optimalities of expectations, choices, performances, and results, which in turn await increases in gain. Outcomes of initial regulatory efforts have disproportionate effects on subsequent adjustments. If that initial effort fails, then the optimalities decline, which further reduces the probability of gain. Just as success can breed success after gain is established, failure can beget failure before gain gets established. This raises interesting questions about the successes of past innovations. What might have happened to the British cotton industry had those first attempts at adopting labor-saving machinery failed? Could they have delayed the industrial revolution?

The mechanisms responsible for these self-perpetuating cycles are the feedback loops. Figure 5.2 illustrates. Causal arrow 1 reflects the cumulative effects of increased or decreased adjustment optimalities on gain. This produces a gain effect, which feeds back to influence subsequent performance (arrow 2), subsequent expectations (arrow 3), and subsequent choices (arrow 4).

Testing New Solutions

Given the structural interdependence of past gains, expectations, choices, and performances, it is surprising we ever pursue new goals. In fact, Chapter 2 chronicled this reluctance to change. Millions of years transpired before our ancestors adopted improved methods of producing food, and thousands of years more before they adopted better methods of producing other goods and services. Only in the last 500 years have rates of innovative output increased. Today there are more innovators and adopters present in the general population than at any time in history. And in technologically advanced countries, self-regulated problem solving toward distant goals is commonplace at work and in personal affairs.

New goal pursuits begin when we identify plausible options, test them, and then adjust subsequent expectations, choices, and performances. The process sorts poorly conceived and executed solutions from those that work. Feedback arrows 2–4 in Figure 5.2 illustrate this recursive testing. Solutions rarely come

Figure 5.2
The Reciprocal Effects of Optimality and Gain

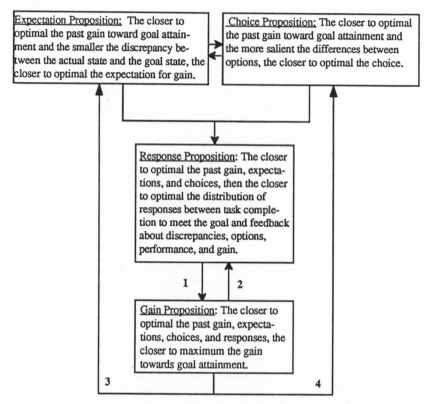

perfectly conceived and fully completed on the first attempt. They appear in bits and pieces, requiring successive attempts to improve and approximate desired ends. The following examples illustrate.

Example 1: Skinner's Bag-Finding Goal. In "An Operant Analysis of Problem Solving," B. F. Skinner demonstrated problem solving by posing the problem of picking up a friend's suitcase from an airport baggage claim:

> You have never seen the suitcase or heard it described; you have only a ticket with a number for which a match is to be found among the numbers on a collection of suitcases. To simplify the problem let's say that you find yourself alone before a large rotary display. A hundred suitcases move past you in a great ring. They are moving too fast to be inspected in order. [Initially you] . . . are committed to selecting suitcases essentially at random, checking one number at a time. How are you to find the suitcase?[68]

One problem is that sampling bags at random wastes time, because you may check some suitcases several times and others not at all. Skinner's solution was to "mark each case as it is checked—say, with a piece of chalk. No bag is then inspected twice, and the number of bags remaining to be examined is reduced as rapidly as possible."[69]

The diagram in Figure 5.3 illustrates the problem solving that might have led to this solution. The discrepancy is the absent bag, and the expectation is to select the correct one. Problem 1 shows how Skinner dispensed with the first expectation "Select Correct Bag" by either matching all bag tags in sequence or by matching them at random. He realized the carousel was revolving too fast to check all bags in sequence. So he didn't follow through. Instead he redefined his expectation. Problem 2 illustrates.

During this phase, Skinner decided to check two bags at a time randomly, which he did. Then he discovered (from the Result box) that he missed many bags because he was checking the same bags repeatedly and this did not increase his chances of finding the bag. So he changed expectations again.

In Problem 3, Skinner chose to use chalk (which he just happened to have with him) because his visual memory was poor. This worked, and soon he found the correct bag. Next time he has a similar problem, he'll expect to find the bag quickly and easily using the chalk method.

Example 2: Pearl Showers's Smoking Goal. Pearl Showers wants to quit smoking and decides to cut down to ten or fewer cigarettes per day. When planning how to reach this goal, she recalls an article that said when the cost of getting cigarettes increased, smokers were less likely to smoke. The article also recommended counting and recording the number of cigarettes smoked, which decreased smoking. Pearl didn't think the counting and recording method would work. She tried the cost method, which she implemented by borrowing cigarettes from her friends. Pearl hated to borrow, so asking for cigarettes would be costly to her. Problem 1 in Figure 5.4 illustrates.

After several days of borrowing, Pearl noticed she was smoking as much as ever. Contrary to expectations, getting cigarettes from her friends was easy and she became accustomed to asking for them. Borrowing wasn't as painful as she thought it would be. So she decided to count and record—as indicated in Problem 2. To determine when to count, Pearl considered after-counts and before-counts. Considering the after-counts seemed logical because then she would be accurate.

But after five days of this procedure, she discovered she often forgot to count. She smoked during office breaks and was in such a hurry to return after smoking that she forgot to count. Pearl switched to the other method—as indicated in Problem 3. This time she counted before she touched a cigarette, which turned out to be an added incentive for recording. After using this method for five days, she smoked nine cigarettes per day. Now Pearl continues to count and record *before* smoking in order to maintain her habit at that level.

Example 3: April Bailey's Reading Goal. April has difficulty understanding what she reads. She gets marginal marks on comprehension tests and wants to raise her reading grade. She set a goal of 80 percent correct on comprehension tests. One reason April doesn't understand what she reads is because she reads

Figure 5.3
Skinner's Bag-Finding Goal

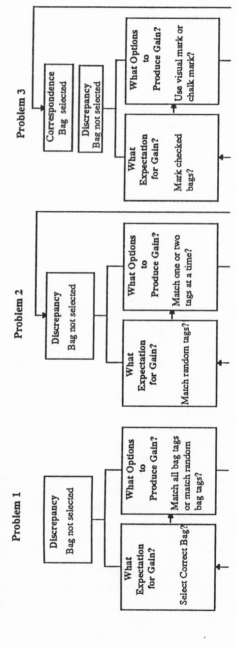

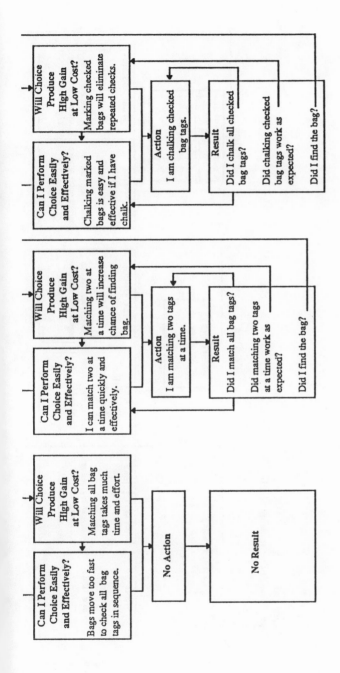

Figure 5.4
Pearl Showers's Smoking Goal

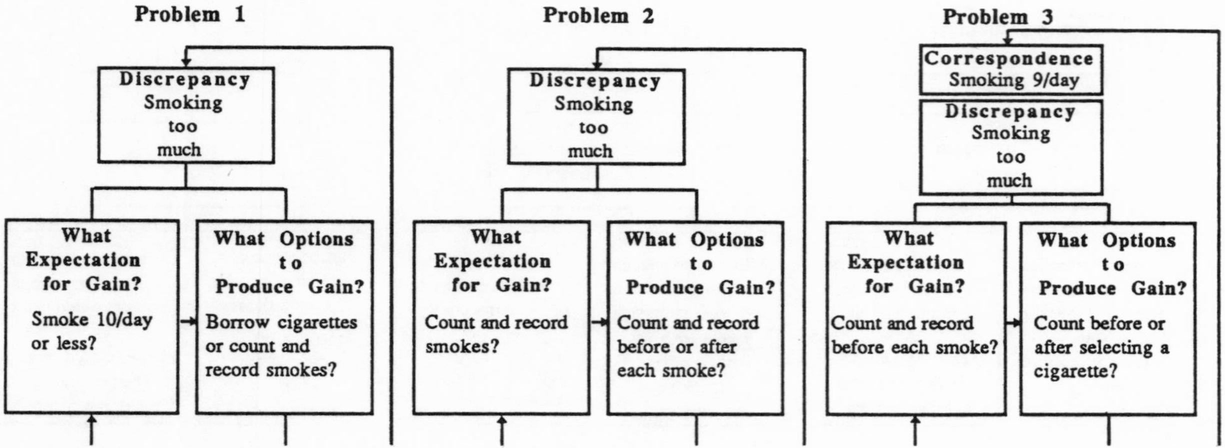

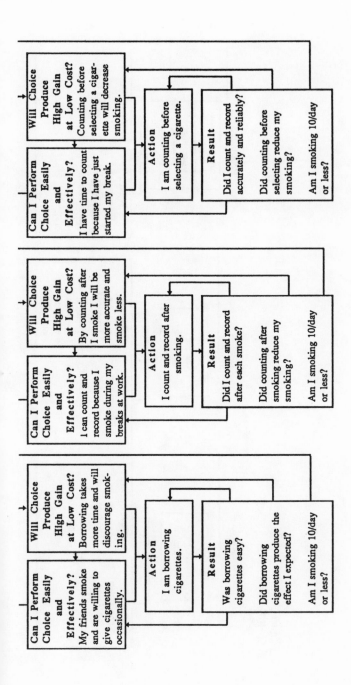

Can I Perform Choice Easily and Effectively?	Will Choice Produce High Gain at Low Cost?	Action	Result
My friends smoke and are willing to give cigarettes occasionally.	Borrowing takes more time and will discourage smoking.	I am borrowing cigarettes.	Was borrowing cigarettes easy? Did borrowing cigarettes produce the effect I expected? Am I smoking 10/day or less?
I can count and record because I smoke during my breaks at work.	By counting after I smoke I will be more accurate and smoke less.	I count and record after smoking.	Did I count and record after each smoke? Did counting after smoking reduce my smoking? Am I smoking 10/day or less?
I have time to count because I have just started my break.	Counting before selecting a cigarette will decrease smoking.	I am counting before selecting a cigarette.	Did I count and record accurately and reliably? Did counting before selecting reduce my smoking? Am I smoking 10/day or less?

Figure 5.5
April Bailey's Reading Goal

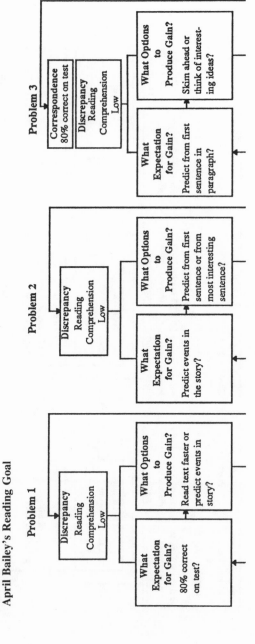

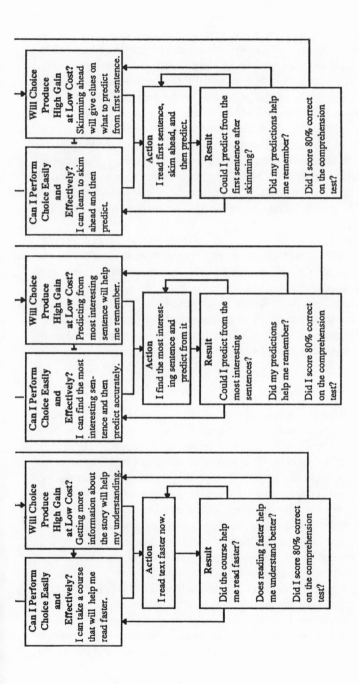

113

so slowly that she doesn't finish soon enough to answer all the comprehension questions on a test. So she decided to learn to read faster—her solution to Problem 1 in Figure 5.5. After three weeks of learning speed reading, April still hadn't improved her scores on comprehension exams, so she decides to follow her teacher's advice and predict events in the story as she reads—the expectation for Problem 2. Next she considers how to make these predictions. Should she predict from the first sentence of the paragraph or the sentence that was most interesting? She chooses the latter. After using this technique for three weeks, April hasn't improved. Again, she follows her teacher's recommendation and changes her method of predicting. This time she predicts events based upon the first sentence in each paragraph—the expectation for Problem 3. She chooses to predict from the first sentence by skimming ahead rather than by thinking of interesting ideas suggested by the first sentence. After using this method for three weeks, April scores an average of 83 percent on comprehension tests. She plans to continue this method.

Self-Regulated Doing. Self-regulated doers test solutions and analyze results in order to discriminate between what is effective and what is not. Skinner watched the field of possible bags diminish when he used the marking procedure; Pearl Showers noticed she smoked less when she counted and recorded before selecting each cigarette; and April Bailey remembered what she read when she predicted story events after reading the first sentence of each paragraph and then skimming ahead. Finding these solutions required choosing, testing, and evaluating. This is self-regulated doing.

Deducing From Old Solutions

Old solutions become so because they produce positive results. They meet our expectations, so we use them again and again. The behavioral explanation is that they are reinforcing. George Homans uses his value proposition to explain repeated use: "The more valuable to a person is the result of his action, the more likely he is to perform the action."[70] According to self-regulation theory, solutions that meet expectations toward reducing discrepancies between goal states and present states are likely to occur again, as indicated in the *response proposition*: "The greater the past gain and the closer to optimal the expectations and choice, then the closer to optimal the distribution of responses between task completion to meet the goal and feedback seeking about goal state-actual state discrepancies, options, task performance, and results."

Solutions that work receive more attention than solutions that don't. Regulators spend more time and behavior performing them and less time and effort searching for other solutions, checking out results, and monitoring progress toward goals. They focus their attention on getting solutions implemented effectively and efficiently. This optimizes performance. It maximizes solution use and minimizes the solution search.

An effective solution is also a candidate for similar problems. We can shortcut problem solving by *deducing* what will work from a rule we *induced* from similar experience. The rule reminds us what works and what doesn't. It tells us the outcomes to expect from different options. We induce it by learning to discriminate about what causes what in a given circumstance.

In the bag-finding problem of Example 1, the solution-rule Skinner induced was that: "To find a strange bag at an airport baggage claim with only the claim ticket, mark all bags you check." The solution-rule that Pearl induced in Example 2 was: "To reduce the number of cigarettes smoked per day, count and record before selecting a cigarette." And the solution-rule that April induced in Example 3 was: "To increase reading comprehension, predict story events by reading the first sentence of each paragraph and then skimming ahead for clues."

These rules reduce the need for testing new solutions. When faced with similar situations, we need only *recall the appropriate rule* and follow it, that is, deduce the action that the rule recommends. For example, if Skinner, Showers, and Bailey were to face similar problems, they might reason as follows:

From Example 1: Skinner's Bag-Finding Goal

1. *Problem*:   I must find someone's bag at the Kansas City airport baggage claim and I only have the claim ticket.

2. *Rule Recall*:   To find a strange bag at an airport baggage claim using only the claim ticket, mark all bags you check.

3. *Deduction*:   Therefore, I will mark all bags I check and examine only unmarked bags.

From Example 2: Pearl Showers's Smoking Goal

1. *Problem*:   My friend wants to quit smoking and has asked for advice on how to quit.

2. *Rule Recall*:   To reduce the number of cigarettes smoked per day, count and record before selecting a cigarette.

3. *Deduction*:   Therefore, I will tell my friend to count and record smokes before selecting a cigarette.

From Example 3: April Bailey's Reading Goal

1. *Problem*:   April must read three chapters in history to prepare for a test on significant facts and trends.

2. *Rule Recall*:   To increase reading comprehension, predict story events by reading the first sentence of each paragraph and then skimming ahead for clues.

3. *Deduction*:   Before reading the chapters, April should read the first sentence of each paragraph, skim ahead for clues, and then predict events.

Deducing what to do from what worked before saves time and effort. Just as feedback seeking on alternatives decreases, so does testing and evaluating results. Skinner, Showers, and Bailey know what works. Faced with similar situations, they need only recall the appropriate rule and deduce the actions it suggests. This optimizes expectations, choices, and responses. The more often a deduction works as expected, the less need for feedback on discrepancies, choices, and results. Eventually solution use becomes habitual, requiring no thinking at all. The problem cue is sufficient to evoke the solution response.

Notes

1. R. R. Palmer, *A History of the Modern World* (New York: Alfred A. Knopf, 1963), 79.

2. Ibid., 79–81.

3. Ibid., 81.

4. Ibid.

5. Robert K. Merton, *Social Theory and Social Structure* (New York: The Free Press, 1957), 578.

6. Max Weber, *The Protestant Ethic and the Spirit of Capitalism*, translated by Talcott Parsons with a Foreword by R. H. Tawney (New York: Charles Scribner's Sons, 1958).

7. Richard T. La Piere, *Social Change* (New York: McGraw-Hill, 1965), 308–309.

8. Ibid., 310.

9. Stephen Kalberg, "Max Weber (1864–1920)," in Adam Kuper and Jessica Kuper (Eds.), *The Social Science Encyclopedia* (New York: Routledge, 1989), 892–896.

10. Weber, *The Protestant Ethic*, 76.

11. Szymon Chodak, *Societal Development: Five Approaches with Conclusions from Comparative Analysis* (New York: Oxford University Press, 1973), 150.

12. Weber, *The Protestant Ethic*, 117.

13. Chodak, *Societal Development*, 151.

14. Max Weber, "Protestantism and the Rise of Modern Capitalism," in Dennis H. Wrong and Harry L. Gracey (Eds.), *Readings in Introductory Sociology* (New York: Macmillan, 1967), 209.

15. Ibid., 210.

16. Ibid., 214.

17. Ibid., 215.

18. Stanislav Andreski, "Method and Substantive Theory in Max Weber," in R. Serge Denisoff, Orel Callahan, and Mark H. Levine (Eds.), *Theories and Paradigms in Contemporary Sociology* (Itasca, IL: F. E. Peacock Publishers, 1974).

19. Ibid., 381–382.

20. Merton, *Social Theory and Social Structure*, 574–606.

21. Ibid., 575.

22. Thomas Sprat, quoted in ibid.

23. Ibid., 582.

24. Ibid., 585.

25. Ibid., 585–587.

26. Christopher Lasch, *The Culture of Narcissism: American Life in an Age of Diminishing Expectations* (New York: Warner Books, 1979), 106.

27. Quoted from Dennis E. Mithaug, *Self-Determined Kids* (New York: Lexington Books, Macmillan, 1991).

28. Napoleon Hill and W. Clement Stone, *Success through a Positive Mental Attitude* (New York: Prentice-Hall, 1987), xv.

29. Napoleon Hill, *The Law of Success* (Evanston, IL: Success Unlimited, 1979), Lesson 2, 32.

30. Napoleon Hill, *Think and Grow Rich* (New York: Fawcett Crest, 1960), 157.

31. W. Clement Stone, *The Success System That Never Fails* (New York: Pocket Books, 1962), 3.

32. George Gallup and Alec M. Gallup, *The Great American Success Story: Factors That Affect Achievement* (Homewood, IL: Dow Jones-Irwin, 1986), 67.

33. B. Eugene Griessman, *The Achievement Factors: Candid Interviews with Some of the Most Successful People of Our Time* (New York: Dodd, Mead & Company, 1987).

34. Charles Garfield, *Peak Performers: The New Heroes of American Business* (New York: Avon, 1986).

35. Anthony Robbins, *Unlimited Power* (New York: Ballantine Books, 1987), 11–12.

36. Other studies cited were as follows: H. C. Lehman and P. A. Witty, "Scientific Eminence and Church Membership," *Scientific Monthly* 33 (1931): 544–549, and S. S. Visher, *Scientists Starred 1903–1943* (Baltimore: Johns Hopkins Press, 1947).

37. Robert H. Knapp and Hubert B. Goodrich, "The Origins of American Scientists," in David C. McClelland (Ed.), *Studies in Motivation* (New York: Appleton-Century-Crofts, 1955), 345.

38. Ibid., 345–346.

39. David C. McClelland, A. Rindlisbacher, and Richard deCharms, "Religious and Other Sources of Parental Attitudes toward Independence Training," in McClelland (Ed.), *Studies in Motivation*, 391.

40. M. Winterbottom, "The Sources of Achievement Motivation in Mothers' Attitudes toward Independence Training," in David C. McClelland, John W. Atkinson, Russell A. Clark, and Edgar L. Lowell (Eds.), *The Achievement Motive* (New York: Irvington Publishers, 1976. Distributed by Halsted Press); also in M. R. Winterbottom, *The Relation of Childhood Training in Independence to Achievement Motivation* (Ann Arbor: University of Michigan, University Microfilms, 1953), Publication No. 5113, 297, 302, 305, 313.

41. David C. McClelland and A. M. Liberman, "The Effect of Need for Achievement on Recognition of Need-Related Words," *Journal of Personality* 18 (1949): 236–251.

42. M. Nieuwsma, "Michener Like His Novels Goes On and On" *Gazette Telegraph* (Colorado Springs, Colorado), 27 December 1988.

43. Richard T. La Piere, *Social Change*, (New York, McGraw-Hill, 1965), 414–415; William Form, "Resolving Ideological Issues on the Division of Labor," in Hubert M. Blalock, Jr. (Ed.), *Sociological Theory and Research: A Critical Appraisal* (New York: The Free Press, 1980), 140–155.

44. Form, "Resolving Ideological Issues," 153.

45. Ibid.

46. Pope Leo XIII, quoted in Paul Meadows, "Industrial Man," in Ephraim H. Mizruchi (Ed.), *The Substance of Sociology: Codes, Conduct and Consequences* (New York: Appleton-Century-Crofts, 1967), 440.

47. In Mizruchi (Ed.), *The Substance of Sociology*, 438.

48. Wilbert E. Moore, "Social Aspects of Economic Development," in Robert E. L. Faris (Ed.), *Handbook of Modern Sociology* (Chicago: Rand McNally, 1964), 898.

49. Raymond S. Nickerson, "On Improving Thinking through Instruction," in Ernst

Z. Rothkopf (Ed.), *Review of Research in Education* (Washington, DC: American Educational Research Association, 1988), 5.

50. John Dewey, *Experience and Education*, (New York: Collier Books, 1963 [1938]), 18–19.

51. Ibid., 86.

52. Ibid., 64.

53. The progressive movement in education in the 1920s, which espoused his philosophy, misinterpreted his ideas and nearly discredited their value. Dewey attempted to correct the record in 1938 in *Experience and Education*.

54. A few psychologists like John B. Watson, Rosalie Rayner, and Mary Cover Jones were developing new research paradigms that would lead to the self-control research of the 1950s. The dominant thinking of that era was Freudian psychoanalysis, which pervaded nearly all the therapeutic and treatment approaches for psychological disorders. See John B. Watson, *Behaviorism* (Chicago: The University of Chicago Press, 1924); John B. Watson and Rosalie Rayner, "Conditioned Emotional Reaction," *Journal of Experimental Psychology* 3 (1920): 1–14; and Mary Cover Jones, "A Laboratory Study of Fear: The Case of Peter," *Journal of Genetic Psychology* 31 (1924): 308–315.

55. As reported by Alexander R. Luria, "Verbal Regulation of Behavior," in Celia Burns Stendler (Ed.), *Readings in Child Behavior and Development* (New York: Harcourt, Brace & World, 1964), 392–403.

56. Luria, "Verbal Regulation of Behavior," 403.

57. Jerome Kagan, "Reflection-Impulsivity," *Journal of Abnormal Psychology* 71 (1966): 17–24.

58. Walter Mischel, "Theory and Research on the Antecedents of Self-Imposed Delay of Reward," in B. A. Maher (Ed.), *Progress in Experimental Personality Research, Vol. 3* (New York: Academic Press, 1966).

59. S. L. Bem, "Verbal Self-Control: The Establishment of Effective Self-Instructions," *Journal of Experimental Psychology* 74 (1967): 485–491; K. Daniel O'Leary, "The Effects of Self-Instruction on Immoral Behavior," *Journal of Experimental Child Psychology* 6 (1968): 297–301.

60. These are only examples of the earliest works.

61. Dennis E. Mithaug, James E. Martin, Martin Agran, and Frank R. Rusch, *Why Special Education Graduates Fail: How to Teach Them to Succeed* (Colorado Springs, CO: Ascent Publications, 1988), 71–76.

62. Dewey, *Experience and Education*, 64.

63. Carl E. Thoresen and Michael J. Mahoney, *Behavioral Self-Control* (New York: Holt, Rinehart and Winston, 1974), 9.

64. George C. Homans, *Social Behavior: Its Elementary Forms*, rev. ed. (New York: Harcourt Brace Jovanovich, 1974), 25.

65. Ibid., 16.

66. George C. Homans, "Bringing Men Back In," *American Sociological Review* 29 (December 1964): 809–818.

67. This formulation is consistent with Vroom's expectancy theory: V. H. Vroom, *Work and Motivation* (New York: John Wiley & Sons, 1964).

68. B. F. Skinner, "An Operant Analysis of Problem Solving," in Benjamin Kleinmuntz (Ed.), *Problem Solving: Research, Method, and Theory* (New York: John Wiley & Sons, 1966), 228–229.

69. Ibid.

70. Homans, *Social Behavior*, 25.

Chapter 6

Maximum Gain

All organisms strive to optimize their adjustments in order to maximize their gains. This is how they survive and thrive. Whether the activity is seeking food, searching for sexual outlets, or exploring environments, the least effort-greatest gain principle applies. The exchanges between organisms and environments that endure conform to this principle.

There are two variation-and-selection theories that explain these end-state outcomes: Darwin's theory of evolution and B. F. Skinner's principles of operant conditioning. The first describes how natural selection of genotypes and phenotypes matches environmental niches over evolutionary time, and the second describes how behaviors match reinforcement contingencies over an organism's lifetime.

Chapter 1 presented the logic common to both—that organismic selections of different environmental conditions produce matches between needs on the one hand and environmental resources on the other. Genotypic-phenotypic changes favor survival of the species when the need-resource match increases; and behavioral changes favor longevity of the individual when response-contingency matches increase. Even though selection and variation occur randomly, accidental matches feed back to increase the chances of subsequent matches. This starts a recursive cycle of matches begetting more matches, as organisms move gradually but inexorably toward successively more adaptive fits.

The principles of variation and selection presented in Chapter 1 explain the evolution of genotypes and phenotypes through natural selection and the shaping of behaviors through reinforcement selection. Matches between organismic needs and environmental resources benefit the species through increased survivability in evolutionary time, and they benefit the individual through increased adaptive responding over its lifetime.

Table 6.1
Other Theories of Human Regulation

George C. Homans's Theory of Social Exchange[1]

1. Value Proposition: The more valuable to a person is the result of his action, the more likely he is to perform the action.

2. Success Proposition: For all actions taken by a person, the more often a particular action of a person is rewarded, the more likely the person is to perform that action.

3. Rationality Proposition: In choosing between alternative actions, a person will choose that one for which, as perceived by him at the time, the value, V, of the result, multiplied by the probability, P, of getting the result, is the greater.

4. Stimulus Proposition: If in the past the occurrence of a particular stimulus, or set of stimuli, has been the occasion on which a person's action has been rewarded, then the more similar the present stimuli are to the past ones, the more likely the person is to perform the action, or some similar action, now.

5. Aggression-Approval Proposition I: When a person's action does not receive the reward he expected, or receives punishment he did not expect, he will be angry; he becomes more likely to perform aggressive behavior, and the results of such behavior become more valuable to him.

6. Aggression-Approval Proposition II: When a person's action receives the reward he expected, especially a greater reward than he expected, or does not receive punishment he expected, he will be pleased; he becomes more likely to perform approving behavior, and the results of such behavior become more valuable to him.

7. Deprivation-Satiation Proposition: The more often in the recent past a person has received a particular reward, the less valuable any further unit of that reward becomes for him.

Albert Bandura's Social Learning Theory [2]

1. Expectation Principle: The greater the expectation for reinforcement, the more likely the attention to modeling cues that precede that reinforcement.

2. Attention Principle: The greater the attention to modeling cues preceding reinforcement, the more likely the cognitive connection between those cues and reinforcement

120

3. Cognitive Effect Principle: The more frequent the cognitive connection between modeling cues and reinforcement, the more likely an imitative response.
4. Social Learning Principle: The greater the expectation for reinforcement and the greater the attention to modeling cues preceding that reinforcement, the more likely an imitative response.
5. Reinforcement Principle: The more often a reinforcing stimulus follows an imitative response, the more likely the imitative response will occur in the future.

Frederick Kanfer and Sue Hageman's Self-Regulation Model [3]

1. Expectation Principle: The more unexpected the consequences of a given behavior, the more likely the occurrence of a problem.
2. Problem-Monitoring Principle: The more often the problem occurrence, the more likely the self-monitoring.
3. Self-Monitoring Principle: The more often the self-monitoring, the more likely the assessment of the situation.
4. Situational Monitoring Principle: The more frequent the assessment of the situation, the more likely the determination of effects of the problem on long- or short-term standards.
5. Self-Evaluation Principle: The more frequent the determination of effects on long- or short-term standards, the more likely the evaluation of the magnitude of the problem.
6. Discrepancy Principle: The greater the magnitude of the discrepancy, the more likely the identification of the problem and the selection of behaviors that can solve it.
7. Reinforcement Principle: The more often a reinforcing stimulus follows the problem solving and solution using will occur in the future. selection of behaviors to solve it, the more likely the problem solving and solution using will occur in the future.

[1] George Caspar Homans, *Social Behavior, Its Elementary Forms* (New York: Harcourt Brace Jovanovich, Inc. 1974)
[2] Albert Bandura, *Social Learning Theory* (Englewood Cliffs, New Jersey: Prentice-Hall, Inc. 1977). The propositions listed for the Bandura theory were derived from an assessment of descriptions of the self-regulatory process in social learning theory.
[3] Frederick H. Kanfer and Sue Hageman, "The role of self-regulation," In Lynn P. Prehm (Ed.) *Behavior Therapy for Depression* (New York: Academic Press, 1981), 143-179. The propositions listed for the Kanfer-Hageman model were derived from an assessment of descriptions of the self-regulatory process in this work.

This analysis gives a new perspective to the problem of adaptation. Darwin and Skinner shared the view that environments, not organisms, determined the structures and behaviors that survive. Although this is valid over the long term, organisms actively define what types of adaptive problems they will solve over the short term. They scan and then select environments best suited to their needs. From one moment to the next, environments are passive presenters of menus of opportunity for organisms to pursue or ignore, as Robert B. MacLeod explains:

> Adaptation, in the Darwinian sense, refers to progressive changes in species in response to changes in an independently definable physical environment. Darwin made his case, and we need not quarrel over his specific hypotheses. The adjustment of the individual to his environment suggests an alluring analogy, but I don't think that the analogy holds. We can plot changes in physical environment (climatic, nutritional, and so forth), and see how organisms adapt themselves in successive generations. But for the individual organism the situation is not really analogous. *The individual selects from its physical (and cultural) environment that to which it will respond. It is thus not only shaped by but also a shaper of its environment.* [italics added][1]

Self-regulation theory is consistent with this analysis. In addition to building upon the correspondence mechanisms described by evolution and operant principles, the theory also shares concepts with other models of human self-regulation—George C. Homans's theory of social exchange; Albert Bandura's social learning theory; and Frederick Kanfer and Sue Hagerman's self-regulation model. Table 6.1 presents these models to illustrate. For example, the theory's *expectation proposition* is similar to Homans's value proposition, Bandura's expectation principle, and Kanfer and Hagerman's expectation principle. The *choice proposition* is comparable to Homans's success proposition. The *response proposition* corresponds to Homans's rationality proposition; and the *gain proposition* serves the function of Bandura's and Kanfer and Hagerman's reinforcement principles.

Self-regulation theory is also different from other theories. Its definitions, assumptions, and propositions describe self-regulatory operations responsible for adaptive success, while its hypotheses predict outcomes from interactions between environmental contingencies and those operations. For example, one set of hypotheses predicts that when contingencies are too favorable (optimal) or too unfavorable (suboptimal), self-regulatory behavior decreases. On the other hand, when self-regulatory behavior occurs during optimal contingencies, it is most likely to maximize gain toward goals. To verify hypotheses such as these, as well as the propositions that support them, the theory needs precisely defined concepts and operations.

Self-Regulation Definitions, Assumptions, and Propositions

The definitions that constitute the theory specify concepts and events that explain adaptation. The *assumptions* identify the untested and possibly untestable

Table 6.2
Types of Terms Used in Self-Regulation Theory

Environmental Indicators	System Indicators	Regulation Indicators

Choice Contingency
Goal Contingency
Moderately Favorable Choice
  Contingency
Moderately Favorable Goal
  Contingency
Optimal Choice Contingency
Optimal Goal Contingency
Suboptimal Choice
  Contingency
Suboptimal Goal Contingency
	Actual State
	Discrepancy
	Gain
	Goal Attainment
	Goal or Goal State
	Maximum Gain
	Optimality
	Result
		Choice
		Cost Responses
		Expected Gain
		Feedback Seeking
		Gain Responses
		Optimal Adjustment
		Optimality of Choice
		Optimality of Performance
		Optimality of Past Gain
		Optimality of Expectation for
		  Gain
		Self-Regulatory Behavior

relationships between events presumed to be true, and the *propositions* describe how the regulatory process works—how expectations, choices, and responses interact to produce gain toward goal attainment.

Definitions

Three types of definitions make up the theory: definitions that describe environmental conditions, definitions that specify the status of the self-regulating system, and definitions about the operations performed by the system. The environmental indicators reflect condition favorability or optimality for goal attainment; the system indicators reflect the system's progress toward goal attainment; and the regulation indicators reflect the optimality of the regulator's expectations, choices, responses, and results. Table 6.2 lists the three types, and Table 6.3 gives their definitions.

Assumptions

Self-regulation theory assumes that the behavior of all living organisms, including humans, is a function of discrepancies between actual and preferred conditions. When discrepancies occur, the organism responds to reduce the discrepancy (Assumption 1 in Table 6.4). The theory also assumes that goal-directed behavior is a function of its success in reducing the discrepancy between actual and preferred conditions. When one set of behaviors or thought patterns produces a greater discrepancy reduction than another, those patterns occur again in the future (Assumption 2). Finally, the theory assumes that when efforts to reduce discrepancies consistently fail, the organism either dies because it cannot fulfill its vital needs or it adjusts by resetting preferred conditions to equal actual conditions (Assumption 3).

Table 6.3
Terms and Definitions in Self-Regulation Theory

1. **Actual State**: most recent gain toward goal attainment.

2. **Choice Contingency**: an event or condition that is necessary to identify operations that produce gain.

3. **Choice**: the distribution of responses between two or more alternatives.

4. **Cost Responses**: responses that do not produce gain toward goal attainment (e.g., feedback responses and incorrect responses).

5. **Discrepancy**: the difference between the actual state and the goal state.

6. **Expected Gain**: the gain toward goal attainment the regulator chooses to produce.

7. **Feedback Seeking**: responding that produces information about goal states, actual states, options, performances, and results.

8. **Gain Responses**: responses that produce gain toward goal attainment.

9. **Gain**: an amount of discrepancy reduction between the goal state and the present state.

10. **Goal Attainment**: the actual state equaling the goal state.

11. **Goal Contingency**: an event or condition that is necessary for the actual state to equal the goal state.

12. **Goal or Goal State**: the gain that makes the actual state equal the goal state.

13. **Maximum Gain**: the possible gain from a given operation.

14. **Favorable Choice Contingency**: an event or condition that increases the probability of choosing the best option.

15. **Favorable Goal Contingency:** an event or condition that increases the probability of performing the operations necessary for goal attainment.

16. **Optimal Adjustment:** when past gains, expectations, choices, and performances are optimal.

17. **Optimal Choice Contingency:** an event or condition that maximizes the probability of identifying the best option.

18. **Optimality of Choice:** ratio of the maximum gain possible from the actual choice to the maximum gain possible from the best choice.

19. **Optimal Goal Contingency:** an event or condition that maximizes the probability of performing the operations necessary for goal attainment.

20. **Optimality of Expectation for Gain:** ratio of gain expected to gain possible from the options available.

21. **Optimality of Performance:** the ratio of gain responses to gain responses plus cost responses.

22. **Optimality of Past Gain:** ratio of actual results to expected results.

23. **Optimality:** the extent to which the goal contingency, choice contingency, past gain, expectation, choice, or performance increases gain toward goal attainment.

24. **Performance:** distribution of responses between gain responses and cost responses.

25. **Self-Regulatory Behaviors:** choosing gain, choosing options to produce gain, performing operations to produce gain, feedback seeking on goal states, actual states, options, performance, and results.

26. **Suboptimal Choice Contingency:** an event or condition that decreases the probability of identifying the best option.

27. **Suboptimal Goal Contingency:** an event or condition that decreases the probability of performing the operations necessary for goal attainment.

125

Table 6.4

Assumptions of Self-Regulation Theory

Assumption 1. All behavior is a function of the discrepancy between a goal state and a current state: the more frequent the discrepancy between an expected state and current state, the more frequent the self-regulatory behavior.

Assumption 2. The closer the match between expected and current states as a consequence of self-regulatory behavior, the more likely similar self-regulatory behavior will occur for discrepancies between similar expected and current states.

Assumption 3. The more persistent the discrepancy between the expected and current state, the more likely the current state will become the expected state.

These assumptions are consistent with the notion that humans are like other living systems that solve problems of survival by searching, selecting, and then maintaining exchanges that maximize correspondence between needs and resources. All living systems expend time, energy, and behavior in return for environment resources. The principle that describes the utility of these exchanges is economic. Systems balance their costs against their gains as they strive to maximize. James Grier Miller describes these functions in *Living Systems*:

> How successfully systems accomplish their purposes can be determined if those purposes are known. A system's efficiency, then, can be determined as the ratio of the successes of its performance to the costs involved. *A system constantly makes economic decisions directed toward increasing its efficiency by improving performance and decreasing cost.* Economic analyses of cost effectiveness are equally important in biological and social science but much more common and more sophisticated in social than in biological sciences. . . . *How efficiently a system adjusts to its environment is determined by what strategies it employs in selecting adjustment processes and whether they satisfactorily reduce strains without being too costly.* [italics added][2]

Miller uses the least-effort-for-maximum-gain principle to explain how systems adjust: "systems tend to reduce the costs, in energy expenditure or other units, of their actions. . . . [They] use least costly adjustments first and more costly ones later. . . . [They] conserve resources by maintaining their subsystem functions efficiently and by keeping down costs."[3]

Of course, not all species are equally capable of minimizing costs and maximizing gains across environments. Most are effective in only one environment. Mammals are more efficient than fish on land, fish are more efficient than mammals in water, and reptiles are more efficient in both land and water, but not as efficient as either fish in water or mammals on land. We humans are the most versatile of all, having found ways to adapt in locations no others have yet attempted. We owe our success to more effective and efficient problem solving. *We can make decisions at the margin*—within that narrow band of opportunity where gains only slightly outweigh costs. We are blessed with internal "Darwin machines'' (our brains), which generate alternatives, test them, and then evaluate possibilities before committing to risky tests.[4] When we choose to do so, we can think it through before we act it out. This maximizes gains and minimizes cost, as Herbert Simon explains in *Reason in Human Affairs*:

> According to the behavioral theory, rational choice may require a great deal of selective search in order to discover adaptive responses. The simplest, most primitive search processes require that possible responses be first generated and then tested for appropriateness. The generator-test mechanism is the direct analogue, in the behavioral theory of rationality, of the variation-selection mechanism of the Darwinian theory. Just as in biological evolution we have variation to produce new organisms, so in the behavioral theory of human rationality we have some kind of generation of alternatives—some kind of combinatorial process that can take simple ideas and put them together in new ways. And similarly, just as in biological theory of evolution the mechanism of natural selection weeds out poorly adapted variants, *so in human thinking the testing process rejects ideas other than those that contribute to solving the problem that is being addressed.* [italics added][5]

The propositions of self-regulation theory build upon this basic assumption that human behavior is a systemic reaction to the problem of change. When we perceive discrepancies between what we expect and what we observe, we pay attention. We gather information to determine the relevance of the discrepancy to ongoing goal pursuits. If the discrepancy suggests an improved opportunity for pursuing an interest or avoiding a setback, we act to reduce the discrepancy.

The propositions do not prove that we act on discrepancies. Rather, they describe how we act to produce gain toward reducing a discrepancy once we perceive it. The hypotheses of the theory presented in a subsequent section address this motivational question. They posit, for example, that moderately favorable goal and choice contingencies increase self-regulatory behavior, while optimal and suboptimal contingencies decrease it.

Propositions

The propositions from self-regulation theory postulate four regulatory functions: (1) the identification of gain that will reduce a discrepancy (expectation proposition), (2) the selection of behaviors or operations that will produce that gain (choice proposition), (3) the distribution of responses between producing gain and gathering information (response proposition), (4) the gain toward goal attainment produced by interactions between past gains, expectations, choices, and responses (gain proposition). Table 6.5 presents these propositions.

The indicator variables that reflect the status of these four operations are (1) optimality of past gain, (2) optimality of past expectations, (3) optimality of choice, (4) optimality of performance, and (5) percent of maximum gain. According to the gain proposition, when the first four are optimal, the percent of maximum gain is 100. Unfortunately, getting all four at their maximum opti-

Table 6.5
Propositions of Self-Regulation Theory

__Expectation Proposition__: The closer to optimal the past gain toward goal attainment and the smaller the discrepancy between the actual state and the goal state, the closer to optimal the expectation for gain.

__Choice Proposition__: The closer to optimal the past gain toward goal attainment and the more salient the differences between options, the closer to optimal the choice.

__Response Proposition__: The closer to optimal the past gain, expectations, and choices, then the closer to optimal the distribution of responses between task completion to meet the goal and feedback seeking about goal state-actual state discrepancies, options, task performance, and results.

__Gain Proposition__: The closer to optimal the past gain, expectations, choices, and responses, then the closer to maximum the gain toward goal attainment.

malities is difficult because changes in one produce changes in others. If optimalities of past gain or expectations decline, then optimalities of choice and performance are likely to decrease as well, which further depresses optimalities of past gain and expectations. The reverse occurs when the optimalities of one or more system indicators increase the optimalities of other indicators. The indicators can also interact in patterns that show no trend toward increased or decreased optimality. Therefore, maximum gain is a product of the four optimality values as indicated by the formula:

$$\% \text{ Max Gain} = (\text{Opt. of Past Gain}) \times (\text{Opt. of Exp.}) \times (\text{Opt. of Choice}) \times (\text{Opt. of Perf.}) \times 100$$

Optimality of past gain is the actual gain divided by the actual gain plus the difference between the actual gain and the expected gain; *optimality of expectations* for gain is expected gain divided by maximum gain possible; *optimality of choice* is possible gain from the actual choice divided by the possible gain from the best choice; and *optimality of performance* is the total responses to complete the choice (gain responses) divided by gain plus cost response.

The product of these optimalities is 100 percent when (1) past gain equals expected gain, (2) expectations for gain are maximum, (3) choice is the best of the options available, and (4) gain responses are maximum and cost responses are minimum. This means the regulator's past gains met expectations, present expectations are as high as possible, choices are the best possible under the circumstances, and the performance is maximally effective and efficient.

In operant studies where "the pigeon 'knows' its pecks bring the food; the rat 'knows' the lever press avoids the shock, and so on . . . [and experimenters] usually make sure that the correlation between response and reinforcement is clear,"[6] past gains, expectations, and choices are optimal, or "1." The rat knows exactly what to expect and how to get exactly what it expects. Therefore, the remaining indicator of gain is the proportion of responses it devotes to pecking (or lever pressing) according to the formula:

$$\frac{\text{Gain Responses (Lever Pressing or Pecking)}}{\text{Total Responses (Gain + Cost Responses)}} = \text{Gain (from choice)}$$

Under these conditions, the greater the distribution of responses toward completing the selected task (for example, pressing the right lever or pecking the right disk), then the greater the gain from that selection. This is equivalent to Herrnstein's matching law, according to which the proportion of reinforced responses on one alternative is to the total responses what the total reinforcements from that alternative is to the total reinforcements from all alternatives:

$$\frac{\text{Reinforced Responses}}{\text{Total Responses}} = \frac{\text{Reinforcement (from selection)}}{\text{Total Reinforcement}}$$

Unfortunately, there are few situations in which we know exactly what to expect and exactly how to get exactly what we expect. Most of the time, we are uncertain what causes what. In fact, much of the struggle to adjust boils down to solving problems of uncertainty. Herrnstein agrees: "It is worth noting, however, that animals (and people) in nature may often be quite confused over what causes what."[7]

Self-regulation theory explains adjustments to these less-than-optimal conditions by adding three variables: optimality of past gains, optimality of expectations, and optimality of choices. Combined with optimality of performance, the product of these variables describes human gain toward goal attainment under all conditions, including those in which regulators are confused and uncertain about what causes what.

A Method of Measuring Self-Regulated Gain

Measurement of gain toward goal attainment is a prerequisite for studying self-regulation. With accurate descriptions of how individuals regulate their expectations, choices, and responses, we can identify with precision the effects of environmental factors on different self-regulatory behaviors. We can determine, for example, if failures to adjust are due to unrealistic (too high or too low) expectations for gain, poor judgements about deciding what to do, or ineffective and inefficient follow-through on decisions. Furthermore, we can observe and record the gain produced by different patterns of regulation during optimal and suboptimal environmental conditions in order to understand why some individuals thrive under conditions that others find impossible to negotiate. Research on self-regulatory operations and their effects may also explain why some education and treatment programs are successful in helping regulators manage their expectations, choices, and behaviors while others are less so.

The following demonstration describes experimental procedures that measure how subjects adjust their expectations, choices, and performances in pursuit of a goal. Figure 6.1 illustrates the simulation. Subjects interact with a microcomputer to (1) set goals indicating the discrepancy reduction that is necessary for goal attainment (Discrepancy Condition box), (2) specify their expectations for gain for each of five attempts to meet the goal (Expectations box), (3) choose a task that will produce the expected gain (Choices box), (4) distribute their responses between performing the task and gathering information on the discrepancy, choices, and results (Responses box), and (5) produce gain toward goal attainment (Results box).

Apparatus and Operations

A Macintosh IIci computer presents self-regulation problems, which subjects solve to earn money by estimating exactly what they can produce. The computer presents "Maximum Gain" procedures and then records subjects' responses and time spent during each phase of the game.

The five computer panels in Figure 6.2 correspond to the five question boxes in Figure 6.1. The panels show up on the computer screen one at a time. A menu panel (not shown) enables subjects to move from panel to panel by clicking the mouse on the number beside the desired panel. Subjects exit the panels by pressing the "Menu" box at the bottom of each panel, which returns to the menu panel for another selection.

Subjects use the "Goal Panel" to specify the number of points expected for a fifteen-minute session ("My Goal") and to specify the goal attainment standard, which is the monetary reward for producing points within an x-point range of expectations. Subjects use the "Options Panel" to learn about the task options and how many points those tasks produce (toward goal attainment). They use the "Choice Panel" to indicate the tasks they plan to work on and the number of points they expect to produce. The "Task Panel" presents the task or problem that subjects will work on in order to earn points. The "Results Panel" provides information on results of the completed periods of the ongoing session.

Depending on the experiment, subjects work non-academic or academic tasks. The non-academic tasks are variations of brick-laying to build a wall. After choosing a task by clicking the "Task Panel," subjects work on tasks by clicking the mouse on the wall image continuously as it "lays" bricks (brick outlines darken) from left-to-right and from bottom-to-top. Academic tasks are variations of math and reading problems with multiple-choice answers in rows that have structural configurations similar to brick-laying to build a wall. Here, however, subjects complete rows of problems from left-to-right and top-to-bottom to fill an assignment page. Like brick-laying, assignments vary according to the number of problems per row and number of rows per assignment.

Subjects gain access to data in the information boxes of the five action panels— "Goal Panel," "Options Panel," "Choice Panel," "Task Panel," and "Results

Figure 6.1
Research Model for Self-Regulation

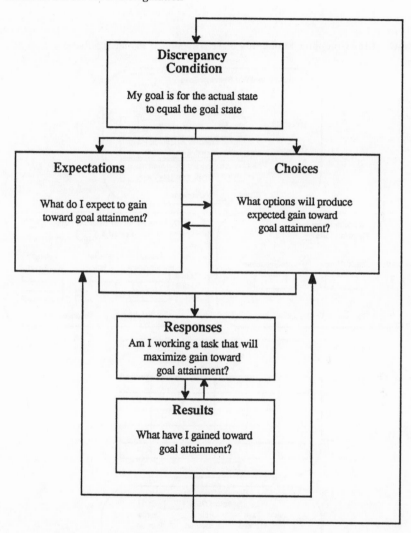

Panel''—by placing the cursor on the information box and clicking it one or more times. This procedure applies to all boxed areas of the panels.

The Self-Regulation Problem

The problem of self-regulation is a problem of managing resources. Given limited time, energy, and behavior, what distribution of resources yields the greatest gain toward meeting a goal? Every session begins with a finite amount

Figure 6.2
Panels of the Computer Simulation of Self-Regulated Problem Solving

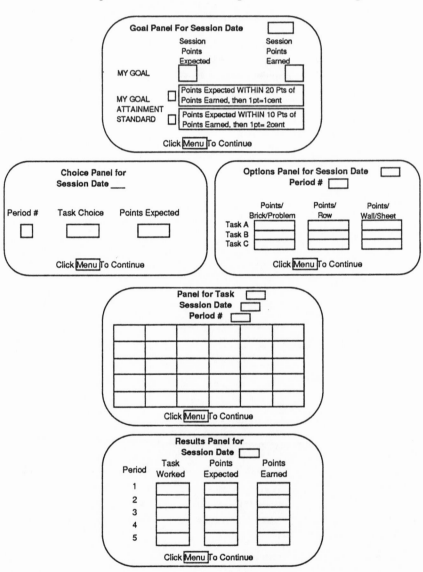

of time and behavior. A session consists of five three-minute periods during which subjects have only 100 responses *to gather information* about goals, standards, choices, and results (feedback seeking); *to choose* goals, standards, and tasks to work on (choosing); and *to work* on chosen tasks to produce points toward goals (task responding). If they wish, subjects can spend all their time and behavior gathering information. The problem with this decision is that it does not produce gain toward the goal. At the other extreme, subjects can choose a task at random and work on it continuously until time runs out. The problem with this decision is that it does not produce gain toward a goal because goal setting is a requisite for points resulting from task responding to count toward a goal.

Between these positions lies a middle option that distributes some time and behavior to gathering information about goals, options, and results, some time and behavior to setting goals and choosing tasks, and as much time and behavior as possible to producing gain toward goals. In general, one would expect that the less time spent choosing and gathering information and the more time spent producing gain, the closer to optimal the expectation for gain. Obviously, when subjects know exactly the gain they can produce in a given session and when they know which task produces that gain, then they can minimize time and behavior spent gathering information and maximize time working on tasks that achieve expected results. And when results meet expectations, they have maximized gain (i.e., their past gain, expectations, choices, and performances equal "1," Proposition IV).

This is more easily said than done, however. Our studies with adults working on complex self-regulation problems (involving three goal standards and five task options varying in profitability along six dimensions) indicated that none was able to improve adjustments and increase gains. Only when the number of goal standards, task options, and task differences decreased significantly were they able to progress toward optimal adjustment and maximum gains.

Experimental Manipulations

Variables in the "Goal" and "Options" panels constitute "inputs" from the environment that make the goal and choice contingencies more or less favorable. In the Goal Panel, the experimenter makes the goal contingency more favorable by increasing the "opportunity band" that defines a match between the expectation and the result. Increasing the band increases optimality, and decreasing the band decreases optimality. It is easier, for example, to produce point totals within 20 of the expected than within 5. A 20-point goal contingency provides a greater chance of matching one's expectations than the 5-point goal contingency. It is a more favorable contingency.

The experimenter alters *choice contingencies* by increasing or decreasing the opportunity to choose optimally. Discriminations between options become more difficult and less favorable when differences between them are small or when distractors prevent their easy detection. Optimality also decreases when there are many options to consider. This increases the cost of finding the best option. By manipulating any of these dimensions, the experimenter can increase or decrease the optimality of the choice contingency. Ironically, the most favorable of all choice contingencies is the single option. It eliminates the need for and cost of discriminating.

Goal Contingencies. A goal contingency is an event or condition that is necessary for goal attainment. In these studies the contingency is matching expectations within plus or minus x points. During baseline conditions for the studies using the setup similar to the one shown in Figure 6.2, there were two goal standards (see the Goal Panel). The first, and most liberal, standard paid off when results were within 20 points of expectations. If a subject set a goal of 60 points, for example, and actually produced between 40 and 80 points, she received a payoff according to that amount at a ratio of one point per one cent. On the other hand, if the subject produced 39 points or less or 81 points or more, she received nothing. The second goal contingency was more constraining but also more rewarding. If results were within 10 points of the goal, the payoff was two cents for each point. Similarly, any result outside that accepted range produced no monetary return.

Goal contingencies are a constancy of life. There is a limited window of opportunity for achieving one's purpose. Failures in meeting deadlines, dates, and assignments, or mistakes in saying too much or doing too little, illustrate the importance of goal standards. Self-regulators avoid these problems of responding too soon, too late, and with too much or too little by learning to *match how much to do and when to do it with what is required when it is required.*

Choice Contingencies. A choice contingency is an event or condition that is necessary to identify the costs and benefits of working on tasks that produce different point totals toward goal attainment (expectations for session points). The Options Panel presents reward values for each task. For brick-laying tasks the values include (1) the ''Points/Brick'' ratio: the number of points earned for each brick laid; (2) the ''Points/Row'' ratio: the number of points earned for each row completed, and (3) the ''Points/Wall'' ratio: the number of points earned for each wall completed.

The contingency is optimal when differences between options are salient and the subject can select the best option from those available. This usually occurs when (1) there are a few options to choose from, (2) the differences between options are in consistent directions, and (3) the differences are large. Consider two options in which one task produces a point-to-brick ratio of 1:1, a point-to-row ratio of 1:1, and a point-to-wall ratio of 1:1, while the second task produces ratios of 2:1, 2:1, and 2:1, respectively. This contingency approaches optimality because there are only two options, all differences are in the same direction (task 2 being more profitable for bricks, rows, and walls), and the differences are large (task 2 being twice as profitable as task one).

Now consider a less favorable choice contingency, one with two task options exhibiting inconsistent differences. The ratios are 1:1, 4:1, and 1:1 for task 1's bricks, rows, and walls, and 1:1, 1:1, and 20:1 for task 2's bricks, rows, and walls. This calculus of profitability is not as obvious. In the short term, Task 1 may be more profitable because the subject completes rows before completing walls, and she can complete more rows than she can complete walls. On the other hand, every time she completes a wall the payoff is five times the payoff for completing a row. More calculations are necessary to determine the relative profitability. For example, how many rows make up the walls of the two tasks? How much time will it take to complete a wall? And so on. Additional feedback seeking is necessary to answer these questions, and this increases the cost of deciding and choosing.

Measuring Regulatory Operations

The measures of self-regulatory behavior are (1) the frequency and pattern of feedback seeking on the information boxes in the Goal Panel, Options Panel, Task Panel, and Results Panel, (2) optimality of expectations, (3) optimality of choice, (4) optimality of performance, (5) optimality of gain, (6) gain toward goal attainment, (7) patterns of choosing, and (8) distribution of responses.

Feedback Seeking. All information about the game comes at a cost. Subjects must position the cursor on an information box and then click it in order for the data display to appear. Recall that each period begins with a finite amount of time and behavior—three minutes and 100 responses or mouse clicks. This means that every minute or mouse click to get information about a goal condition, task option, or result is one minute less to complete tasks that produce gain toward the goal. This too is a constancy in life. Solutions to problems incur the cost of searching, thinking about what turned up in the search, and analyzing data finds to make rational choices. In self-regulation studies, subjects must wrestle with the same economic forces as in everyday life. No information is free. However, once retrieved, information can be of great service in setting goals, choosing tasks to attain them, and monitoring results to match the expectations required for goal attainment.

The measures of feedback seeking used in these studies are similar to those reported by Hake and Vukelich,[8] Hake, Vukelich, and Kaplan,[9] Mithaug,[10] and Mithaug and Wolfe[11] on social influence effects during cooperation and competition. The apparatus used in those studies (which were conducted over a decade ago) allowed subjects to press a button, which illuminated a light behind an opaque mirror displaying an electromechanical counter, which tabulated self's and others' point totals. This procedure enabled the researchers to record feedback seeking as rigorously as task responding. When information on a counter was important (reinforcing), subjects demonstrated their interest by pressing the light switches repeatedly to view the data.

With its multiple information boxes, the computer screen provides an equivalent, though more elegant and flexible, measure of feedback seeking. In addition to recording subjects' mouse clicks for each viewing of an information box, the computer records real time for each response occurrence. The types of feedback seeking that are tracked are labeled according to the information boxes they target. Feedback on the "Session Points Expected" box of the Goal Panel is known as goal expectation feedback, while feedback on the "Session Points Earned" box of that panel is known as goal points earned feedback, and so on for the remaining information boxes.

Expecting. Subjects set a goal for each session and then set expectations for gain toward meeting that goal for each period. To earn the maximum points each session, they must set expectations for a maximum during goal setting, choose the most profitable task, and then spend maximum responses to generate points and minimum responses gathering information. In these experiments the maximum possible is 550 points. *Optimality of expectations* for gain toward goal attainment (points converted into money) is actual points expected divided by that maximum. When subjects expect the maximum points possible, their expectations are optimal, or "1."

Choosing. Subjects select tasks using the Choice Panel. Each option has a different capacity to produce points according to the ratio described previously. One task option is more favorable than the rest, producing from 25 to 50 percent more points. *Optimality of choice* is the point production or gain possible from the selected task divided by the point production possible from the most productive task. When a subject selects the most productive task, the choice is optimal, or "1."

Task Responding. Optimal choices translate into maximum gain when subjects distribute the most responses possible completing tasks that generate gain toward goal attainment. This means laying bricks on the Task Panel (for the non-academic task) or clicking the mouse on correct answer choices on the Task Panel for math problems (for the academic task). Optimality of performance is the total number of task responses divided by the maximum number of responses possible. This number is 475 per session, which leaves 25 responses for feedback seeking to monitor the goal state-actual state discrepancy, select best task options, and check results. When subjects use all 475 responses to complete tasks, their performance is optimal, or "1".

Results. Optimality of gain is the match between points expected and points produced. The calculation is actual points earned divided by actual points earned plus the difference between the actual and expected points. When expected points equal actual points, optimality is "1."

Gain. Self-regulated gain is the product of the four optimality factors: (1) optimality of past gain (results), (2) optimality of expectations for gain, (3) optimality of choice, and (4) optimality of performance. When all four equal 1, gain is maximum. Gain is the product of these four indicators: optimality of past gain × optimality of expectations × optimality of choice × optimality of performance.

Patterns of Feedback Seeking. Our pilot research on adults indicates that patterns of information seeking affect this success in matching results with expectations. We found four patterns. One concentrates all responding on task performance at the expense of gathering information on goal states, options, or results. This is common when subjects begin the self-regulation problem. It is also resistant to extinction, as some subjects complete many sessions without earning anything because they fail to match results with their expectations. A second pattern—also slow to goal attainment (monetary results)—involves concentrating responses on gathering information (feedback seeking) about options, though it is not as resistant to extinction. A third pattern involves feedback seeking only on results and goal states. This is the most effective in the short term because it permits subjects to calculate what they must do in order to produce a match with their expectations. But this takes time, and it may contradict initial perceptions that the solution is to work fast and produce as many points as possible. The fourth pattern is a combination of feedback seeking on options and results. This is probably the most effective in the long term because it solves two problems at once: matching results with expectations and choosing the most profitable task. Unfortunately, it is also the most challenging to master because a change in one condition may affect the others, which makes determining what causes what more difficult. The computer tabulates the frequency of these responses for subsequent analysis.

Response Distributions. Another variable that describes regulatory strategies is the distribution of resources between gathering information and task responding. Our preliminary data suggest that during the early stages of self-regulation, subjects allocate more responses to feedback seeking and less to task responding. Once they figure a solution, however, they eliminate unnecessary information searches and concentrate resources on producing gain. Although this pattern generally holds, there is much variation between subjects. Some invest substantially more in information searches than others.

Results of Measuring Self-Regulated Gain

The propositions of self-regulation theory specify four variables affecting self-regulatory gain toward goal attainment. They are the optimalities of past gain, expectations, choices, and performances. According to the gain proposition, gain toward goal attainment increases as these indicators approach "1." Table 6.6 lists these propositions and the operational definitions they imply.

It follows from this that the consequences of goal attainment also vary directly with gain toward goal attainment. As gain approaches maximum, the consequences of goal attainment approach maximum, too. Of course, this is consistent with the theoretical notion of adaptive organisms fitting within environmental niches. As gain toward goal attainment approaches the maximum, adjustment to environmental contingencies approach the optimal.

Experimentally, this translates into a correlation between self-regulated gain

Table 6.6
Measures of Self-Regulation

I. The Expectation Proposition: The closer to optimal the past gain toward goal attainment and the smaller the discrepancy between the actual state and the goal state, the closer to optimal the expected gain.

$$\text{Optimality of Past Gain} = \frac{\text{Results}}{\text{Results} + \text{Discrepancy Between Results and Expected Gain}}$$

$$\text{Optimality of Expected Gain} = \frac{\text{Expected Gain}}{\text{Maximum Gain Possible}}$$

II. The Choice Proposition: The closer to optimal the past gain toward goal attainment and the more salient the differences between options, the closer to optimal the choice.

$$\text{Optimality of Choice} = \frac{\text{Maximum Gain Possible from Choice}}{\text{Maximum Gain Possible from Best Choice}}$$

III. The Response Proposition: The closer to optimal the past gain, expectations, and choices, then the closer to optimal the distribution of responses between task completion to meet the goal and feedback seeking about goal state-actual state discrepancies, options, task performance, and results.

$$\text{Optimality of Performance} = \frac{\text{Gain Responses}}{\text{Gain Responses Plus Cost Responses}}$$

IV. The Gain Proposition: The closer to optimal the past gain, expectations, choices, and performance, the closer to maximum the gain toward goal attainment.

$$\begin{pmatrix} \text{Percent of} \\ \text{Maximum} \\ \text{Gain} \end{pmatrix} = \begin{pmatrix} \text{Optimality} \\ \text{of} \\ \text{Past Gain} \end{pmatrix} \times \begin{pmatrix} \text{Optimality} \\ \text{of} \\ \text{Expected} \\ \text{Gain} \end{pmatrix} \times \begin{pmatrix} \text{Optimality} \\ \text{of} \\ \text{Choice} \end{pmatrix} \times \begin{pmatrix} \text{Optimality} \\ \text{of} \\ \text{Performance} \end{pmatrix} \times 100$$

(as measured by the product of the four optimality states) and the consequences of goal attainment (money earned from the game). As the optimality of subjects' game play improves, gain toward goal attainment increases, which in turn increases the consequences of goal attainment—money. The consequences of goal attainment are a direct function of self-regulated gain, which is a direct function of the optimalities of gain, expectations, choices, and performances.

Therefore, optimalities of adjustment determine progress toward goal attainment. In maximum gain, they also predict the consequences of goal attainment. Subjects who regulate expectations, choices, and response distributions optimally produce the greatest gains and earn the greatest returns from goal attainment.

It follows from this that the best measure of adaptive fit is the correlation between the organism's adjustments or self-regulated gains and environmental consequences. The higher the correlation between gains and consequences, the more adaptive the fit; the lower the correlation, the less adaptive the fit. When the fit is perfect, adjustment is optimal, the gain is maximum, and the correlation is 1.00.

Of course, few of us achieve perfect fits with our environments, and when we do, it is because we have chosen goals that we can competently pursue. Then

Figure 6.3
The Adaptive Fits of Three Maximum Gainers

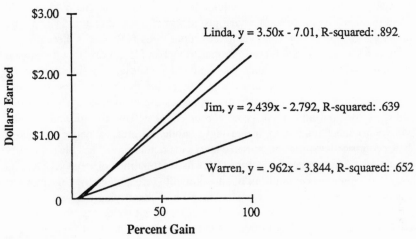

we know the maximum gain to expect. We know how to choose wisely and how to perform competently. So we routinely achieve exactly what we expect. In maximum gain, some subjects developed these competencies better than others. Figure 6.3 presents results of three "Gainers" who worked an average of twelve hours on maximum gain. Linda earned money on 45 percent of her sessions and received an average of $.79 per session; Jim earned money on 44 percent of his sessions and received an average of $.21 per session; and Warren earned money on only 25 percent of his sessions and received an average of $.07 per session.

Linda was the most efficient adaptor because she produced greater earnings with less effort—$.79 per session compared to Jim's $.21 per session and Warren's $.07 per session. Self-regulated gain predicted this more adaptive fit. The correlation between gain and outcome for Linda was .94, but Warren's was .81 and Jim's was .80. In addition, Linda produced gain at a more rapid rate than either Jim or Warren. The regression equations reflect these differences. Note also that although correlations between gain and earnings were the same for Jim and Warren, their rates of producing gain were not. Regression lines for the three subjects represent those different adjustments. Linda's self-regulated gain was 1.64 times more adaptive than Jim's and 3.64 times more adaptive than Warren's; and Jim's gains were 2.54 times more adaptive than Warren's.

Implications of Self-Regulation Theory

Assessing and evaluating adaptive fits is a first step toward understanding self-regulation and its interaction with the environment. A second step is to identify factors that influence when and how the self-regulating system produces gain. What conditions increase the probability that it will adjust optimally and gain maximally? According to the self-regulation propositions, internal and external factors influence its success. We have just analyzed internal factors. The phrase "the closer to optimal the past gain" in Propositions I–III tracks these effects.

Now we turn to external factors. Propositions I and II indicate that the greater the discrepancy between the goal state and actual state and the less salient the differences between options, then the less favorable the optimalities of expectations and choices. With greater discrepancies come increased chances that conditions for goal attainment (goal contingency) will be too difficult for the regulator to meet; and with increasingly subtle differences between options (choice contingency) come decreased chances the regulator will be able to identify best options. These external factors affect the optimalities of expectations and choices. At some maximum limit of suboptimality (e.g., when the regulator has no chance of meeting the goal contingency or of identifying the best option), regulatory activity toward that pursuit will cease altogether as the regulator switches to another goal. The converse logic applies to the limits of environmental optimality. When regulators have near-guarantees from optimal expectations and choices, they are similarly unlikely to change because current patterns of thinking and doing already produce expected gains. At the same time, decreased regulatory activity has different gain effects during the two conditions. Minimal change in regulatory behavior maintains gain production during optimal contingencies, whereas it has no gain effect during suboptimal conditions.

By implication one would expect that while optimal or suboptimal environmental conditions reduce regulatory activity, environmental conditions intermediate between these limits will maximize activity. From the regulator's perspective, there is no reason to regulate differently during optimal contingencies because present expectations, choices, and performances are sufficient to produce expected gain. During suboptimal conditions, there is no reason to regulate because no amount of change in expectations, choices, and performances will be sufficient to produce gain. Meeting those contingencies is just too difficult. Only during optimally challenging goal and choice contingencies will regulators have a reasonable chance of improving gain by making a change. During these moderately favorable contingencies, a new expectation, a different choice, or an alternative pattern of distributing responses may prove effective. The two hypotheses below summarize these deductions:

Hypothesis 1: The closer to optimal or suboptimal the goal and choice contingencies, the less frequent the self-regulation.

Hypothesis 2: Self-regulation is more likely during moderately favorable goal and choice contingencies than during optimal or suboptimal goal and choice contingencies.

Now consider how these relationships appear in the perceptions of the regulator. Doris is a student who has learned to regulate her behaviors to achieve distant goals. She is an experienced achiever and she gets good grades. She knows what results to expect for a given amount of work. She knows how to choose study strategies and how to distribute her time and effort to complete assignments. She also disciplines herself to follow through on tasks that are necessary to get what she wants.

Doris sets her own goals, strives to achieve them, and then experiences satisfaction when she makes progress. Doris expects to achieve goals that are beyond what she achieved in the past (moderately favorable goal and choice contingencies), which often requires more work and better methods of producing gain than what she had done previously. No one tells her what goals she should set or how she should meet them—although she often seeks advice when she gets confused and does not know where to begin. Doris has the habit of performing at or near her potential in most of what she does. After meeting one goal she sets a more challenging goal next time. This increases her potential as well as her expectations for gain.

Now consider Carey, who is a poor student, dislikes school, avoids homework, and spends much of her time watching television and hanging out with friends. She dreams about what she might be when she grows up but has no idea of what steps are necessary to fulfill her dreams. When asked what grades she expects to earn each semester, she says she expects to fail all her courses. Carey's goals are either so high she cannot achieve them (suboptimal contingencies) or so low she is certain of achieving them (optimal contingencies). When expectations are too high, no amount of planning and working will make any difference; when they are too low, any amount of planning and working will be effective. Consequently, there is no connection between what she expects and what she does. Frequently Carey feels depressed and helpless. She depends so much on external events for stimulation and entertainment that she doesn't know what to do or how to improve her situation. Carey is a poor self-regulator.

Doris pushes herself to greater and greater challenges. At the same time she regulates her expectations, choices, and performances to maximize gain toward what she wants. When she succeeds, she feels good about herself, and depending upon the level of challenge, she concludes that she is either competent or intelligent. She thinks she's competent when she accomplishes goals she has met in the past, and she concludes she is intelligent when she accomplishes challenging goals.

Carey, on the other hand, avoids challenge and repeats patterns of expecting, choosing, and doing that fail to produce results. She rarely gets what she wants, however modest her expectations are. Her infrequent ability to produce expected results on easy goals leads her to conclude she is incompetent, which further depresses her motivation to achieve. When she occasionally produces gain toward a challenging goal (suboptimal contingencies), she concludes she is lucky.

Doris and Carey are at opposite ends of the gain continuum. Doris makes

Table 6.7
Self-Regulation Attributions for Gain during Optimal and Suboptimal Contingencies

	Optimal Goal & Choice Contingencies	Suboptimal Goal & Choice Contingencies
Frequent Gain	Competent Self-Regulation	Intelligent Self-Regulation
Infrequent Gain	Incompetent Self-Regulation	Lucky Self-Regulation

regular progress in her goal pursuits, which leads her to conclude she is competent and occasionally intelligent—depending upon the problems she solves and obstacles she overcomes. Carey, on the other hand, rarely produces gain toward goals. When she fails to achieve what she perceives to be within her grasp, she concludes she is incompetent; when she succeeds occasionally on difficult tasks, she concludes she is lucky. Hypotheses 3–6 describe these predictions, and Table 6.7 illustrates the gain-contingency patterns that produce them.

Hypothesis 3: The more frequent the gain during optimal goal and choice contingencies, the more likely the regulator will perceive the regulation to be *competent*.

Hypothesis 4: The less frequent the gain during optimal goal and choice contingencies, the more likely the regulator will perceive the regulation to be *incompetent*.

Hypothesis 5: The more frequent the gain during suboptimal goal and choice contingencies, the more likely the regulator will perceive the regulation to be *intelligent*.

Hypothesis 6: The less frequent the gain during suboptimal goal and choice contingencies, the more likely the regulator will perceive the regulation to be *lucky*.

Conclusion

This chapter has presented definitions, assumptions, and propositions to explain how optimal adjustments maximize gain. Furthermore, it has described experimental procedures for measuring past gain, expectations, choices, and responses and then illustrated how these factors interact to produce gain toward goal attainment. This demonstration showed that increased correlations between

Figure 6.4
Four Models of Adaptive Responding

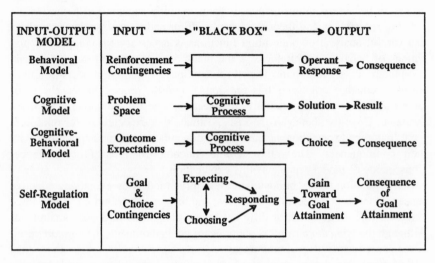

self-regulated gain and consequences of goal attainment reflect greater "adaptive fits" with environmental contingencies. Finally, deductions from the propositions of the theory led to two sets of hypotheses.

The first set predicted that regulatory behavior is more likely during moderately favorable goal and choice contingencies than during optimal or suboptimal contingencies, and the second set predicted how regulators perceive their efforts under different goal and choice contingencies. When regulators produce frequent gain during optimal contingencies, they are likely to perceive their regulation as competent; when they produce frequent gain during suboptimal contingencies, they will perceive their regulation as intelligent. On the other hand, if they experience infrequent gains during optimal contingencies, they will perceive their regulation as incompetent, and if they rarely produce gains during suboptimal contingencies, they will perceive their regulation as being lucky when they are finally successful.

Although these deductions and predictions are substantially different from those emanating from other theories of adjustment, self-regulation theory is not at variance with basic notions that anchor those explanations. Nevertheless, there are significant differences in the structure and focus that bear noting. The four input-output models in Figure 6.4 identify key variables that differentiate between behavioral, cognitive, cognitive-behavioral, and self-regulation explanations.

All models postulate environmental influence via a stimulus effect or input indicated on the left of each model. They also posit outputs indicated on the right. The variables intervening between input and output constitute the "substance" of each explanation. Note that behavioral theory posits no intervening variables, claiming that stimuli representing reinforcement contingencies at input and reinforcing consequences at output fully explain response patterns and frequencies. The intervening "black box" connecting inputs with outputs is unnecessary because stimulus-response chains lawfully account for themselves.

Other researchers and theorists disagree. Information-process theorists claim that careful analysis of brain-mind functions is necessary for complete explanations of behavior. Their focus is the black box. Inputs and outputs depend upon the processes it harbors. The "Problem Space-Cognitive Process-Solution-Result" sequence represents this position. Cognitive process affects the regulator's ability to choose rationally, to select the "best" alternative from those available. Cognitive-behavior theorists postulate that expectations for reinforcement (outcome expectations) connect environmental stimuli and cognitions with their consequences. The "Expectation Outcome-Cognitive Process-Choice-Consequence" model represents this explanation.

Self-regulation theory builds upon these three models by explaining adaptive success in terms of expectations, choices, and response distributions. These three variables interact to produce different levels of gain toward goal attainment. Although the *immediate* result is gain toward goal attainment, the *ultimate* result is the consequence of goal attainment.

Self-regulation theory connects with behavioral theory by postulating that expectations for gain are a function of the distribution of responses between task responding and feedback seeking. Performance becomes optimal when individuals minimize time and effort in seeking information or responding incorrectly and maximize time and effort in completing tasks that reduce discrepancies. Optimality occurs when responding is maximally efficient: all responding is toward goal attainment. There are no wasted responses.

Self-regulation theory extends cognitive theory by postulating that optimal choosing between alternatives affects the effectiveness of efforts to reduce the discrepancy. When individuals choose the best option from those available, they increase the effectiveness of their regulation. Although the theory does not postulate what cognitive strategies facilitate rational choice, it does indicate that difficulty in discriminating essential differences between options will affect one's ability and willingness to choose optimally.

The theory also borrows from cognitive-behavioral theory, which describes the influence of outcome expectations on subsequent choices and performances. Social learning theory, for example, postulates that expectations for reinforcement determine if a response will occur and have an opportunity to be reinforced. Self-regulation theory claims, via the expectation proposition, that the optimality of one's expectations for gain toward goal attainment influences response distributions and, ultimately, gain toward goal attainment.

Of course, these borrowings and connections alone are insufficient to explain what self-regulation is, how it operates, and what factors influence its effectiveness and efficiency. The input-output representation of self-regulation in Figure 6.4, for example, fails to capture how past gain feeds back to affect

Figure 6.5
Self-Regulation Theory's Causal Model

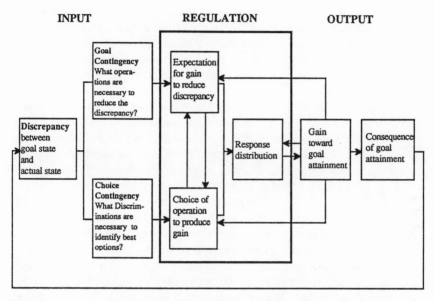

subsequent expectations, choices, and performances. Figure 6.5 illustrates this feature.

The causal model in Figure 6.5 also differentiates between environmental influences or inputs on the one hand and adaptive gain or output on the other. Environmental conditions influence expectations for gain and choices to produce that gain via the goal and choice contingencies that define discrepancy conditions. The *goal contingency* is an event or condition that is necessary for the actual state to equal the goal state, and the *choice contingency* is an event or condition that is necessary to select an option that will satisfy the requirement for goal attainment. Figure 6.5 shows how changes in goal and choice contingencies affect self-regulation, which in turn affects gain resulting from the regulatory effort.

When a regulator expects gain from a perceived environmental opportunity (goal contingency) and when she can discriminate sufficiently well between options to determine what actions will meet the requirement for goal attainment (choice contingency), then regulation is likely. According to the input-output model, goal and choice contingencies affect optimalities of expectations and choices, which affect action follow-through, which in turn affects gain. The input condition affects regulation and the output of regulation affects the continuation or termination of its pursuit.

External conditions determined by the environment (goal and choice contingencies) and internal conditions determined by the system (self-regulation) interact to affect the value of the pursuit and the progress toward its attainment. When changes in the environment produce discrepancies between expectations and observations, and when reducing those discrepancies is expected to be valuable and successful, then the regulator will attempt to reduce them. Moreover, when gain from past regulatory action meets expectations, then progress toward goal attainment is sufficiently reinforcing to maintain regulatory effort in the future.

The model shows self-regulators to be active, reactive, or inactive, depending upon their understanding of the environmental contingencies in effect as well as their perception of the regulatory effects. They may ignore discrepancies because gains required to reduce them are too great for the time and effort available. Or, after committing to a pursuit, they may decide to quit because the enterprise is too expensive compared to alternatives that are available.

The theory provides a framework for understanding these limits of self-regulation. Its explanation for optimal adjustment and maximum gain is consistent with real-world phenomena of optimization, as the next two chapters will show. For example, optimizers are persons who know what they want, how they can get it, and what knowledges and abilities they must employ to maximize gain. They interact with environmental opportunity *to make suboptimal conditions optimal* by gradually improving the match between what they can do and what the environment demands in return for gain toward goal attainment. Optimizers shape themselves and their environments by learning what works and what doesn't, remembering what doesn't, and using what does. They use *self-determination strategies* to regulate their thinking and doing toward valued ends. They self-direct and self-correct their way to self-determined gain.

Notes

1. Robert B. MacLeod, "Retrospect and Prospect," in Howard E. Gruber, Glenn Terrell, and Michael Wertheimer (Eds.), *Contemporary Approaches to Creative Thinking: A Symposium Held at the University of Colorado* (New York: Atherton Press, 1962), 203.

2. James Grier Miller, *Living Systems* (New York: McGraw-Hill, 1978), 41.

3. Ibid., 436.

4. William H. Calvin, *The Cerebral Symphony* (New York: Bantam Books, 1990), 261–273.

5. Herbert A. Simon, *Reason in Human Affairs* (Stanford, CA: Stanford University Press, 1983), 41.

6. Richard J. Herrnstein, "Formal Properties of the Matching Law," *Journal of the Experimental Analysis of Behavior* 21 (1974): 160.

7. Ibid.

8. D. F. Hake and R. Vukelich, "Analysis of the Control Exerted by a Complex Cooperation Procedure," *Journal of the Experimental Analysis of Behavior* 19 (1973): 3–16.

9. D. F. Hake, R. Vukelich, and S. J. Kaplan, "Audit Responses: Responses Maintained by Access to Existing Self or Coactor Scores during Nonsocial, Parallel Work, and Cooperation Procedures," *Journal of the Experimental Analysis of Behavior* 19 (1973): 409–423.

10. Dennis E. Mithaug, "Development of Procedures for Identifying Competitive Behavior in Children," *Journal of Experimental Child Psychology* 8 (1973): 443–460.

11. Dennis E. Mithaug and Mark S. Wolfe, "The Development of Peer Influence Effects in Dyads," *The Mexican Journal of Behavior Analysis* 4 (1978): 93–100.

Chapter 7

Self-Determined Gain

Although all humans self-regulate, not all do so with equal success. Some regulate needs and behaviors to survive from one moment to the next; others self-regulate to maximize gain toward long-term goals. Those who maximize control their destinies by deciding what they want and then selecting the optimal route for getting it. They are happy, fulfilled, self-determined gainers who know how to achieve optimal experience from maximum pursuits. Mihaly Csikszentmihalyi described their experiences in *Flow: The Psychology of Optimal Experience:*

> Contrary to what we usually believe . . . the best moments in our lives . . . are not the passive, receptive, relaxing times—although such experiences can also be enjoyable, if we have worked hard to attain them. The best moments usually occur when a person's body or mind is stretched to its limits in a voluntary effort to accomplish something difficult and worthwhile. Optimal experience is thus something that we *make* happen. For a child, it could be placing with trembling fingers the last block on a tower she has built, higher than any she has built so far; for a swimmer, it could be trying to beat his own record; for a violinist, mastering an intricate musical passage. For each person there are thousands of opportunities, challenges to expand ourselves.[1]

Optimal experience is a byproduct of transforming suboptimal conditions into optimal opportunities. Writer May Sarton discovered it in writing poetry: "I'm absolutely alone then and I'm in a state of great intensity of feeling and intellect. I'm perfectly balanced and nothing else exists. Time doesn't exist."[2] Composer Burt Bacharach found it in writing music: "The music is hard, but I like going back to the room and writing. I'm happy because I push myself into a discipline. I get into a groove where I'm playing the piano and melodies start to flow and I'm happy."[3] And futurist writer John Naisbitt found it while fulfilling his potential: "People who work for a sense of personal worth keep working at it. They want to push and stretch. They want to experience their potential. They want to get right out there to the edge, and that's what they keep pushing for."[4]

Of course, optimal experience doesn't last long, probably because it requires a perfect match between expectations and performance on the one hand and environmental demands and personal gains on the other. Propositions from self-regulation theory capture this delicate balance. It is not surprising the experience is so difficult to achieve.

Recall Carey from the previous chapter who dreamed what she might be when she grew up but had no idea how to realize those dreams. In fact, Carey never connected expectations with plans and actions. When she set expectations that were too high, *no amount* of planning and working could meet them; when she set them too low, *any amount* of planning and working would achieve them. Carey never learned to connect what she expected with what she could do. Carey was a poor self-regulator. She lacked the self-determination skills needed to regulate herself effectively and efficiently.

Today, many youth are like Carey. They don't know how to self-regulate. They leave school without knowing what they like, what they want, or what they can do. They drift and postpone adulthood for years.

Failures to Self-Determine

According to Skinner, "The evolution of culture is a gigantic exercise in self-control."[5] This statement is especially true today. Lack of self-control is at the epicenter of youth's malaise and dependence. In *Adult Children Who Won't Grow Up*, Larry Stockman and Cynthia Graves write:

> it would not be unreasonable to estimate that at least 40 percent of the current group of young adults (eighteen to forty years of age) are excessively dependent. This would mean that approximately 36 million young adults are taking an unhealthy length of time to sever the ties of adolescence. . . .
> The scope of the problem is enormous, and the need to cope with it is urgent. For if we have a generation of unhealthy and overly dependent young adults beginning to raise their own children, they are unlikely to be able to teach their children how to be independent. And the problem will snowball.[6]

Adrienne Miller and Andrew Goldblat call these un-determined youth "Hamlets, Overthinkers Who Underachieve":

> Almost every Hamlet has at least one personality trait that predisposes him to the syndrome. He may never have developed the taste for risk required for success in a free market economy. He may have been humiliated by defeat once too often to engage in competition. He may have little patience for details or knotty problems. He may lack self-confidence. He may hate work. He may be a procrastinator,

figuring that he'll get around to a career sometime in the future. Or he may be passive by nature, counting himself a victim of forces beyond his control.[7]

Susan Littwin, author of *The Postponed Generation*, says that increased dependence of youth is a consequence of growing up in the 1980s. They never learned the self-determination skills that are necessary for independent thinking and doing:

It seems almost impossible to untangle the real and practical problems from the emotional ones. Perhaps it is best to look at it as a social problem that arises from their history. These were the special children of perfect parents, and they've had very little practice in dealing with failure or rejection. But fate has taken these bright, charming middle-class aristocrats and dumped them into a rude, tightfisted world. They tried independence; it didn't work, and that sapped their confidence and sent them home crying.[8]

In "Young beyond Their Years," Kenneth L. Woodward reported that

something happened on the way to the 21st century: American youth, in a sharp reversal of historical trends, are taking longer to grow up. As the 20th century winds down, more young Americans are enrolled in college, but fewer are graduating—and they are taking longer to get their degrees. They take longer to establish careers, too, and longer yet to marry. Many, unable or unwilling to pay for housing, return to the nest—or are slow to leave it. They postpone choices and spurn long-term commitments. Life's on hold; adulthood can wait.[9]

Woodward concluded that American youth lack the self-control and self-discipline that are necessary for mature adulthood:

[Adulthood] *implies the development of character, competence and commitment, qualities essential for self-discipline, cooperation and taking care of others.* By these standards, young Americans entering the 21st century are far less mature than their ancestors were at the beginning of the 20th. The difference is evident in all areas of youthful development: sex, love, marriage, education and work. [italics added][10]

In *Self-Determined Kids: Raising Satisfied and Successful Children*, I myself chronicled a similar set of problems.[11] In the last decade over 70 percent of high school seniors with jobs spent little or none of their earnings for their education or for long-term savings;[12] sexually transmitted diseases increased 318 percent for 15- to 24-year-olds from 1950 to 1986;[13] births to unmarried 15- to 19-year-old mothers increased 251 percent during the same period;[14] arrests for drunk driving and drug abuse for 14- to 17-year-old youth increased over 1,300 percent from 1965 to 1985;[15] homicides involving youth between 15 and 19 years of age increased 215 percent and suicides for the same age group increased 278 percent between 1960 and 1985.[16]

Reports on youth progress at school have been equally disturbing. In 1981 an international math comparison placed eighth graders in the U.S. thirteenth among eighteen countries;[17] in science, U.S. elementary and high school students knew less in 1983 than their counterparts did in 1970;[18] in a survey of economic knowledge conducted in 1988, only 34 percent of U.S. high school students could correctly define "profits," and only 39 percent knew the definition of "gross national product."[19]

In 1983 the National Commission on Excellence in Education reported our "Nation at Risk": high school achievement scores were lower than when the Soviet Union launched Sputnik over thirty years ago, Scholastic Aptitude Test scores for college-bound high school seniors had decreased dramatically during those years, and remedial math courses in public four-year colleges had increased 72 percent. Business and military learners have spent millions of dollars on remedial programs to teach math and reading skills to young workers and recruits.[20] Former Colorado governor Richard Lamm, author of *Megatraumas: America in the Year 2000,* said:

> America is not replacing itself with a skilled enough workforce to keep it economically healthy and socially stable. By no standards are American students and young adults coming close to having the skills, motivation and talents of our economic competitors. Our children are in the bottom third of industrial nations on all education comparisons. Our major economic competitors have children who are ahead of ours from the moment they enter the first grade and these nations graduate far more of their 18-year-olds from high school than we do. Additionally, those they graduate are better educated, more knowledgeable and more motivated.[21]

Apparently, allocating more money for schooling is not the answer. From 1955 to 1986, per student expenditures in public elementary and secondary school *increased* 168 percent in constant 1985–1986 dollars while pupil-teacher ratios *decreased* 23 percent during that same period. Even the nation's sacred cow, special education, reported disappointing results. After more than a decade of special testing, special placements, and special instruction, students leaving school showed few benefits that one could attribute to their educational experiences. In *Why Special Education Graduates Fail*, my colleagues and I reported results from state-wide followup studies of special education graduates that indicated the following:

1. 30 percent dropped out of school; and dropouts had less chance of employment than those who completed school;
2. Only 30 percent of graduates found full-time work;
3. 67 percent earned less than five dollars per hour;
4. Females had a lower probability of employment than males;
5. Only 40 percent lived independently of parents six to eight years after leaving school;

6. Special education programs had no demonstrated effects on post-school adjustments;
7. The probability of unemployment increased over time;
8. Graduates lacked understanding of their needs, interests, and abilities;
9. Graduates lacked self-confidence;
10. Graduates lacked problem-solving skills.[22]

Another study assessing parental perceptions of their adult children's needs after they left schools in Colorado found that students needed to develop self-confidence, problem-solving skills, and an awareness of their own interests, needs, and abilities. Parents were concerned about their adult children's capacities for self-direction.[23]

Whether today's students are college-bound, remedial, or special, they all face serious difficulties after they leave school. Those in regular education suffer from "Postponement," "Boomerang," or "Hamlet" syndromes, and those in remedial and special education programs suffer from excessive dependence. All seem to lack self-direction, self-confidence, and independent problem-solving skills. How different these assessments are from the turn-of-the-century prototypic American who sacrificed to achieve. Recall Christopher Lasch's description of the archetypical embodiment of the American dream:

> [The self-made man] owed his advancement to habits of industry, sobriety, moderation, self-discipline, and avoidance of debt. He lived for the future, shunning self-indulgence in favor of patient, painstaking accumulation; and as long as the collective prospect looked on the whole so bright, he found in the deferral of gratification not only his principal gratification but an abundant source of profits.[24]

Self-Determined Gainers

Although today's shrinking breed of self-determined gainers may subscribe to the same tight-fisted, sacrificial values of fifty years ago, they continue to use *strategies* similar to those employed then. Interviews with leading musicians, politicians, scientists, religious leaders, businessmen, celebrities, and sports stars[25] led Eugene Griessman to identify thirty factors that accounted for their achievements. The three most important were (1) *doing what you enjoy*, (2) *competence*, and (3) *persistence*—the same ones Hill identified in 1937 and Gallup and Gallup described in 1986.

The first factor, doing what you enjoy, received 9.9 of 10 points on Griessman's importance scale. Persons who understood their needs, interests, and abilities directed themselves with the conviction and passion needed to succeed. They were intrinsically motivated. They had the desire that Napoleon Hill called the "starting point of all achievement."[26]

Today's superachievers depend no less upon inner passion and intrinsic motivation to move them forward. Malcolm Forbes, former editor of *Forbes* magazine, said that success depended upon doing what you enjoy:

People often ask me, "How do I become successful?" I say, "Whatever you like to do, just find a way to do it."

The biggest mistake people make in life is not trying to make a living at doing what they most enjoy. There's no job that's all joy. But to work at a job you hate is probably the biggest waste in life. If you don't care about it or you can get by with it and if you're not really consumed to do anything else, fine. But that's a waste. We're all responsive to something and we do our best when we're doing something that has a turn-on to it. There is no other way to go.[27]

In *Do What You Love, The Money Will Follow,* Marsha Sinetar described a vocationally integrated person as one for whom "[work] becomes a devotion, a labor of love, and indeed—whatever the person himself might call it—a spiritual exercise because the individual's concentrative powers, his choices, actions and values, are motivated, prompted and fueled by love, and his service, as it were, is simply the enactment of this positive life-force. His being or essential self lives in all he does."[28]

The second factor emerging from Griessman's study was competence; it received a factor rating of 9.8. According to Griessman:

Competence—to use the language of logic—is not a *necessary and sufficient* cause of high achievement. That is, competence by itself does not always lead to success. There are other very important factors that are essential to high achievement—timing, discovery, mentors, innovation.

But competence probably comes closer than any of the achievement factors to being a *necessary* cause. No one becomes a high achiever without becoming competent at something. Some individuals become high achievers without some of the other factors. Some are persistent but not very focused; others are highly motivated but not particularly good managers of their time. There even seems to be a kind of interchangeability of factors, so that an individual may fall back on determination or sheer grit when the joy of working begins to wane. But all the high achievers know something well, or they learn to *do* something well.[29]

Hill also found competence to be necessary for success: "The accumulation of great fortunes calls for power and power is acquired through highly organized and intelligently directed specialized knowledge."[30] Gallup and Gallup studied the successful people appearing in Marquis's *Who's Who in America* and found that *special knowledge* of one's field was one of three essential factors for success, the other two being common sense and self-reliance.[31]

Griessman's third success factor was persistence, which received an importance average rating of 9.3. "Clearly, high achievers possess the ability to keep at the tasks and careers they choose. They finish the jobs that they consider important and they stick by their guns when attacked. . . . They think about the future, but not too much. Mainly they are intent on doing well what comes to them each day."[32] Hill said that persistence was the *only* factor that could adequately account for the unfathomable successes of a Henry Ford or a Thomas

Edison,[33] and Gallup and Gallup also found that "will power to *persevere* and realize those goals" was important.

Contemporary superachievers testify to its value. "Captain Outrageous," Ted Turner, founder of Cable News Network (CNN) and Turner Broadcast System (TBS), said: *"The secret to my success is that I never quit.* Winners never quit, and quitters never win. You might go bankrupt, you might lose everything, but as long as you're out there still duckin' back, as long as you haven't given up, you're not beaten" (italics added).[34] Jacques Cousteau agreed: "I am obstinate— when I have something in mind . . . I make a list of things I like to play with: the Amazon, Haiti, the windship. I try, and I don't get the money. I try again, and I don't get the money, and after ten years I get it."[35] General Albert C. Wedemeyer said: "I have not given up easily. . . . I've kept on striving to accomplish my objectives. I've met with disillusionments; I met with disappointments. Sometimes I was confronted with deceit, but I kept on anyway along the avenue that I'd selected, and tried to reach the goals."[36] Senator William Proxmire—father of the Golden Fleece Award and holder of the longest string of roll-called votes in Congress—said the secret to success is: "Persistence. Sticking with an objective, accepting defeat, coming back and hammering away at it until you've succeeded."[37]

These factors—*intrinsic motivation*, *competence*, and *persistence*—affect one's ability to match needs, interests, and abilities with environmental opportunity in order to maximize gain. Self-determined gainers build upon strengths and interests. This reduces their costs and maintains their pursuits. Optimizers enjoy gains toward goal attainment as well as the consequences of goal attainment. According to the former president of the American Institute for Psychoanalysis, Dr. Theodore Isaac Rubin:

> Part of what destroys our appreciation of happiness and happiness itself is that we have become product-oriented rather than process-oriented. If you're doing something you enjoy, which gives you satisfaction, the doing is more important than the accomplishment. For me, the process of writing a book is really exciting. When the book is finished, that is another kind of satisfaction. However, if the end result is my only satisfaction, and the process is looked upon with disdain and contempt and is arduous, then I'm missing all the time and energy I put into writing that book waiting for the product. The result of the product is infinitesimal. The joy and happiness from the process lasts much longer and is more involving and more satisfying over an extended period of time in your life.[38]

Our ability to act from intrinsic motive rather than from external control depends upon how intelligently we match up with environmental opportunity. It also depends on how competently and persistently we select and test options to meet those needs. Although each factor contributes to self-determined gain, the centerpiece of effective self-regulation is competence. From it springs intelligent matching and persistent adjusting. As Edward Deci and Joseph Porac explained:

The human organism is in constant interaction with the environment. Humans are active in this process, operating on the environment and adapting to it. By nature they strive to be competent and self-determining in these interactions, because competence and self-determination have important survival value. People need to be effective, to feel like they can bring about desired outcomes. This need for competence and self-determination is the psychological basis of intrinsic motivation.[39]

The Competence Factor

Competence is the single most influential factor in producing gain. As it increases, confidence in setting expectations for gain also increases, which promotes intrinsic interest in the domain. Intrinsic interest, in turn, increases the value of the activity, which increases persistence. Confident people believe in their plans and feel good about following them through. They get their thoughts, feelings, and actions "in sync" to act effectively. This produces positive results, which feed back to reinforce confidence and persistence.

Figure 7.1 illustrates. Confidence and competence interact during thinking and doing to produce gain toward goal attainment. For example, positive feeling and effective thinking about setting expectations for gain affect and are affected by confident and effective thinking during decision making. Moreover, confident and competent expecting and choosing combine to influence actions to follow through confidently and effectively. When actions produce positive results, information about those results feeds back to further increase confidence in thinking and doing.

The cycle works in reverse, too, when negative feelings and disruptive thoughts reduce effective thinking and performance, which in turn decrease confidence and expectations for gain. Peak performers say the most important ingredient to effective action is confidence. When they believe in what they do and how they do it, they don't fail. Feelings and thoughts produce positive or negative expectations for gains. This is the principle behind Norman Vincent Peale's positive thinking philosophy.[40] According to Herbert Benson, author of *Your Maximum Mind*:

> In many ways, the positive-thinking attitude is the *sine qua non* of any successful self-improvement effort. In other words, you must *think* you can achieve a self-help goal before you can expect to reach that goal.
>
> Why should this be?
>
> There are a number of reasons positive thinkers prevail over negative thinkers. For one thing, if you think you can do something, you're more likely to attempt it and then keep on trying until you have given your goal a decent try. Of course sometimes you may very well be wrong. You may try several things and fail. But at least the *possibility* is there that you'll be able to achieve something worthwhile. Conversely, if you think you can't do something, you're likely not to try at all. Or you may try so halfheartedly that you give up at the first sign of difficulty.[41]

Figure 7.1
The Confidence Cycle

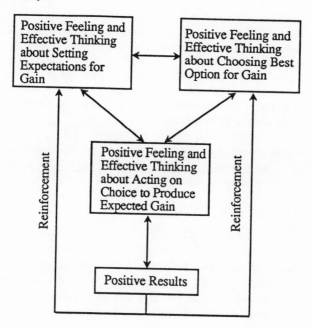

As competence develops, confidence in predicting gains increases, which affects the intrinsic value of performing the activity in the future. Competent people find ways of expressing their talents in the absence of external inducements. They maintain commitment because they enjoy completing tasks and performing activities that occasionally meet their expectations. The next two hypotheses describe how the competence-confidence cycle affects intrinsic interest in the goal pursuit.

Hypothesis 7: The greater the competence in choosing and performing an activity, the greater the confidence that actual gains will match expected gains for that activity.

Hypothesis 8: The more confident and more accurate the prediction of gain toward goal attainment, the greater the intrinsic interest in activities that produce that gain.

Competence increases one's sense of control because it increases capacity to predict. In *Human Nature and Predictability*, Miles Friedman and Martha Willis argue that humans strive for optimal predictability, which is midpoint between

total unpredictability (which threatens) and total predictability (which bores).
Optimal predictability maximizes interest and maintains motivation:

> A major reason the ability to predict contributes to adaptation is because it generates
> self-confidence. As individuals are able to confirm their predictions, they develop
> self-confidence in their ability to predict. And as they develop confidence, they
> anticipate success in predicting and become more persistent in pursuing the con-
> firmation of a prediction. Also, they become more adventurous and less afraid of
> the unknown. Their confidence compels them to believe that sooner or later they
> will be able to confirm their predictions.[42]

This explanation is similar to the one David McClelland uses to account for
the effects of optimal challenge in his theory of achievement motivation.[43]

The Persistence Factor

Confidence and competence increase persistence on tasks otherwise considered
tedious, strenuous, and enervating. World-class pianists spend hours practicing
each day. Writers, artists, National Football League players, professional golfers,
and other competent superachievers persist, too. Why? Because they enjoy improving, accomplishing, and surpassing. George Sheehan, medical editor for
Runner's World magazine and author of *Personal Best*, said:

> I recall toiling up a mountain in a 10-mile race in Durango and having the runner
> beside me say, 'It's so beautiful here.' I took a brief look at the peaks around us
> and the river in the canyon a thousand feet below, said 'Yes' and got back to
> work. My end is not simple happiness. My need, drive, and desire is to achieve
> my full and complete self. . . . The problem in motivation is not the dedication and
> effort and sacrifice needed to get what we want, it is knowing what it is we could
> and must want to begin with.[44]

Lee Trevino, who started golf at age twenty-one, said, "I don't think success
is very difficult to achieve. I think that when the good Lord puts you on this
earth, you are gifted with some type of talent. The biggest problem is that people
are not willing to sacrifice what it takes to achieve their potential in the field
they are talented in."[45]

Griessman's research found similar dedication:

> The amount of time that really great performers, whether musicians or athletes,
> devote to practice is mindboggling. . . . Practice, for writers, means writing and
> rewriting. Albert Payson Terhune used to say that *an aspiring writer should write
> one million words and throw them into the wastebasket. Only after a million words
> is an aspirant qualified to make a beginning in the art of authorship*. The message
> is that any writer who manages to become successful prior to writing a million
> words is well ahead of the game. [italics added][46]

Andy Rooney is persistent, too: "I work quite hard . . . that's one of the things I didn't know about myself until later in life. . . . But when it comes to writing, I work hard. I get in here early every morning *and I stick at it*" (italics added).[47] Charles Schulz begins at 9 A.M. every day to draw pictures for more than 2,000 newspapers; James Michener writes every morning from 7:30 to 12:30; and Louis L'Amour, who authored 101 of the world's most popular westerns, wrote five pages a day, including Sundays and holidays. Isaac Asimov claimed that the principal factors responsible for his success are persistence and industry.

What drives prodigious effort? One answer is self-improvement. In *Intrinsic Motivation and Self-Determination in Human Behavior*, Edward Deci and Richard Ryan reported studies describing how competence and motivation interact:

> The few surveys that have explored the reasons why people engage in sports suggest that for the average amateur, intrinsic factors are dominant in their motivation. . . . [Several studies] found evidence from youths in amateur sports that the most important factors influencing their sports enjoyment and participation were *improvement of skills, sense of personal accomplishment*, and excitement derived from the activity. Consistently less important were the more extrinsic factors such as rewards, uniforms, and social approval. . . . [Other research] found that the primary motivators for young hockey players were the *desires for competence, challenge*, and affiliation. At least in the minds of the young participants, the satisfactions and purposes of sports seem to be intrinsic. [italics added][48]

When producing gain toward goal attainment is enjoyable apart from the consequence of goal attainment, it is more likely to persist. This is intrinsic motivation. It is not surprising that competent, "gain-producing" thinking and doing is intrinsically reinforcing.

Of course, meeting the discrepancy-reduction expectations is also reinforcing and will affect similar striving when problems arise. In fact, the schedule of success one experiences affects persistence. Intermittent discrepancy reductions produce more consistent responding than continuous success. Hence, the occasional discrepancy reduction maintains more problem solving and solution testing than consistent discrepancy reductions. The persistence hypothesis summarizes:

Hypothesis 9: The greater the interest in activities that produce intermittent gain toward goal attainment, the greater the persistence in performing those activities.

The Intelligence Factor

Persons who consistently maximize gain across different goal and choice contingencies appear to be more intelligent than those who only occasionally succeed, and according to Hypothesis 5 (from Chapter 6), they feel more intelligent, too: "The greater the gain during suboptimal goal and choice contingencies, the more likely the regulator will perceive the regulation to be intelligent.'' Although the hypothesis describes how results of self-regulation affect the intelligence attribution, it does not explain what regulators do in order to produce gain during suboptimal contingencies. It does not explain, for example, why people engage in unlikely pursuits in the first place or, once engaged, why they persist until they produce the gain they need and want.

People who adjust intelligently to their environments transform suboptimal goal and choice contingencies into optimal ones. Then they optimize their adjustments and maximize their gains. They do this by choosing environments and goal pursuits that match their needs, interests, and abilities, which increases their chances of success.

Intelligent adjustment begins by finding the harmonious fit between needs, opportunities, interests, and abilities. The closer these match, the more likely an intelligent adjustment. According to Robert Sternberg, author of *The Triarchic Mind*: ''Intelligence is essentially a cultural invention to account for the fact that some people are able to succeed in their environment better than others. We define as 'intelligence' those *mental self-management* skills that enable these people to do so'' [italics added].[49] Sternberg's triarchic theory defines everyday intelligence ''as the *purposive adaptation to, selection of, and shaping of real-world environments relevant to one's life and abilities.*''[50]

Intelligence is effective self-regulation, or, in Sternberg's words, effective ''mental self-management.'' It involves (1) matching what we like and can do with what we want and need to do to get it; (2) determining how best to transform actual states (what we have) into goal states (what we want); (3) implementing the best solutions to produce this transformation; (4) comparing gains with expectations, and (5) adjusting subsequent expectations for gain and estimations of opportunity. Miles Friedman and Martha Willis call this *rational self-regulation* because it increases predictability:

> Successful individuals select goals they wish to pursue and make plans that they predict will achieve the goals. They then proceed to implement, test, and revise the plans in pursuit of the goals. The successful football coach conceives of a plan to win the game and revises it, as conditions dictate, to maximize the probability of winning the game. The successful business executive projects an amount of profit as the goal of the enterprise for the year, makes plans to achieve the goal, mobilizes the resources of the organization, implements the plan, and adjusts it to maximize the chances of achieving the goal.
>
> Thus the prediction motive impels individuals to behave rationally. The practice of rationality improves their ability to predict, and accurate prediction results in adaptation.[51]

Hypothesis 10 describes these matches. The first match is between the goal contingency and the gain we must produce for goal attainment. When the goal contingency matches our interests and abilities to produce required gain, we have achieved the first match. We expect to generate a gain we enjoy and are capable of producing. Our interests and abilities are compatible with the environmental requirement for goal attainment.

Hypothesis 10: During suboptimal contingencies, the closer the match between (1) goal and choice contingencies, (2) interests and abilities, and (3) expectations, choices, and performance, then the more intelligent the adjustment and the more likely the gain.

The second match is between the choice contingency and the discriminations we must make in order to identify options that produce expected gain. Again, when the choice contingency matches our interests and abilities to choose optimally, we have achieved the second match. We enjoy searching for operations to produce gain and we have the talent and skills necessary to make the discriminations that will identify the best option.

The third match is between the choice and the tasks we must perform in order to follow through on that choice. When our interests and abilities match the requirements for completing tasks necessary for choice follow-through, we have achieved the third match. We enjoy working and have the ability to complete essential tasks well enough to produce expected gain.

Matching those three conditions harmonizes needs, interests, and abilities. What we need and want is concordant with our motivation and ability for fulfillment. Figure 7.2 illustrates these match conditions in self-regulated problem solving.

Competence and persistence affect the regulator's progress toward these end-state attainments. Obviously, the more competent and persistent the regulatory effort, the more likely the match between needs, opportunities, interests, and abilities. The effects of these regulatory efforts appear intelligent to the extent that the regulator transforms suboptimal contingencies into optimal ones as suggested in Hypothesis 10.

Self-Determination Strategies

Young children learn strategies for intelligent matching slowly over time. At first they depend upon adults to transform suboptimal conditions into optimal conditions so they can get what they want. Parents clarify and define ill-defined situations by teaching rules and guidelines for what to expect, how to choose, and when to adjust. Gradually children learn self-determination strategies that produce situationally specific expectations, choices, and performances. Then they can transform suboptimal conditions into optimal ones on their own. They can self-regulate their own problem solving to meet goals. This decreases their dependence upon others and increases their intrinsic orientation and motivation to self-direct.

Susan Harter's research on elementary students documented some of these changes from extrinsic to intrinsic classroom orientation, which she described

Figure 7.2
Match Conditions that Affect Intelligent Adaptation

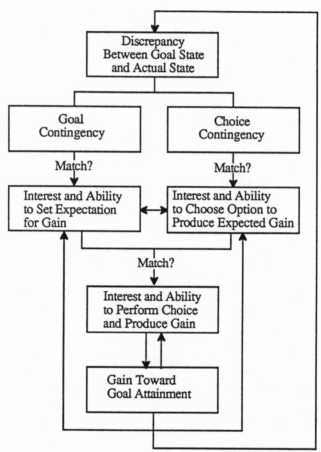

as a shift from reliance on external reward to internalized self-reward.[52] She said that the shift to intrinsic motivation involved "enjoyment in the basic mastery process itself—being curious, seeking challenge, and figuring things out on one's own. They tap one's desire to engage in mastery attempts, to exercise one's cognitive skills, and to be in control of these events. As such, they are more akin to intrinsic motivation in the sense of the effectance-like process identified."[53]

Parents who nurture early competency training may be inadvertently building their children's intrinsic motivation to pursue personal goals. Research conducted by Benjamin Bloom and his colleagues found that early competency training led to increased mastery, self-confidence, and intrinsic motivation:

> As they [young prodigies] began to receive recognition for the talent in the early years of instruction, the children's investment in the talent became greater. No longer was the prime motivation to please parents and teachers. It now became the individual's special field of interest. The child became more capable and outstanding in this talent field than he or she was in other areas, such as particular school subjects, other social and extracurricular activities, or other talent fields. The child was identified by others as having special qualities in the talent field and became known to himself as well as to others in terms of his involvement in that field.[54]

Self-knowledge about strengths and weaknesses developed at the same time. One child reported: "[I was] better at tennis. . . . I knew I'd be a good professional in tennis. Whereas in basketball . . . I wasn't physical enough. Those guys, they're big. They're physical. . . . They were bigger. I was maybe smarter. But I didn't have the raw physical assets."[55] Another young athlete said: "I played basketball, baseball, and a little football. . . . I played baseball regularly, and that was probably my first love . . . besides tennis. And it was a problem because it's played at the same time of year. . . . And I couldn't do both after a while. I did do both for a couple of years, [but] I just didn't have the time for it. [I chose tennis], I guess, [because of] the uniqueness of the sport maybe. And I had done well in it. . . . And while I liked playing team sports, I guess maybe the individual aspect did something for me."[56]

Youth with competencies soon develop their own self-determination strategies because they know what they need and want and how to set expectations and choose options that are consistent with those needs and wants. These conditions combine to produce follow-through on their choices. By the time they reach their teens, they self-direct and self-correct in many areas of their lives. They are effective and efficient self-regulators.

Unfortunately, not all students have such robust starts toward self-determined gain. Many don't know what they like or what they can do, so they depend upon their parents and teachers to tell them. Although adult-directed problem solving may be effective and efficient, it delays learning to self-regulate. Eventually all students must direct their own thinking and doing in pursuit of personal goals. Parents and teachers would serve young people better by teaching them self-determination strategies that facilitate self-regulated problem solving to meet goals.

This has been the approach employed at the Center for Educational Research at the University of Colorado,[57] where my colleagues and I developed procedures to teach adults with disabilities self-determination strategies to facilitate self-regulated problem solving to meet employment goals.

Figure 7.3 shows the discriminations these problem solvers learn in order to discover for themselves what they like and what they can do. To "Find Best

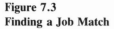

Figure 7.3
Finding a Job Match

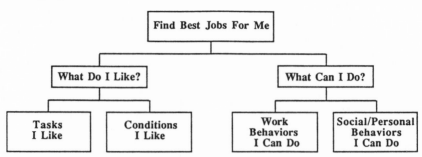

Jobs for Me,'' they discriminate between "What Do I Like?" and "What Can I Do?" To answer "What Do I Like?" they break the problem into: "Tasks I Like" and "Conditions I Like." To answer "What Can I Do?" they identify "Work Behaviors I Can Do" and "Social/Personal Behaviors I Can Do." These questions help them match their interests with their abilities.

Figures 7.4 and 7.5 demonstrate how self-regulated thinking and doing determine "What I Like." In Figure 7.4 participants *regulate their thinking* by asking means-ends questions that connect the goal state—finding "What I Like"—with specific actions that will achieve the goal state. They ask themselves: "What do I need to do?" "Can I do it now?" and "What will help me do it now?" In Figure 7.5 participants *regulate their doing* by asking means-ends questions that connect actions with plans to act: "What do I need to do?" "What am I going to do?" "What am I doing now?" "What have I done?" and "What do I need to do next time?"

The staff facilitate learning by requiring participants to specify what they expect they will like and be able to do *before* going into the community for hands-on tryouts. Immediately after work in the community, they assess their reactions by comparing them with expectations. Then they identify discrepancies and decide what they will do next time to reduce those differences. They repeat the process until they agree with themselves about tasks and conditions they like.

A similar procedure helps participants discover what they do best. After completing their work, they circle their strengths and weaknesses on the top half of a one-page self-assessment form. Next they give it to their supervisor, who completes the same evaluation on the bottom half and returns it. Then they compare their self-assessments with their supervisors' evaluations. They note discrepancies and decide what to do next time to increase correspondence. After many self-assessments and comparisons, participants learn to evaluate themselves according to supervisor expectations at the workplace.

These procedures are simple, practical, and effective. They help persons who have never made intelligent matches become more effective self-regulators on the job. The procedures also demonstrate how to teach strategies necessary for self-regulated problem solving: (1) setting an expectation (Do I like this task? Can I perform it?), (2) seeking feedback about that expectation (going to job sites to experience tasks and getting evaluations from supervisors), (3) comparing that information with expectations, (4) identifying discrepancies between expectations and results, and then (5) identifying operations to reduce the discrepancy (change expectations and/or behaviors next time).[58]

The Means-Ends Mechanism

Goal attainment requires analytic thinking and systematic responding. In recent decades, cognitive researchers have described a variety of metacognitive strategies that increase competent thinking,[59] and behavioral researchers have introduced a wide range of self-control procedures to increase competent follow-through.[60] These research efforts represent the two major approaches to teaching self-determination strategies: *self-instruction*, which directs thinking toward action-oriented solution behaviors (such as the means-ends questions in Figure 7.4), and *self-management*, which increases the self-monitoring, self-evaluation, and self-reinforcement skills to improve follow-through (as illustrated in Figure 7.5).

Self-determination strategies like self-instruction and self-management catalyze self-regulation by improving thinking and doing. They help regulators solve problems to meet distant goals. Figures 7.4 and 7.5 illustrate how these procedures help persons with severe mental and physical disabilities direct their own job searches. The procedures are effective because they jumpstart the means-ends mechanism for self-regulation.

It is worth recalling once again that means-ends problem solving is not unique to self-regulation theory. Analogous cybernetic mechanisms have been around for decades. In 1960 George A. Miller, Eugene Galanter, and Karl H. Pribram formulated the ''TOTE'' to account for the organization of all behavior—from the simplest reflex response to the most complex problem-solving behavior.[61] The TOTE—meaning test-operate-test-exit—describes how the nervous system responds to discrepancies between expected and observed signals. Incoming signals undergo neurologic (or perceptual-cognitive) tests for consistency with expected values. If results indicate a discrepancy, the system initiates operations to return the system to congruence. The TOTE is a non-teleological explanation for purposeful behavior.

Allen Newell and Herbert Simon used a similar device to develop computer simulations of human problem solving. The algorithm for those programs was finding the discrepancy between goal states and actual states, finding an operation to reduce the discrepancy, and then testing the operation. If the program could not test the operation, it searched for conditions that enabled that test. The program repeated the process until it found an operation it could perform or it gave up the search. Once it found an operable means, the program reversed

Figure 7.4
Competent Thinking "To Find Jobs I Like"

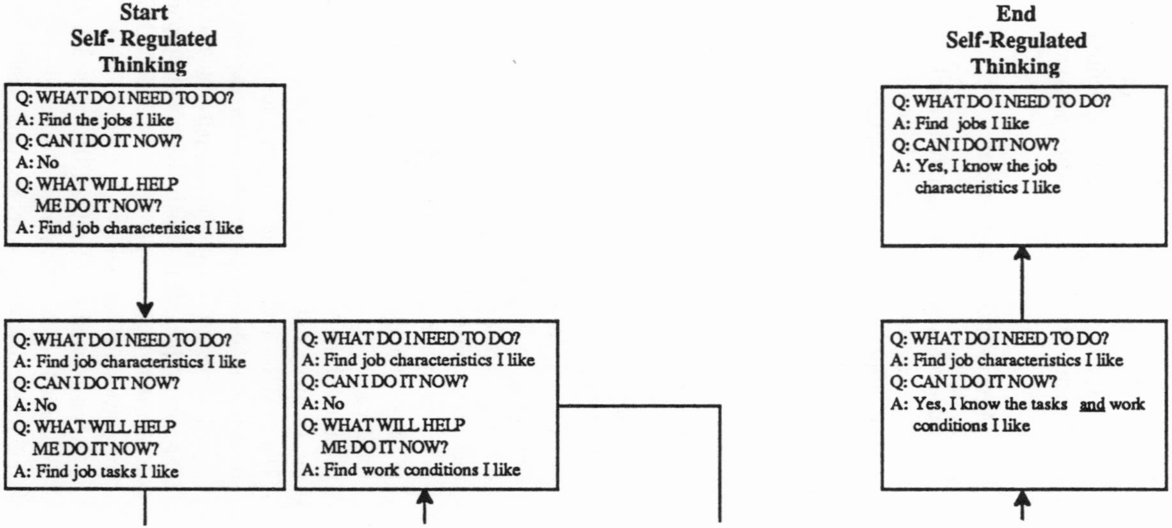

Start
Self-Regulated
Thinking

Q: WHAT DO I NEED TO DO?
A: Find the jobs I like
Q: CAN I DO IT NOW?
A: No
Q: WHAT WILL HELP
   ME DO IT NOW?
A: Find job characteristics I like

Q: WHAT DO I NEED TO DO?
A: Find job characteristics I like
Q: CAN I DO IT NOW?
A: No
Q: WHAT WILL HELP
   ME DO IT NOW?
A: Find job tasks I like

Q: WHAT DO I NEED TO DO?
A: Find job characteristics I like
Q: CAN I DO IT NOW?
A: No
Q: WHAT WILL HELP
   ME DO IT NOW?
A: Find work conditions I like

End
Self-Regulated
Thinking

Q: WHAT DO I NEED TO DO?
A: Find jobs I like
Q: CAN I DO IT NOW?
A: Yes, I know the job
   characteristics I like

Q: WHAT DO I NEED TO DO?
A: Find job characteristics I like
Q: CAN I DO IT NOW?
A: Yes, I know the tasks and work
   conditions I like

166

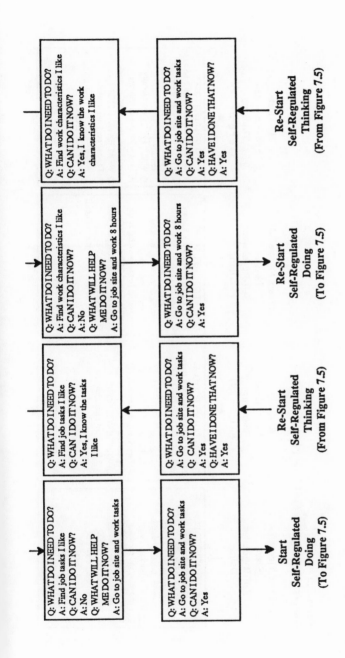

Q: WHAT DO I NEED TO DO?
A: Find job tasks I like
Q: CAN I DO IT NOW?
A: No
Q: WHAT WILL HELP ME DO IT NOW?
A: Go to job site and work tasks

Q: WHAT DO I NEED TO DO?
A: Find job tasks I like
Q: CAN I DO IT NOW?
A: Yes, I know the tasks I like

Q: WHAT DO I NEED TO DO?
A: Find work characteristics I like
Q: CAN I DO IT NOW?
A: No
Q: WHAT WILL HELP ME DO IT NOW?
A: Go to job site and work 8 hours

Q: WHAT DO I NEED TO DO?
A: Find work characteristics I like
Q: CAN I DO IT NOW?
A: Yes, I know the work characteristics I like

Q: WHAT DO I NEED TO DO?
A: Go to job site and work tasks
Q: CAN I DO IT NOW?
A: Yes

Q: WHAT DO I NEED TO DO?
A: Go to job site and work tasks
Q: CAN I DO IT NOW?
A: Yes
Q: HAVE I DONE THAT NOW?
A: Yes

Q: WHAT DO I NEED TO DO?
A: Go to job site and work 8 hours
Q: CAN I DO IT NOW?
A: Yes

Q: WHAT DO I NEED TO DO?
A: Go to job site and work tasks
Q: CAN I DO IT NOW?
A: Yes
Q: HAVE I DONE THAT NOW?
A: Yes

Start
Self-Regulated
Doing
(To Figure 7.5)

Re-Start
Self-Regulated
Thinking
(From Figure 7.5)

Re-Start
Self-Regulated
Doing
(To Figure 7.5)

Re-Start
Self-Regulated
Thinking
(From Figure 7.5)

Figure 7.5
Competent Doing "To Find Jobs I Like"

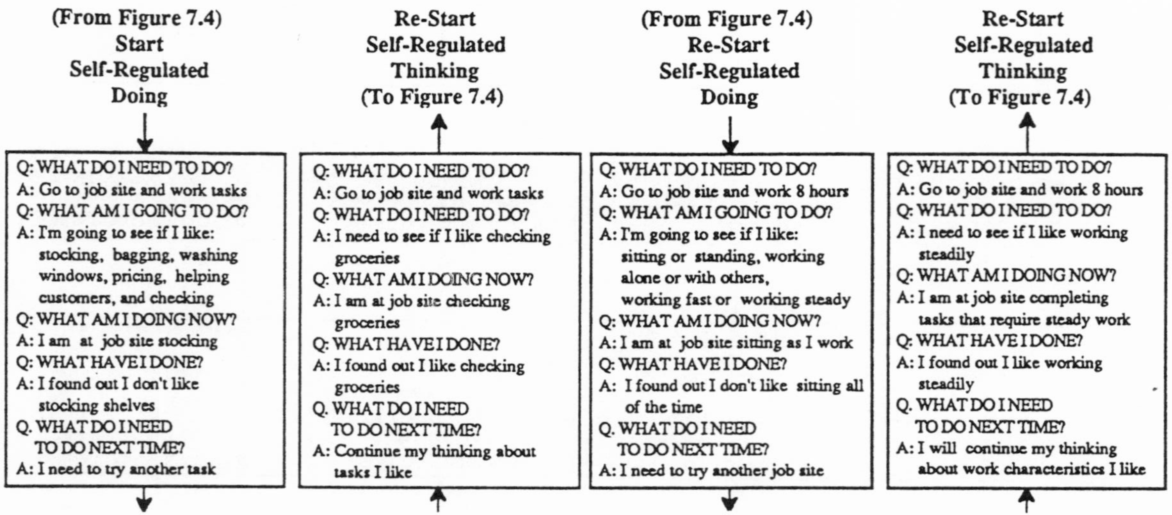

(From Figure 7.4) Start Self-Regulated Doing	Re-Start Self-Regulated Thinking (To Figure 7.4)	(From Figure 7.4) Re-Start Self-Regulated Doing	Re-Start Self-Regulated Thinking (To Figure 7.4)
Q: WHAT DO I NEED TO DO? A: Go to job site and work tasks Q: WHAT AM I GOING TO DO? A: I'm going to see if I like: stocking, bagging, washing windows, pricing, helping customers, and checking Q: WHAT AM I DOING NOW? A: I am at job site stocking Q: WHAT HAVE I DONE? A: I found out I don't like stocking shelves Q: WHAT DO I NEED TO DO NEXT TIME? A: I need to try another task	Q: WHAT DO I NEED TO DO? A: Go to job site and work tasks Q: WHAT DO I NEED TO DO? A: I need to see if I like checking groceries Q: WHAT AM I DOING NOW? A: I am at job site checking groceries Q: WHAT HAVE I DONE? A: I found out I like checking groceries Q: WHAT DO I NEED TO DO NEXT TIME? A: Continue my thinking about tasks I like	Q: WHAT DO I NEED TO DO? A: Go to job site and work 8 hours Q: WHAT AM I GOING TO DO? A: I'm going to see if I like: sitting or standing, working alone or with others, working fast or working steady Q: WHAT AM I DOING NOW? A: I am at job site sitting as I work Q: WHAT HAVE I DONE? A: I found out I don't like sitting all of the time Q: WHAT DO I NEED TO DO NEXT TIME? A: I need to try another job site	Q: WHAT DO I NEED TO DO? A: Go to job site and work 8 hours Q: WHAT DO I NEED TO DO? A: I need to see if I like working steadily Q: WHAT AM I DOING NOW? A: I am at job site completing tasks that require steady work Q: WHAT HAVE I DONE? A: I found out I like working steadily Q: WHAT DO I NEED TO DO NEXT TIME? A: I will continue my thinking about work characteristics I like

168

Q: WHAT DO I NEED TO DO?
A: Go to job site and work tasks
Q: WHAT AM I GOING TO DO?
A: I'm going to see if I like bagging, washing windows, pricing, helping customers, and checking groceries
Q: WHAT AM I DOING NOW?
A: I'm at job site bagging groceries
Q: WHAT HAVE I DONE?
A: I found out I like bagging groceries
Q: WHAT DO I NEED TO DO NEXT TIME?
A: I need to try another task

Q: WHAT DO I NEED TO DO?
A: Go to job site and work tasks
Q: WHAT AM I GOING TO DO?
A: I am going to see if I like helping customers and checking groceries
Q: WHAT AM I DOING NOW?
A: I am at job site helping customers
Q: WHAT HAVE I DONE?
A: I found out I like helping customers
Q: WHAT DO I NEED TO DO NEXT TIME?
A: I need to try another task

Q: WHAT DO I NEED TO DO?
A: Go to job site and work 8 hours
Q: WHAT AM I GOING TO DO?
A: I am going to see if I like standing, working alone or with others, working fast or working steady
Q: WHAT AM I DOING NOW?
A: I am at job site standing as I work
Q: WHAT HAVE I DONE?
A: I found out I like standing while I work
Q: WHAT DO I NEED TO DO NEXT TIME?

Q: WHAT DO I NEED TO DO?
A: Go to job site and work 8 hours
Q: WHAT DO I NEED TO DO?
A: I need to see if I like working fast or working steadily
Q: WHAT AM I DOING NOW?
A: I am at job site completing tasks that require fast work
Q: WHAT HAVE I DONE?
A: I found out I don't like working fast
Q: WHAT DO I NEED TO DO NEXT TIME?
A: I need to try a different job site

Q: WHAT DO I NEED TO DO?
A: Go to job site and work tasks
Q: WHAT AM I GOING TO DO?
A: I am going to see if I like washing windows, pricing, helping customers, and checking groceries
Q: WHAT AM I DOING NOW?
A: I am at job site washing windows
Q: WHAT HAVE I DONE?
A: I found out I don't like washing windows
Q: WHAT DO I NEED TO DO NEXT TIME?
A: I need to try another task

Q: WHAT DO I NEED TO DO?
A: Go to job site and work tasks
Q: WHAT AM I GOING TO DO?
A: I am going to see if I like pricing canned goods, helping customers, and checking groceries
Q: WHAT AM I DOING NOW?
A: I am at job site pricing canned goods
Q: WHAT HAVE I DONE?
A: I found out I like pricing canned goods
Q: WHAT DO I NEED TO DO NEXT TIME?
A: I need to try another task

Q: WHAT DO I NEED TO DO?
A: Go to job site and work 8 hours
Q: WHAT AM I GOING TO DO?
A: I am going to see if I like working alone or with others, working fast or working steady
Q: WHAT AM I DOING NOW?
A: I am at job site working alone
Q: WHAT HAVE I DONE?
A: I found out I like working alone
Q: WHAT DO I NEED TO DO NEXT TIME?
A: I need to try another job site

Q: WHAT DO I NEED TO DO?
A: Go to job site and work 8 hours
Q: WHAT DO I NEED TO DO?
A: I need to see if I like working with others, working fast or working steadily
Q: WHAT AM I DOING NOW?
A: I am at job site working with others
Q: WHAT HAVE I DONE?
A: I found out I like working with others
Q: WHAT DO I NEED TO DO NEXT TIME?
A: I need to try a different job site

Figure 7.6
Derivation of Self-Regulated Thinking and Doing

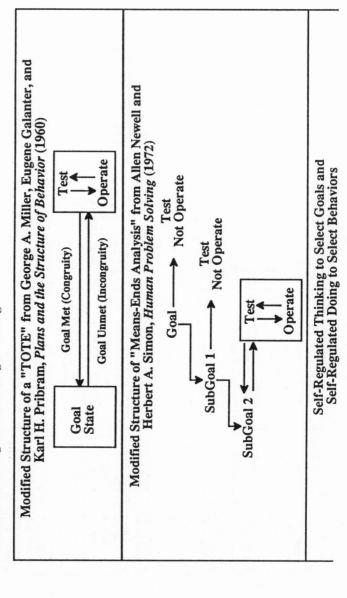

Modified Structure of a "TOTE" from George A. Miller, Eugene Galanter, and
Karl H. Pribram, *Plans and the Structure of Behavior* (1960)

Modified Structure of "Means-Ends Analysis" from Allen Newell and
Herbert A. Simon, *Human Problem Solving* (1972)

Self-Regulated Thinking to Select Goals and
Self-Regulated Doing to Select Behaviors

170

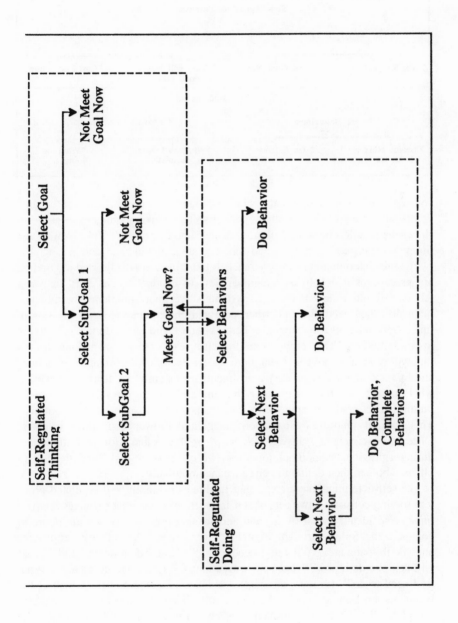

Figure 7.7
Self-Instructions for Self-Regulated Thinking and Doing

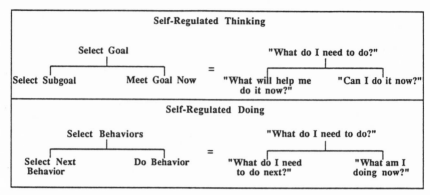

course because completing that operation produced an end, which then became an operable means to yet another end and so on to goal attainment. Figure 7.6 shows the parallels between Miller, Galanter, and Pribram's TOTE, Newell and Simon's means-ends program, and self-regulated thinking and doing.

The self-determination strategies such as those used in self-directed job finding are procedures that help us remember how to conduct means-ends analyses. Although biologic and neurologic systems solve many problems for us automatically, they need direction when goal and choice contingencies are suboptimal. Self-determination strategies help us choose and respond more effectively in these situations. They provide cues for setting expectations and making choices that will gradually move us toward our goals. By following strategic guidelines and by recycling self-regulatory adjustments persistently, we learn what works, what doesn't, and how to improve thinking and doing over successive opportunities. This gradually transforms contingencies from suboptimal to optimal. This gradually improves expectations for gain and lowers estimations of costs. Once we discover the "answer," "rule," or "guideline" for goal attainment during a previous suboptimal condition, we can pass on that "knowledge" to others who can then define the circumstance optimally.

The self-determination strategy that facilitates persistent self-regulated problem solving consists of two sets of self-instructions—one that regulates *analytic thinking* to identify what to do, and another that regulates *systematic doing* to complete the follow-through. Figure 7.7 illustrates. The self-instructions for analytic thinking are: "What do I need to do?" "Can I do it now?" and "What will help me do it now?" The self-instructions for systematic doing are: "What do I need to do?" (to meet the goal), "What am I doing now?" (which of the behaviors am I doing to meet the goal), and "What do I need to do next?" (to complete all the behaviors needed to reach my goal). Figure 7.8 illustrates the use of these phrases to find a job.

Of course, these are examples of a search and select strategy that helps identify the best combination of expectations, operations, and behaviors for a given pursuit. Figure 7.9 illustrates. We analyze (break down) gain expectations until we find one with an operation we can perform, we analyze gain operations until we find one that is affordable, and then we search and select response operators until we perform all the behaviors required by the choice.

Successful self-regulators know how to search, they remember where they are in their searches, and they know how to persist to the completion of those searches. This moves them from self-regulated thinking through self-regulated doing. They rarely get stuck thinking in circles about what they want to accomplish and how they will accomplish it. Once they decide what to do, they rarely stall with procrastination. They take action, learn from its consequences, and regulate toward gain.

Self-Determined Gain

Interactions between competence and persistence accelerate self-determined gain. As competence increases, so does persistence; and as persistence increases, so does competence. Success in meeting expectations increases, too, which elevates expectations for future success. Albert Bandura calls this self-efficacy: "Self-percepts of efficacy influence thought patterns, actions, and emotional arousal. In causal tests the higher the level of induced self-efficacy, the higher the performance accomplishments and the lower the emotional arousal."[62]

Prior to goal pursuit, we assess our ability to achieve. Past experience tells us what's likely to succeed and what's not. We pursue goals with high-efficacy percepts and avoid those with low-efficacy percepts. We also persist longer when our efficacy percepts are positive. Bandura explains:

> Judgments of self-efficacy also determine how much effort people will expend and how long they will persist in the face of obstacles or aversive experiences. When beset with difficulties people who entertain serious doubts about their capabilities slacken their efforts or give up altogether, whereas those who have a strong sense of efficacy exert greater effort to master the challenges. . . . High perseverance usually produces high performance attainments.[63]

This is another way of saying that past experience with success and failure affects expectations for future engagement. This is consistent with the expectation proposition: "The closer to optimal the past gain toward goal attainment . . . the closer to optimal the expectation for gain." As Bandura pointed out, failure is costly. It reduces expectations for gain. Disappointment in the search for solutions decreases expectations. Persons who fail repeatedly remember their failures when they set subsequent expectations.

Consider Jonathan, a pianist who hates to fail. Simply remembering lost competitions arouses negative feelings. These are emotional costs he must suffer in order to win. Occasionally he asks, "Is the joy of winning worth the fear of losing?" As his cost estimations rise relative to gains he expects, his expectations for gain become suboptimal. As expectations decline, his chances of entering future competitions decline as well.

Figure 7.8
Self-Regulated Problem Solving for Thinking and Doing

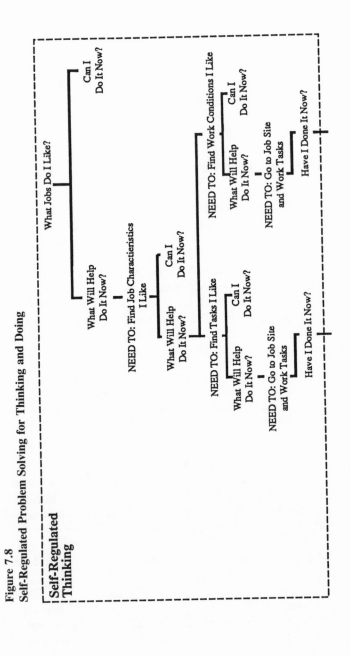

174

Self-Regulated Doing

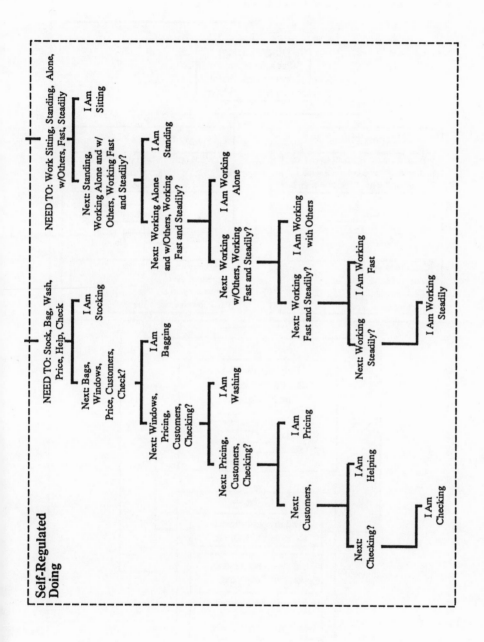

Figure 7.9
Self-Regulated Thinking and Doing during Self-Regulation

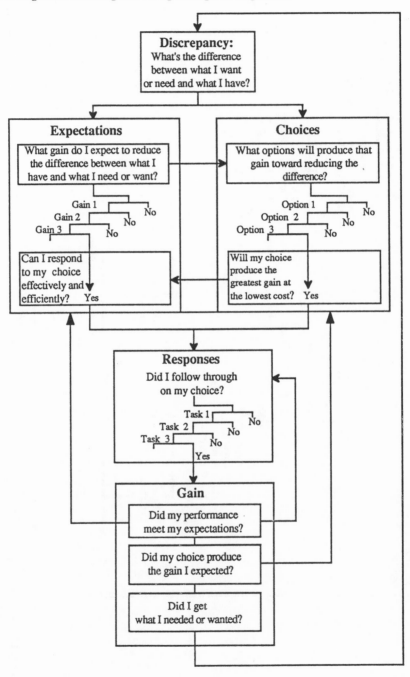

Now consider Mary, who is intrinsically motivated. She has had positive experiences competing, and she enjoys practicing and performing. Competing gives her a "high" and stimulates "flow." Her experiences are rewarding. She competes for challenge rather than outcome. Mary's expectations for gain increasingly approximate optimality because she enjoys the *process* (gain toward goal attainment) as well as the *outcome* (consequence of goal attainment). The journey is her reward. The enjoyment of practicing to become more competent interacts with persistence to accelerate the probability of success, which further reinforces commitment to goal attainment. At the same time, Mary's expectations for gain and chances of producing it increase. Mary feels self-determined.

The expectation proposition shows how the end of one self-regulatory episode affects the beginning of the next. It summarizes past regulatory effort. Expectations depend upon baselines of past gain. This explains why past gain toward goal attainment increases expectations for success and past failures decrease expectations. At the extremes, success brings success and failure brings failure.

In addition to affecting expectations for gain, competence and persistence also influence choosing and doing, as Propositions II and III indicate. Competent individuals make better discriminations between alternatives. They know what information to look for, and once they find that information, they know how to translate it into actions that meet goals. They also self-manage themselves effectively and efficiently by completing required behaviors. In other words, they are competent and persistent means-ends analysts during thinking and doing (as illustrated in Figure 7.8).

The choice proposition indicates how competent discriminations affect optimal selections:" . . . the more salient the differences between options, the closer to optimal the choice." The response proposition shows how optimal past gain, optimal expectations, and optimal choices affect the effectiveness and efficiency of performance: "The closer to optimal the past gain, expectations, and choices, the closer to optimal the distribution of responses between task completion to meet the goal and feedback seeking about goal state-actual state discrepancies, options, task performance, and results."

Competent and persistent regulators perform essential tasks effectively and efficiently because (1) they have the skills necessary to be effective, and (2) they have practiced those skills sufficiently to perform them in a timely manner. They know how to complete essential tasks quickly and accurately, which further reduces the costs of goal attainment.

Competence and persistence affect all phases of self-regulation. Their effects show up with expectations that are realistic and achievable, with choices for options that work best, and with performances that are effective and efficient. Their cumulative effects are increased matches between gain and expectations along with increased sense of control over those outcomes. Hypothesis 11 describes these relationships. It states that competent and persistent regulators who are successful are more likely to perceive their efforts as self-determined than persons who are less competent, less persistent, and less successful.

Hypothesis 11: The more frequent the gain from competent and persistent self-regulation, the more likely the regulator will perceive the gain to be self-determined.

As costs decrease and gains increase, regulators are less discouraged by failure. In fact, occasional setbacks reaffirm resolve, which accelerates the success cycle of competence begetting competence and persistence begetting persistence. Expectations become more accurate, judgements more perceptive, and adjustments more effective. Occasionally, regulatory activity and gain occur simultaneously, which intensifies the sense of control. Mihaly Csikszentmihalyi calls this "flow."

Self-determined regulators experience flow more frequently than others because they immerse themselves in their pursuit. They adjust expectations, choices, and performances continuously in response to feedback about the gain their activities produce. They are at "one" with their pursuit, "so involved in an activity that nothing else seems to matter."[64] This increases their chances of experiencing simultaneous regulation and gain, as Csikszentmihalyi explains:

> The optimal state of inner experience is one in which there is *order in consciousness*. This happens when psychic energy—or attention—is invested in realistic goals, and when skills match the opportunities for action. The pursuit of a goal brings order in awareness because a person must concentrate attention on the task at hand and momentarily forget everything else. These periods of struggling to overcome challenges are what people find to be the most enjoyable times of their lives. . . . A person who has achieved control over psychic energy and has invested it in a consciously chosen goal cannot help but grow into a more complex being. By stretching skills by reaching toward higher challenges, such a person becomes an increasingly extraordinary individual."[65]

Notes

1. Mihaly Csikszentmihalyi, *Flow: The Psychology of Optimal Experience* (New York: Harper & Row, 1990), 3.

2. May Sarton, quoted in Dennis Wholey, *Are You Happy?* (Boston: Houghton Mifflin, 1986), 109.

3. Burt Bacharach, quoted in ibid., 175.

4. John Naisbitt, quoted in ibid., 66.

5. B.F. Skinner, "Can Psychology Be a Science of Mind?" *American Psychologist* 45, No. 11 (1990), 1206.

6. Larry Stockman and Cynthia Graves, *Adult Children Who Won't Grow Up* (New York: Contemporary Books, 1989), 23–24.

7. Adrienne Miller and Andrew Goldblat, *The Hamlet Syndrome: Overthinkers Who Underachieve* (New York: William Morrow, 1986), 133.

8. Susan Littwin, *The Postponed Generation: Why American Youth Are Growing Up Later* (New York: William Morrow, 1986), 133.

9. Kenneth L. Woodward, "Young beyond Their Years," *Newsweek, Special Issue: The 21st Century Family* (1990), 54.

10. Ibid., 55.

11. Dennis E. Mithaug, *Self-Determined Kids: Raising Satisfied and Successful Children* (New York: Lexington Books, Macmillan, 1991).

12. U.S. Department of Education, Office of Educational Research and Improvement, *Youth Indicators 1988* (Washington, DC: Author, 1988), 86.

13. Ibid., 94.

14. Ibid., 14.

15. Ibid., 116.

16. Ibid., 102.

17. Ibid., 64.

18. Associated Press, "Barometer Shows Drop in U.S. Pupils' Science Knowledge: Americans Subpar in All Categories," *Gazette Telegraph* (Colorado Springs, Colorado), 11 September 1987.

19. Associated Press, "Test Shows Lack of Economic Knowledge: Students Stumped by 'Profit,' " *Gazette Telegraph* (Colorado Springs, Colorado), 29 December 1988.

20. National Commission on Excellence in Education, *A Nation at Risk: The Imperative for Educational Reform* (Washington, DC: Author, 1983).

21. Richard Lamm, "Young Americans Don't Measure Up," *Rocky Mountain News* (Denver, Colorado), 24 September 1989.

22. Dennis E. Mithaug, James E. Martin, Martin Agran, and Frank R. Rusch, *Why Special Education Graduates Fail: How to Teach Them to Succeed* (Colorado Springs, CO: Ascent Publications, 1988), 23.

23. Dennis E. Mithaug, Chiyo N. Horiuchi, and Brian A. McNulty, *Parent Reports on the Transitions of Students Graduating from Colorado Special Education Programs in 1978 and 1979* (Denver, CO: Colorado Department of Education, 1987), 56.

24. Christopher Lasch, *The Culture of Narcissism, American Life in an Age of Diminishing Expectations* (New York: Warner Books, 1979), 106.

25. B. Eugene Griessman, *The Achievement Factors* (New York: Dodd, Mead, and Company, 1987).

26. Napoleon Hill, *Think and Grow Rich*, (New York: Fawcett Crest, 1960), 33.

27. Malcolm Forbes, quoted in ibid., 295.

28. Marsha Sinetar, *Do What You Love, the Money Will Follow: Discovering Your Right Livelihood* (New York: Dell Publishing, 1987), 208.

29. Griessman, *The Achievement Factors*, 37.

30. Hill, *Think and Grow Rich*, 77.

31. George Gallup and Alec Gallup, *The Great American Success Story: Factors That Affect Achievement*, (Homewood, IL: Dow Jones-Irwin, 1986), 67.

32. Griessman, *The Achievement Factors*, 103.

33. Hill, *Think and Grow Rich*, 163–164.

34. Ted Turner, quoted in Michael Meyer, *The Alexander Complex: The Dreams that Drive Great Businessmen* (New York: Times Books, 1989), 219.

35. Jacques Cousteau, quoted in Griessman, *The Achievement Factors*, 82.

36. Albert C. Wedemeyer, quoted in ibid., 89.

37. William Proxmire, quoted in ibid., 87.

38. Theodore Isaac Rubin, quoted in Wholey, *Are You Happy?* 57.

39. Edward L. Deci and Joseph Porac, "Cognitive Evaluation Theory and the Study of Human Motivation," in Mark R. Lepper and David Greene (Eds.), *The Hidden Costs*

of Reward: New Perspective on the Psychology of Human Motivation (Hillsdale, NJ: Lawrence Erlbaum Associates, 1978), 151.

40. Norman Vincent Peale, *The Power of Positive Thinking* (New York: Fawcett Crest, 1988).

41. Herbert Benson, *Your Maximum Mind* (New York: Avon Books, 1987), 59–60.

42. Miles I. Friedman and Martha R. Willis, *Human Nature and Predictability* (Lexington, MA: Lexington Books, 1981), 31.

43. David C. McClelland, John W. Atkinson, Russell A. Clark, and Edgar L. Lowell, *The Achievement Motive* (New York: John Wiley & Sons, 1976).

44. George Sheehan, *Personal Best* (Emmaus, PA: Rodale Press, 1989), 21.

45. Lee Travino, quoted in D. L. McCoy, *Megatraits* (Plano, TX: Woodware Publishing, 1988), 208–209.

46. Griessman, *The Achievement Factors,* 53.

47. Ibid., 35.

48. Edward L. Deci and Richard M. Ryan, *Intrinsic Motivation and Self-Determination in Human Behavior* (New York: Plenum Press, 1985), 314.

49. Robert J. Sternberg, *The Triarchic Mind: A New Theory of Human Intelligence* (New York: Penguin Books, 1988), 71.

50. Ibid., 65.

51. Friedman and Willis, *Human Nature and Predictability*, 26.

52. Susan Harter, "A Developmental Perspective on Some Parameters of Self-Regulation in Children," in Paul Karoly and Frederick H. Kanfer (Eds.), *Self-Management and Behavior Change: From Theory to Practice* (New York: Pergamon Press, 1982), 182–183.

53. Ibid., 183.

54. Benjamin S. Bloom, "Generalizations about Talent Development," in Benjamin S. Bloom (Ed.), *Developing Talent in Young People* (New York: Ballantine Books, 1985), 517.

55. Judith A. Monsaas, "Learning To Be a World-Class Tennis Player," in Bloom (Ed.), *Developing Talent in Young People*, 247.

56. Ibid., 247–248.

57. The Center for Educational Research at the University of Colorado–Colorado Springs conducts research and demonstration projects that help persons with disabilities learn the self-determination skills described in this section. The participants in these projects exhibit a full range of handicapping conditions, including mental retardation, learning disabilities, emotional/behavior disorders, mental illness, traumatic brain injury, and physical disabilities.

58. The methods and procedures are explained in Dennis E. Mithaug, James E. Martin, James V. Husch, Martin Agran, and Frank R. Rusch, *When Will Persons in Supported Employment Need Less Support?* (Colorado Springs, CO: Ascent Publications, 1988). Similar procedures for use at home and at school are explained in Dennis E. Mithaug, James E. Martin, Eva Frazier, and Michael Allen, *What Special Education Teenagers Must Learn at Home* (Colorado Springs, CO: Ascent Publications, 1988), and Dennis E. Mithaug, James E. Martin, Martin Agran, and Frank R. Rusch, *Why Special Education Graduates Fail: How to Teach Them to Succeed* (Colorado Springs, CO: Ascent Publications, 1988).

59. See, for example, Michael Pressley and Joel R. Levin (Eds), *Cognitive Strategy Research: Psychological Foundations* (New York: Springer-Verlag, 1983), and Andrew

W. Meyers and W. Edward Craighead (Eds.), *Cognitive Behavior Therapy with Children* (New York: Plenum Press, 1984).

60. See, for example, Paul Karoly and Frederick H. Kanfer (Eds), *Self-Management and Behavior Change: From Theory to Practice* (New York: Pergamon Press, 1982).

61. George A. Miller, Eugene Galanter, and Karl H. Pribram, *Plans and the Structure of Behavior* (New York: Holt, Rinehart and Winston, 1960).

62. Albert Bandura, "Self-Efficacy Mechanism in Human Agency," *American Psychologist* 37 (1982): 122.

63. Ibid., 123.

64. Csikszentmihalyi, *Flow: The Psychology of Optimal Experience,* 4.

65. Ibid., 6.

Chapter 8

Innovative Gain

Optimal adjusters stay in touch with change, anticipate its direction, and then maintain what they are doing or switch. In the last half century these decisions have become more difficult because the rate of change has accelerated, forcing individuals to take more risks. Peter Drucker says:

> Something, surely has happened to young Americans—and to fairly large numbers of them—to their attitudes, their values, their ambitions, in the last twenty to twenty-five years. Only it is clearly not what anyone looking at the young Americans of the late 1960s could possibly have predicted. How do we explain, for instance, that all of a sudden there are such large numbers of people willing both to work like demons for long years and to choose grave risks rather than big organization security? Where are the hedonists, the status seekers, the 'me-too-ers,' the conformists?[1]

Contrast this with the social conditions that preceded the Reformation and industrial revolution. The Middle Ages, for example, produced little innovation. Feudal society discouraged it, even punished it. Conformity to manorial ways and Church doctrine dominated. This changed when a few risk-takers cracked the shell of conformity that had encased and encrusted minds and spirits for centuries. In 1514 Nicholas Copernicus's heliocentric theory questioned man's central position in nature. Three years later, Martin Luther challenged the Church by posting ninety-five theses on the door of the Schlosskirche Church in Wittenberg, Germany. After that, "I-think" replaced "group-think" in an explosion of innovative activity unmatched in human history.

Although sweeping generalizations about factors responsible for this epic transformation make exciting drama, they overlook the part played by nitty-gritty problem solvers who plodded, probed, and persevered. Propelling any fast-paced, fully packed roller coaster of change is usually a lone individual—thinking, questioning, searching, and finding. Group-think is fine, but individual thought proves divine.[2] Martin Luther did not get ninety-five theses from brainstorming. And Copernicus did not formulate the heliocentric theory with co-authors. Individual minds create what group minds imitate.

How did these great thinkers think? What was special about Darwin, Mozart, Picasso, Bach, or Einstein? Were they instruments of a higher force, or were they "simply" more effective and more efficient self-regulators?

Innovators in Science

Kepler, Darwin, Einstein, and Planck are among the elite in scientific achievement. Johannes Kepler's laws of elliptical orbits corrected Ptolemaic and Copernican theories of circular orbits; Charles Darwin's theory of evolution revolutionized theoretical paradigms in natural and social science; Albert Einstein's theory of relativity explained Newton's laws of gravitation and laid the foundation of modern physics; and Max Karl Ernst Ludwig Planck's quantum theory introduced the world to quantum mechanics and atomic energy. What started these men on their paths to discovery? Was it divine inspiration or opportunity for gain? Once committed to pursuit, what maintained them? What emboldened their challenges to centuries of contrary thought and practice?

Since ancient times, astronomers had assumed that planets moved in circular orbits. Kepler challenged that view with mathematical proofs that planets moved in elliptical orbits. In the 1800s Lamarck theorized about evolution, as did Herbert Spencer. But Darwin found a better explanation. Why? When Albert Einstein learned physics, scientists believed the speed of light was variable. But to formulate the theory of relativity, Einstein had to reject that assumption, claiming that the speed of light was constant. When Planck learned physics he accepted the inviolability of its nineteenth-century laws. They were absolutes to which all other principles complied. Yet Planck's quantum theory explained radiation emission by challenging those sacred laws.

What propelled these audacious challenges? Was it an inconsistency—a discrepancy between expectations and observations that undermined assumptions about an orderly universe? While working for Danish astronomer Tycho Brahe, Kepler learned that Brahe's measurements of the positions of stars and planets showed Mars to be off as much as eight minutes of arc from the position predicted by Ptolemaic theory of circular motion. Kepler knew Brahe's measurements were accurate, which meant that Ptolemaic theory was inaccurate. He refused to accept the third possibility—that God's universe was mathematically cacophonous. So Kepler searched for a better explanation. And he found one: elliptical, not circular, orbits predicted the positions of planets.

Charles Darwin's interest in evolution was heightened during a voyage to the Galapagos Islands, where he took voluminous notes on different species inhabiting the islands. The controversy dominating the attention of scientists at that time was between geologic theories of evolution on the one hand and biblical accounts of creation on the other. The geologic evidence so impressed Darwin that he accepted the evolutionary perspective. But this too created an inconsistency. How could unchanging organisms live harmoniously in evolving environments? Howard E. Gruber described Darwin's thinking:

> He began with a notion of a stable, harmonious natural order, in which all organic beings were adapted to each other and to their physical environment in a fashion ordained by the Creator. As he came to accept modern geological views of a constantly changing order in the physical world, *a contradiction within his point of view developed* as follows: each species was adapted to its milieu; the milieu was undergoing constant change; and yet the species were changeless. Darwin probably began to feel this contradiction during the final months of the voyage, as he was going over his notes and organizing his materials. It was not until July 1837, ten months after returning to England, that he began his first notebook on "Transmutation of Species." It was over a year after that in September 1838, that the role of natural selection in evolution began to be clear to him.[italics added][3]

Inconsistencies like these also disturbed Albert Einstein. A case in point was the electrodynamic theory for why current is induced when magnets rotate about a wire. The theory claimed that when the magnet rotates, an electric field develops that induces current. But when the wire rotates about the magnet, the theory postulated no electric field (apparently, stationary magnets don't create electric fields), yet current still flows. This inconsistency was unacceptable to Einstein. So he modified the laws of electrodynamics to include the idea of relative rather than absolute motion. This permitted the theory to use the same explanation for both phenomena: relative motion between magnet and wire created electric fields, which induced currents.[4]

But this formulation created yet another inconsistency. In order to derive mathematical explanations for relativity, Einstein had to assume that the velocity of light was constant regardless of its source or state of motion at that source. This too was an audacious step, as Richard Morris explained: "After all, the velocity of ordinary objects do not exhibit this kind of constancy. If a jet plane is traveling at a speed of 1,000 kilometers per hour, and if it fires a rocket that has a velocity of 800, the rocket will streak toward its target at 1,800 kilometers per hour; the two speeds must be added."[5]

Einstein's theories reshaped twentieth-century physics. His assumption about the speed of light also accounted for the mysterious results of the Michelson-Morley experiment in 1887. Prior to that study, physicists had assumed that light was a wave phenomenon mediated by "space ether." Theoretically, wave-like properties occurred because when light passed through the ether its direction was altered. But when Michelson and Morley measured light rays traveling to and from earth, they found no evidence of an ether wind. Einstein's assumption about the constancy of the speed of light cleared up the mystery. There was no need for positing an ether because the speed of light was constant.

Relativity also explained the apparent contractions reported for an object traveling away from a stationary observer at 90 percent of the velocity of light. Scientists had thought the contraction effect was real—that any observer could verify it, including those on the speeding spaceship. Einstein's explanation was that the contraction was only relative. It did not occur on the spaceship. In fact, persons on the ship perceived contraction of objects at the launching pad. The theory also predicted the relativity of observations in time: no two observers at different locations in space could observe exactly the same sequence of events. The theory also postulated that mass was relative: the faster an object travels, the greater its mass becomes, Therefore, no object ever reaches the speed of light, because then mass would be infinite.

Like Kepler, Einstein was driven by a fundamental belief in an orderly, harmonious universe. Inconsistencies demanded resolution. According to Morris:

> The Einsteinian universe was a strange one. At least it appeared strange to physicists accustomed to the "commonsense" views that were embodied in nineteenth-century physics. . . . Physicists who studied his theories in detail soon recognized that Einstein had introduced his new ideas about the nature of time and space not because he was in love with the bizarre, but because he wanted to weld physics into a harmonious whole. He had propounded his theories of relativity because *he had felt that the old physics was not as logical or consistent as it should be.* [italics added][6]

Although Max Karl Ernst Ludwig Planck understood relativity and accepted its principles, he was less confident about other deviations from Newtonian physics, especially his own. Unlike Einstein, who never hesitated challenging hallowed laws, Planck believed in classical physics and tried to fit his findings to its predictions. Unfortunately, one finding would not fit—the blackbody radiation effect. When a perfectly black object is heated, it emits radiation in a manner similar to radiation emitted from a stone or piece of iron placed in fire. Classical physics could not account for the amount of radiation emitted in blackbox experiments. Measurements always showed less radiation than what theory predicted. Planck wanted to know why.

Like Einstein, he worked the problem backwards. Rather than beginning with accepted theory and its attendant assumptions, Planck constructed a mathematical model describing the quantities of light actually emitted in blackbody experiments. Then he formulated assumptions necessary for those equations to work. His results indicated that blackbody radiation only occurred in discrete packets of one, four, and 165,007,713,982 units, never in quantities in between.[7] What a shock! Nothing in existing theory accounted for this phenomenon. In fact, if light were truly a wave, it should emit continuous energy bursts rather than stratified, categorical strata. In 1900 Planck announced his quantum theory of light, which postulated bundles or quanta emissions to explain blackbody radiation.

Planck was a reluctant innovator. The last thing he wanted was to alter theory. He said that quantum theory was "an act of desperation," and for years afterward he labored to account for quantum phenomena using traditional physics.[8] But in the final call, he transcended conservative allegiance to clear up another inconsistency that challenged belief in cosmic harmony.

Innovators In Music, Literature, and Art

While the great innovators in science struggled to affirm harmony, their artistic and musical counterparts struggled to create harmony. Johann Sebastian Bach, one of the world's most prolific composers, is an example. He came from a family of musicians who participated in church and town bands in central Germany for over one hundred years. Demand for new music from audiences and churchgoers kept music writing alive. As cantor of St. Thomas Church in Leipzig in 1723, Bach wrote a cantata (sacred text set to music) for each Sunday service— 60 per year and 300 over five years. How did he do it?

Like other composers, Bach used rules of composition to build musical structures; he borrowed themes, melodies, and chord progressions from other compositions; and occasionally he even produced new combinations of his own. Rules for composing fugues offered two structural components: the exposition and the episode. The exposition was a pattern of voice entries that expressed the subject or main theme as well as an answer or an imitation of that theme. The episode consisted of one or more passages in free counterpoint connecting two expositions. Fugue composers—including Franz Joseph Haydn, Ludwig van Beethoven, and Wolfgang Amadeus Mozart—produced original compositions simply by rearranging these structural units in different musical lines.

In addition to following basic rules, Bach and his peers borrowed heavily from themselves and each other. Then he recombined those borrowings into novel structures that gave the appearance of originality. According to Robert W. Weisberg:

> Norman Carrell has attempted to trace every instance of such borrowing. . . . Over 225 of Bach's nonvocal works contain borrowings from his own earlier works. In his nonvocal works, Carrell traces more than eighty cases of borrowing from other composers. . . . Carrell finds Vivaldi's influence in much of Bach's work, and believes that Bach owed Vivaldi much in the way of inspiration, in addition to the works which are based directly on Vivaldi's compositions.[9]

What seems like plagiarism by today's standards was accepted practice then. Bach's borrowings provided foundations for subsequent rearrangement and elaboration. Though hardly created from whole cloth, the results were still new, as Weisberg explains: "Bach's use of borrowed material usually involved such elaboration and extension that an essentially new composition was produced. Indeed, one aspect of Bach's genius was his ability to borrow a piece from another and turn it into something immeasurably finer."[10] Other composers were equally adept revisionists. George Frideric Handel borrowed so extensively that his "borrowees" complained publicly.[11] Even Mozart was an accomplished imitator. After competing with Clementi in a composition contest (and winning), he borrowed a Clementi theme from that competition for one of his later compositions. One scholar estimated that 80 percent of Mozart's melodies were from works of others. Beethoven borrowed too, but usually from himself. However, some claim that his *Eroica* Symphony was inspired by a theme by Carl Philipp Emanuel Bach.[12]

According to these accounts, innovation is more often variation on a theme than origination of a theme. Creative works in art, poetry, and literature exhibit a comparable birthright. According to Weisberg's analysis of Alexander Calder's mobile, Pablo Picasso and Georges Braque's collage, Samuel Taylor Coleridge's *Kubla Khan*, Fyodor Dostoyevky's *The Idiot* and *Crime and Punishment*, and Pablo Picasso's *Guernica*: "[the] evidence revealed that the initial ideas an artist uses as the basis for the evolution of a new work come from his or her earlier work or that of other artists."[13]

Self-Regulated Innovation

Innovation is incremental problem solving that successively approximates an evolving expectation. It is a special case of self-regulated problem solving to reduce discrepancies between goal states and present states. What distinguishes innovation from routine problem solving is attention to unusual discrepancies. Innovators are attracted by ill-defined discrepancies that often go unnoticed by others. Only persons with relevant experience and competence notice their occurrence and recognize their significance. Recall the inconsistencies that attracted Kepler, Darwin, Einstein, and Planck.

Experts make hundreds of thousands of associations between discrepancies, expectations, options, and their effects. These vast resources sensitize their perceptions about what is consistent and what is not, what might work and what might not. The ill-defined discrepancy that arouses suspicion also affects the direction and result of problem solving. Innovators search for solutions to problems not yet clearly defined. This permits problem perceptions and solution expectations to evolve together, which yields unpredictable patterns of search and unusual solutions to test.

Only in recent centuries have interactions between expectation defining and solution finding occurred with sufficient frequency to impact social conditions. Prior to the industrial revolution, only a tiny fraction of the population tinkered with new ideas and new products. There was no incentive to innovate during that period, and the knowledge base necessary for it to be effective was contaminated by myth, fear, and superstition. Much has changed since. In many countries of the world today there has been a veritable explosion of innovative activity, due in part to the exponential growth in the scientific and technological knowledge base that spawns new variations on tested themes.

Contemporary innovation requires enormous investments in time and energy in order to master disciplinary activity and then push back its frontiers. Would-be innovators must invest to become competent. Then they must persist in their quests to express that competence with purpose and wit. Unfortunately, this requires long bouts with ambiguity, uncertainty, and risk—experiences too unpleasant for many to tolerate.

The Competence Factor

Innovators are competent. More than that, they are experts. They have stored hundreds of thousands of knowledge units and patterns that map the significant causal connections defining their subject domains. According to Herbert Simon: "The expert has stored in memory a large number of patterns, which he recognizes when they occur in the situation around him. The grand master chess player, for example, has stored a large number of patterns, which he recognizes when they occur on a chess board before him."[14] Even educators recognize that expert thinking depends upon content-specific competence. The term "generalized expertise" may be oxymoronic. Innovative thinking presumes expert knowledge about something, as Raymond Nickerson explains:

> It is a truism to note that without some conception (or misconception) of a domain, one cannot think about it at all. If one lacks the concepts that define quantum electrodynamics, one really cannot think about that subject. On the other hand, a head full of facts about a domain does not guarantee that one will *think* effectively about the domain. Indeed, there is a sense in which knowledge may sometimes make thinking unnecessary. This would be true, for example, when what appears to be a difficult problem is solved quickly by someone who happens to know the solution because he encountered precisely the same problem a short time ago. *Perhaps on the first occasion finding the solution required much thought, but on the second it did not.* In the most productive marriages of domain knowledge and thinking ability, knowledge serves as a stimulus to discover more.[italics added][15]

Indeed, contradictions between knowledge stored in memory (expectations) and observations of the environment can stimulate creative and innovative thought. Adrian de Groot's research on chess masters showed surprising differences between expert and novice playing. Contrary to myth that masters "see" more moves in advance, de Groot found that the expert's advantage is perceptual memory of "best moves" for different board configurations. He concluded that "although it is very difficult to show that chess masters are superior to lesser players in the structural qualities of their operational thinking they are easily superior in *perceptual achievement*; and . . . the basis of chess mastership (that is, again, the superiority of the master over lesser players) is to a very large extent a matter of *memory* (the 'highly differentiated system of immediately available, specific playing methods,' and other problem transformation dispositions.''[16] In other words, expert chess players select better patterns of play, *based upon their experience*. They respond quickly and effectively to routine chess problems they have encountered before. This leaves time to consider novel and less familiar board patterns. Other research has found similar differences between expert and novice problem solving in mathematics, bridge, physics, social science, athletics, and teaching.[17]

Experts spend less time on the routine and more time on the unusual. For them, "knowing" is recognizing a pattern and the solution it implies, as Simon and his colleagues explained:

> In every domain that has been explored, considerable knowledge has been found to be an essential prerequisite to expert skill. The expert is not merely an unindexed compendium of facts, however. Instead, large numbers of patterns serve as an index to guide the expert in a fraction of a second to relevant parts of the knowledge store. This knowledge includes sets of rich schemata that can guide a problem's interpretation and solution and add crucial pieces of information. This capacity to use pattern-indexed schemata is probably a large part of what we call physical intuition.[18]

John Bransford and Nancy Vye described similar pattern-indexed schemata for experts:

> Experts in a domain often encounter familiar problems. They are able to rely on automatized skills to recognize these problems. This fluent pattern recognition requires only a minimum of attention so *the expert is free to deal with other aspects of the problem*. In contrast, novices often feel overwhelmed because their lack of fluency or automaticity causes attentional strain. . . . Overall, fluency in motor skills and pattern recognition skills seems important for effective performance in all domains. Of course, experts exhibit fluency that is backed by understanding. For example, their pattern recognition seems to be organized around meaningful principles that derive from core concepts in the field. [italics added][19]

Stimuli suggested by "other aspects of the problem" are the *discrepancy signals* that motivate searches for solutions to inconsistencies.

Experts don't become so overnight. They spend years mastering content for split-second access, nimble manipulation, and effective application. Simon indicated that it takes an average of ten years to master content and become an expert: "Using simple probability models, as well as a computer simulation of the chess perception process, quantitative estimates were made of the 'vocabulary' of familiar chunks in a master's memory. The estimates obtained by several different procedures all fall in the range of twenty-five thousand to one hundred thousand chunks—that is, a vocabulary of roughly the same size as the vocabulary of an educated adult in his native language."[20] Simon concludes: "Research done by my colleague John R. Hayes and I indicates that nobody reaches world class in less than ten years of diligent application. Bobby Fischer became a chess grand master in slightly less than ten years. 'It took a bit more than ten years for Mozart,' Simon added facetiously. 'Mozart was a slow learner.' ''[21]

In *Developing Talent in Young People*, Benjamin S. Bloom chronicled the training regimes of gifted young artists, athletes, musicians, and scholars.[22] These prodigious talents spent long, difficult hours of dedicated concentration in their talent areas in order to master demands. The average time gifted pianists took to win their first major international competition like the Chopin International Piano Competition or the Tchaikovsky International Competition was 17.14 years. World-class tennis players required a decade of training, which began as early as age three or four. Research mathematicians and neurologists usually took much longer than athletes or performers.[23] Even Jack Nicklaus, the golden bear of golf, took ten years to reach experthood. According to B. Eugene Griessman:

> When I interviewed Jack Nicklaus, I wondered if perhaps he would be an exception to the ten-year rule. Nicklaus, after all, was sensational as a youngster. When he played his first nine holes at age ten, he carded a 51. At age thirteen, he won the Ohio State Junior Championship. At age fifteen, he qualified for the U.S. Amateur, and at age seventeen qualified for the U.S. Open, missing the cut.
>
> However, my question was laid to rest when I came upon a definitive article on Nicklaus, written by Herbert Warren Wind for the New Yorker. Wind writes: "When old golf hands discuss when it was that it first occurred to them that Nicklaus might turn out to be not just a first-class golfer but a rare champion, more often than not they cite his performance in one or another of three events that took place early in his career: the 1960 World Amateur Team Championship, the 1960 U.S. Open at Cherry Hills, outside Denver, in which he was second, only two strokes behind Arnold Palmer; then the premier golfer in the world, and the 1962 U.S. Open at Oakmont, outside Pittsburgh, where he caught Palmer with an almost flawless last round of 69 and defeated him the next day in their playoff." ...
>
> In 1960, Nicklaus was twenty years old—ten years older than when he played his first game.[24]

The Persistence Factor

Of course, it matters little exactly how long it takes to become competent, because all mastery demands sustained effort. This translates into commitment and perseverance—unlikely characteristics of the very young. Consequently, persistence awaits maturity unless other circumstances intervene—like Mozart's father, who guided and directed, or Jean-Paul Sartre's passion, which captured and fulfilled: "By writing I was existing. . . . My pen raced away so fast that often my wrist ached. I would throw the filled notebooks on the floor, I would eventually forget about them, they would disappear. . . . I wrote in order to write" (At age nine).[25]

A consequence of persistent effort is prodigious production. Consider the innovation rates of giants like Sigmund Freud, who produced 330 publications in his 45-year career; Albert Einstein, who published 248 works in 53 years; and Charles Darwin, who published 119 papers and books in 51 years.[26] Thomas Edison holds the record for the most patents—1,093; Alfred Binet published 277 works; Francis Galton published 227; Mozart completed 600 compositions before his death at age 33; Schubert wrote 500 compositions before he died at age 31; Bach produced over 1,000 compositions; Rembrandt constructed nearly 3,000 paintings, etchings, and drawings; and Picasso completed more than 20,000 works.[27]

Not all creators and innovators are that prolific, although the most productive usually dominate. Wayne Dennis counted the creations of innovators in secular music, books, gerontology and geriatrics, geology, research on infantile paralysis, chemistry, and linguistic research and found that 10 percent of these producers accounted for 50 percent of the creative works. Most innovators (61 percent) made single contributions, while the most productive created 9 percent of the total.[28] This is consistent with other studies. Dean Keith Simonton says that although there are thousands of composers, only 250 are ever heard in concerts: "A mere 36 composers account for three-quarters of all works performed, and just 16 provide half of all music listening. The top 10 composers give us 40 percent of the master works, while the top three composers—Mozart, Beethoven, and Bach—offer about 6 percent each or almost 20 percent taken together. In sum, fewer than 1 percent of the composers with extant compositions provide most of the classical repertoire."[29]

The elite also dominate qualitatively, which suggests that those who produce the most impact their disciplines the most. Wayne Dennis examined the lifetime productivity of American scientists elected to the National Academy of Sciences who reached the age of 70, and he found that the least productive published 27 works—considerably more than the single publication rate of the less distinguished sample. The average production of the elite was 203 per person, with 36 percent having fewer than 100 and 27 percent having at least 300.[30]

Dennis also studied the records of scientists from the *Catalog of Scientific Literature 1800–1900* published by the Royal Society of London and found that this less prestigious group was also less productive. Its productive range was from 1 to 458, with 30 percent publishing a single piece and 60 percent having fewer than 7 publications. In an analysis of factors affecting entry into the *Encylopaedia Britannica*, Dennis found that the most productive 10 percent with more than 50 publications had a 50 percent chance of being listed, while the remaining 90 percent had only a 3 percent chance of being listed. Simonton concluded: "This stark difference converts to a correlation coefficient of .46 between being in the top decile in productive rank and being acclaimed by posterity about a half-century later. . . . Hence quality, as measured by eminence, is linked with quantity of output."[31] Other studies report similar findings: American Nobel Prize winners publish twice as many papers as matched samples drawn from *American Men of Science*; and scientists who publish the most receive the greatest number of literature citations by other researchers.[32]

Persistent production may be essential for innovation because those who produce consistently have a greater chance of influencing their fields than those who dabble intermittently. According to Allen Newell, J. C. Shaw, and Herbert Simon: "[innovative] thinking requires high motivation and persistence, taking place either over a considerable span of time (continuously or intermittently) or at high intensity."[33] Richard Mansfield and Thomas Busse agree:

> Creative accomplishments in science do not come easily. In the case of a major discovery, there is almost always an *extended period of persistent effort* before a solution begins to emerge. Francis Crick and James Watson, for example, spent a year and a half trying to discover the structure of DNA before developing the model that won them a Nobel prize. Einstein spent seven years working on the problem of the velocity of light in relation to different frames of reference before he hit upon the key to the solution and developed his theory of special relativity. Many other examples of persistent effort could be mentioned. The amount of effort and time required in this phase of the creative process varies within wide limits, but it is probably great enough to deter all but the most highly motivated scientists. [italics added][34]

Napoleon Hill studied eminent industrial giants of the nineteenth century and concluded that persistence was the only characteristic that explained their accomplishments:

> What mystical power gives to men of persistence the capacity to master difficulties? Does the quality of persistence set up in one's mind some form of spiritual, mental or chemical activity which gives one access to supernatural forces? Does Infinite Intelligence throw itself on the side of the person who still fights on, after the battle has been lost, with the whole world on the opposing side?
> I had the happy privilege of analyzing both Mr. Edison and Mr. Ford, year by year, over a long period of years, and therefore, the opportunity to study them at close range, so I speak from actual knowledge when I say that I found no quality save persistence, in either of them, that even remotely suggested the major source of their stupendous achievements.[35]

Of course, persistence alone is insufficient to explain innovative gain. Working hard and staying on track helps, but stubborn pursuits down dead-end paths still lead nowhere. All innovators must revise thinking and adjust doing occasionally in order to succeed. This can be difficult even for great ones. Einstein persisted for seven years on special relativity and for seven more after that on general relativity. He was less successful the third time when he tried to formulate a unified field theory that combined the laws of gravity and electromagnetism. Nevertheless, he persisted, as Richard Morris described: "Einstein . . . pursued the chimera with such single-minded purpose that he had little time to consider the problems that other scientists thought to be much more important. Einstein was still seeking a unified field theory when he died at the age of seventy-six; at that time he was not much nearer his goal than he had been at the age of forty."[36]

The Interaction Factor

Persistence and competence interact during incremental problem solving to gradually approximate ultimate ends. Final products appear ingenious, even awesome, when compared with their origins, which cloud the meandering, back-tracking, and oscillating that finally conclude with a discovery. According to Weisberg: "The creative product comes about as a result of modification and elaboration of earlier work; and the new product evolves in a series of small steps as the thinker moves slowly away from earlier work."[37]

Ideas about what problems to define and what solutions to find are an outgrowth of the most recent solution incrementally added to an evolving thought chain, as Donald T. Campbell explained in an article entitled "Blind Variation and Selective Attention in Creative Thought as in Other Knowledge Processes." Thought creations function in accordance with principles of variation and selection similar to those proposed by Darwin. The only difference is that this variation and selection occurs in our heads rather than in the environment. Random variation of "thought trials" provides the raw material for selecting the best match with evolving problem definitions and solution selections. By "selectively attending" to the thoughts that are most relevant to the latest addition to the solution chain, we alter the frequency and type of thoughts subsequently generated. Campbell calls this "blind-variation-and-selective-retention." Thought production is the blind variation, and attention selection is selective-retention.

Similar explanations have existed for over a century, beginning with A. Bain's *The Senses and the Intellect* (1874), E. Mach's "On the Part Played by Accident in Invention and Discovery" (1896), P. Souriau's *Théorie de L'invention* (1881), and H. Poincaré's "Mathematical Creation" (1913).[38] Campbell postulated six conditions to explain the mechanism:

1. Mnemonic representations of the environmental discrepancy.
2. Mnemonic searches for "thought-trials" to reduce the discrepancy.
3. Thought-trial generations that randomly produce alternative solutions.
4. Selection criteria for determining the match between thought-trials and discrepancy reduction.
5. Maintenance of thought-trials that approximate a match with selection criteria.
6. Test operations that compare thought selections with environmental events to identify matches.[39]

Campbell concluded that "all processes leading to expansion of knowledge involve [these] blind-variation-and-selective retention procedures."[40] More recently, neurobiologist William H. Calvin proposed a similar variation-and-selection mechanism called the Darwin Machine:

> The Darwin Machine can account for much: for imagination, for generating a broad range of choices, narrowing them down, imagining again, and so creating more and more sophisticated thoughts in much the same way as the better-known biological evolution creates fancier and fancier species. The Darwin Machine theory accounts for how this explanation was generated, its sentences constructed and revised, and for how criticism of the proposal can be listened to, analyzed, and amalgamated into a new view.
>
> Indeed, one wonders if alternative explanations for thought will not simply turn out to be mechanistic equivalents to Darwin Machines, once reduced to such an elementary neurophysiological level. What else is there besides *randomness for generating imaginations, for innovating, for finding the best fits?* That is not to say that explanations at other levels might not turn out to be more useful for some purposes, just as equation-solving algorithms are extremely handy for dealing with a restricted class of phenomena (when you learned long division, you learned an algorithm—a routine procedure guaranteed to provide an answer). A directed search of an ordered list of possibilities, as in expert systems that attempt to diagnose a patient's disease by asking a series of key questions, may be far more efficient than randomly spinning hypotheses. But when we start talking of innovation, imagination, our own stream of thought, and how we initially arrive at an algorithm, we may well be talking Darwin Machines but simply in various "languages."[italics added][41]

Innovators generate thought-trials persistently, combining, matching, recombining, and matching again and again until they find approximations worth trying. Then they test. They learn what works and what doesn't, and they repeat the generation-selection-testing again. Over repeated trials, solutions gradually approximate test criteria until there is a match.

Persistent innovators have an advantage because they give themselves more opportunities to improve testing criteria through reality checks. Each product tells them if their generation-selection-testing mechanism is on target. What works in the environmental test (as opposed to what seems to work in the mental test) resets mental criteria for subsequent thought generations, selections, and tests. New thoughts now center on the latest criteria reinforced and revised by the environmental check. What differentiates great innovators from also-rans is not the persistence of their innovative behaviors per se, but rather the *persistence of interactions between thought-trials and the actions they produce*. This suggests that the greater the number produced, then the more frequent their environmental tests and the more frequent feedback to adjust subsequent thoughts and subsequent tests. Probability logic translates this into greater chances of success. According to Richard Mansfield and Thomas Busse: "One reason for the importance of a period of extended effort is that it increases the likelihood that

Figure 8.1
Routine Solution Finding and Testing

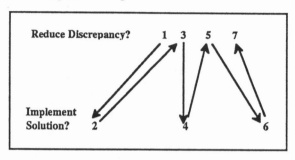

chance association will provide clues to the solution of the problem.''[42] Dean Simonton agrees:

> This demonstrated connection between quantity and quality is consistent with a "constant probability of success" model of creative productivity. Perhaps the odds that any single contribution will prove successful are constant across all creators and so those creators who are most likely to produce a masterpiece are precisely those who produce more works altogether. As W. H. Auden once observed, since major poets are so prolific, "The chances are that, in the course of his lifetime, the major poet will write more bad poems than the minor." . . . Or as Dennis more formally conjectured in the realm of science, "the correlation between fame and fecundity may be understood in part in terms of the proposition that the greater the number of pieces of scientific work done by a given man, the greater the likelihood that one or more of them will prove to be important. . . . *Other things being equal, the greater the number of researches, the greater the likelihood of making an important discovery that will make the finder famous.*"[italics added][43]

Examples of Self-Regulated Innovation

All innovators are determined gainers, but not all determined gainers are innovators. The factors that set innovators apart are quantitative and qualitative. Innovators engage in quantitatively more solution searches and tests to reach their goals. This yields greater depth and breadth in discovery and generates greater chance for unusual outcomes. Innovators also engage in qualitatively different pursuits. They strive for ill-defined goals by redefining purposes while finding ways to fulfill them. Innovators follow unpredictable discovery trails toward occasional gains.

Figures 8.1 through 8.3 contrast routine and innovative decision paths of two determined gainers. Figure 8.1 shows the routine path Pearl Showers followed to reach her smoking goal (from Chapter 5). She searched for and tested three solutions. First she selected the borrow-cigarettes procedure—solution 1 in Figure 8.1. When she tested it (2) and discovered she smoked as much as ever,

Figure 8.2
Innovative Solution Finding and Testing

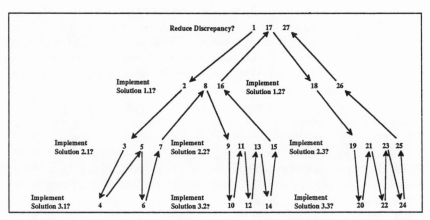

she decided to count cigarettes immediately after each smoke (3). When she implemented this procedure (4), she discovered it didn't work either because she was rushed after her smoke break and forgot to count. Finally, she decided to count each cigarette before lighting up (5). When she implemented this procedure (6), she smoked less than ten per day, which met her goal (7). The procedure reduced the discrepancy between the number of cigarettes she expected to smoke per day and the number she actually smoked each day.

Pearl's problem solving was routine self-regulation because it required only a few means-ends analyses to identify operations to reduce the discrepancy. It was quantitatively simple—both in depth (number of levels/rows of analysis) and breadth (number of different solutions attempted per level). Now consider John Hustle's quest for a larger house.

John Hustle's Quest for a Larger House

John Hustle wants a larger, more expensive house but doesn't have sufficient monthly income to qualify for the loan it requires (Discrepancy 1 = $500; Figure 8.2). So he decides to start his own business, which he will operate in addition to his regular job (Solution 1.1: Decision 2). His first problem is that he can't start a business until he decides what he likes and what might be successful for him. So he reads books on how to start a business and learns that selling real estate can be profitable. This appeals to him. He is good at sales and enjoys it. So he decides to become a real estate broker (Solution 2.1: Decision 3). To learn more about real estate, John attends a one-day seminar on "How to Make a Fortune in Real Estate in Your Spare Time" (Solution 3.1: Decision 4). There he discovers he needs a license, so he enrolls in a community college course that will prepare him for the qualifying exam (Decision 5). After completing the course John passes the exam and obtains his license (Decision 6).

Now John is a broker (Decision 7) and can start his business (Solution 1.1). But he needs customers. So he decides to advertise (Solution 1.1: Decision 8). This presents a new obstacle. What will he say? How will he target his message? John has no knowledge of advertising, and he cannot get his business off the ground without it. He decides to learn more about marketing and advertising (Solution 2.2). He takes another course at the community college, this one entitled "Marketing Yourself in Real Estate" (Solution 2.2: Decision 9), where he learns that he needs a marketing message to be delivered to the residences of different neighborhoods (Decision 10). John signs up for a two-day workshop on "Advertising Messages that Sell" (Solution 2.2: Decision 11). At the workshop, he prepares a message that is consistent with the principles of effective sales (Decision 12). Now he can format the message in a brochure. To solve this problem John consults with his friend who is a commercial artist at an advertising agency (Decision 13). After working with her to develop a brochure, he has advertising copy ready to print (Decision 14). Now he knows enough about advertising (Decision 15) to begin his campaign (Solution 1.1: Decision 16) and start his business.

After six months of selling real estate on weekends, John realizes that the best he can expect is an extra $300 per month. This leaves him $200 short of qualifying for the larger house (Discrepancy 17 = $200). He considers other options for increased income and decides that he needs a partner to invest in the house with him (Solution 1.2: Decision 18). John doesn't know anyone who might be interested, so he decides to develop prospects (Solution 2.3). His first prospect is his father, who likes to invest and usually has money available for new enterprises (Decision 19). John presents the idea to his father but gets an unfavorable response. The real estate market is bad, and houses aren't appreciating. Next John considers his sister (Decision 21), who is also investment-wise and has extra funds. Her reaction is similar to that of her father (Decision 22). Finally John talks with his commercial artist friend, who happened to be looking for a place to rent (Decision 23). While proposing the investment idea, he asks her to marry him (they have been getting along so well in recent months). She accepts both offers (Decision 24), which enables John to satisfy his problem of finding a co-investor (Decisions 25 and 26), which gives him added income to meet the $500 discrepancy goal (Discrepancy 27 = 0).

Figure 8.2 diagrams the decision path John followed to meet his goal. It resembles a logic tree because John used means-ends analysis on each step of his quest. He began with the goal to reduce the $500 per month income discrepancy to 0. Then he asked what actions would reduce that discrepancy. Next he asked himself if he could perform those behaviors now. When he could not,

Figure 8.3
John's "Innovative" Gain from Self-Regulation

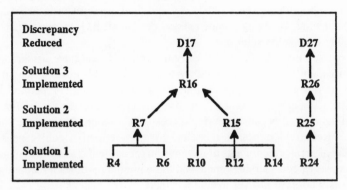

he asked what behaviors or conditions would permit him to perform those behaviors. Then he repeated the means-ends analysis until he could act. This led
him to discover six actions necessary for goal achievement. They were (1)
attending a workshop on selling real estate (Decision 4); (2) completing a community college course for the real estate license (Decision 6); (3) taking a course
on how to develop a marketing plan (Decision 10); (4) attending a workshop to
develop an effective sales message (Decision 12); (5) developing a brochure to
deliver the sales message (Decision 14); and (6) finding a partner who was
willing to co-invest in the house (Decision 24). Two actions were ineffective.
Discussions with his father and sister to co-invest did not yield expected gains
(Decisions 20 and 22).

What did John learn? He learned the solution sequence illustrated in Figure
8.3: (1) responses 4 and 6 led to solution 7; responses 10, 12, and 14 led to
solution 15; response 24 led to solution 25; (2) responses 7 and 15 led to solution
16; and response 25 led to solution 26; and (3) response 16 led to discrepancy
17 = \$200, while response 26 led to discrepancy 27 = 0. He learned the number
and type of gains that were necessary to reduce the discrepancy and meet his
goal.

The Quantitative Difference

Figures 8.1 through 8.3 show *quantitative* differences between routine and
innovative regulation. Routine regulation requires only a few selections and tests
to find what works. Pearl Showers conducted one means-ends analysis and three
tests. John Hustle, on the other hand, conducted three means-ends analyses and
eight tests. Relatively speaking, John's higher rate of searching and testing gave
him a greater chance of finding an innovative solution, which he did.

In addition to this frequency difference, innovators engage in other types of
behaviors more often. They exhibit more frequent feedback seeking of alter-

natives, more frequent testing of new solutions, and more frequent feedback seeking on results of those new responses. Consequently, they experience more frequent suboptimal expectations, choices, and performances and for longer periods of time. By being competent and persistent, they increase their chances of finding acceptable solutions.

Of course, any encouragement early in the search will have sustaining effects for subsequent searching. Dean Simonton describes this effect when young scientists submit papers for publication. Even though initial competition between submitters is equal, the scientist whose paper gets accepted is more likely to submit again, and because of prior success, she is more likely to be successful again.[44] Robert Merton calls this "the Matthew effect [which] consists in the accruing of greater increments of recognition for particular scientific contributions to scientists of considerable repute and the withholding of such recognition from scientists who have not yet made their mark."[45]

Persistent submissions for publication are also more likely as a consequence of the occasional acceptance. Research on schedules of reinforcement indicates that intermittent reinforcement produces more sustained responding than continuous reinforcement. Scholars who have a proportion of articles accepted for publication are more likely to sustain than those who get every submission accepted at first and then have a dry spell or who always fail. Both get discouraged easily. Not so for the intermittent succeeder who perseveres for long droughts, always expecting the next attempt to succeed. This pattern is conducive to innovative gain, given the uncertainty of results from unpredictable decision trails. Einstein invested seven years of problem solving to formulate his theory of special relativity, and another seven to formulate his theory of general relativity. Then he tried unsuccessfully for another forty years to formulate a unified field theory.

The Qualitative Difference

The second difference between innovators and routinizers is qualitative. One can analyze problems and test solutions with care, precision, and detail and still never produce creative gain. The problem being solved may be too difficult or the goal it enables insignificant. In order for an idea or product to qualify as innovative, it must be novel *and* significant—it must involve the modification or rejection of previously accepted ideas.[46] Competence increases these chances. For example, expert sensitivity to ill-defined inconsistencies frequently signals what is worth examining, as B.F. Skinner noted:

> The major result of this experiment was that some of my rats had babies. I began to watch young rats. I saw them right themselves and crawl about very much like the decerebrate or thalamic cats and rabbits of Magnus. So I set about studying the postural reflexes of young rats. Here was a first principle not formally recognized by scientific methodologists: *when you run onto something interesting, drop everything else and study it.*[italics added][47]

Newell, Shaw, and Simon agree. The following conditions represent their analysis of the innovative process:

1. The product of the thinking has novelty and value (either for the thinker or for his culture).
2. The thinking is unconventional, in the sense that it requires modification or rejection of previously accepted ideas.
3. The thinking requires high motivation and persistence, taking place either over a considerable span of time (continuously or intermittently) or at high intensity.
4. *The problem as initially posed was vague and ill-defined, so that part of the task was to formulate the problem itself.*[italics added][48]

Ill-defined goals produce innovative results because both purpose and problem solving evolve together. Mihaly Csikszentmihalyi illustrated:

> In a recently concluded longitudinal study of painters and sculptors, for instance, we found that young artists who usually knew what they wanted to do before they started to work ended up producing art that was considerably less original than the paintings made by artists who approach each canvas without knowing in advance what they were going to do. This latter group, who succeeded in becoming recognized as artists, *typically discovered their goal in any given painting only after they had become involved with the painting itself.* Their emotions and thoughts coalesced into a plan of work only after they had seen the results of their initial almost random and tentative brush strokes. In fact, original artists usually discovered the plan of their work after the work itself was half over. Less original artists, by contrast, have an aesthetic plan from the very beginning: They know how the finished picture should look. . . . In the first case, the approach is *emergent: The goal arises out of a unique interaction between person and environment.* In the second case, it is programmed by cultural conventions. The same relationship holds as far as rewards are concerned. The conventional artist is rewarded when the painting matches recognized criteria of style. The original artist must discover his or her own rewards. Because the goal he or she sets has never quite existed before, it is difficult to know whether it has been achieved; in fact, only the artist can know. [underscore added][49]

Research on ill-defined problems indicates that expectations for gain or loss affect how we perceive problems. When expectations for gain are low, discrepancy signals from ill-defined problem areas go unnoticed and unattended. Even when signals get through, lowered expectations depress interest in goal pursuit, as Robert Abelson and Ariel Levi pointed out: "Simply perceiving that there is a discrepancy between the existing and a desired state does not necessarily lead the individual to take action. . . . [Other researchers have pointed out] that the individual must also be motivated to resolve the problem and must perceive that there exist the necessary abilities and resources to do so."[50]

Rewards for attending to a discrepancy must outweigh the costs of determining what it is, what it means, and what, if anything, to do about it. This is consistent with the self-instructions suggested by the expectation and choice propositions: "Will my choice produce the greatest gain at the lowest cost?" "Can I respond to my choice effectively and efficiently?"

Prolific innovators are sensitive to subtle and unusual cues. In addition, their competence and intrinsic interest reduce cost estimations and increase gain expectations. This motivates feedback seeking to specify precise expectations for resolution. Furthermore, successful innovators are more discriminating about what is unusual and significant because they have logged hundreds of thousands of thought-trials, solution tests, and causal inferences. They know what is worth pursuing as well as how best to commence pursuit. According to G. Steven Tuthill and Susan Levy, authors of *Knowledge-Based Systems:*

> Experience enables domain experts to function at higher levels of abstraction than their colleagues. This abstraction level permits more rapid sorting and indexing between and among models. Further, experts compile and store a larger number of compiled domain-specific links. Using these links, they can rapidly recognize patterns, eliminate possibilities, and form hypotheses. . . . Thus, the characteristic of mature experts is a well-developed metacognitive awareness. These people demonstrate a greater awareness of the requirements needed to perform a given task, the materials to be acquired, and the activities essential to complete the task. As a result, they are aware of the interactions among the knowledge elements and form a plan according to the need. Novices, however, are aware of the major factors; while experts have a sharp focus, novices have only an indication of the need.[51]

Experts are more likely to take on ill-defined discrepancies than novices because they know how to proceed. They can make fine distinctions between what is important and what is not. They recognize how the "unusual" fits in the terrain of the domain. Past success with similarly ill-defined discrepancies encourages pursuit.

The Innovation Hypothesis

Innovation and self-determination are variants of self-regulation. Although both depend upon high levels of self-regulatory activity, they have different relationships with gain. Perceptions of self-determination are likely when regulatory activity and gain occur together frequently. Innovative gain, by contrast, usually requires long periods of regulation in the absence of gain.

Another difference is that perceptions of self-determination can occur during optimal and suboptimal goal and choice contingencies, whereas innovative gain is most likely to occur during suboptimal contingencies that are ill-defined. Conditions of uncertainty redefine expectations during continuously evolving interactions between solution selecting and solution testing. Of course, self-determination and innovation are similarly influenced by competence and persistence, as indicated in Hypothesis 12.

Hypothesis 12: The more competent and persistent the self-regulation during suboptimal and ill-defined goal and choice contingencies, the more
likely the innovative gain.

The intelligence factor is absent from the innovation hypothesis because it is
possible to perceive oneself as being intelligent but not innovative, or conversely,
innovative but not intelligent. Given that perceptions of intelligence depend upon
the frequency of gain during suboptimal goal and choice contingencies (Hypothesis 5), would-be innovators who exhibit great persistence and competence
but produce no gain probably do not regard their regulation as being intelligent,
even though their results may later prove to be innovative. Conversely, regulators
who consistently produce gain when goal attainment is improbable are likely to
regard themselves as being intelligent because they adjusted well under difficult
circumstances. Their gain, however, need not be innovative for them to perceive
themselves as being intelligent.

Conclusion

In this book I set out to explain how optimal adjustment maximizes gain. The
underlying assumption was that under ideal conditions, humans are rational
adaptors. They optimize their adjustments in order to maximize their gain. They
think and behave in their best interests over the long term.

But this occurs only under ideal conditions — in the best of all possible worlds
where (1) access to information is complete, (2) knowledge about its use is valid,
and (3) performance of its dictates is competent. Under these circumstances, we
never decide without data or act without knowledge. We always think rationally,
perform competently, and adjust optimally. The correspondence between our
past experience, expectations, choices, and performance is perfect.

The definitions, assumptions, and propositions of *self-regulation theory* (see
Appendix) explain the mechanisms that are responsible for these optimal adjustments and maximum gains. The *terms* and *definitions* provide the language
necessary to describe essential variables of self-regulation; the *assumptions* describe the nature of self-regulating systems — that they are purposeful, self-
correcting (they learn), and evolving; and the *propositions* describe how the
variables of self-regulation (past gains, expectations, choices, and responses)
interact to affect gain toward goal attainment. As past gains, expectations,
choices, and responses optimize, gain toward goal attainment maximizes.

The central question addressed by the theory is how discrepancies between
expectations and observations get resolved. How do humans adjust to a world
that frequently fails to live up to expectations? During ideal conditions, when
the world does exactly as we expect, there is no need to adjust thinking or doing.
All that is necessary is that we think how we thought in the past and do what
we did before. Unfortunately, stability like this is short-lived. Unexpected events
occur, our plans don't turn out as expected, and our behaviors don't always

produce the results we need. So we adjust. We seek new methods of thinking and doing.

The propositions in self-regulation theory describe conditions that affect how successfully we reduce discrepancies between present states and goal states. According to the expectation and choice propositions, the factors affecting how well we adjust are (1) past gain toward goal attainment, (2) the discrepancy condition, and (3) the choice condition. When our experience adjusting to those discrepancies is minimal, when discrepancies between actual states and goal states are large, and when the operations that will reduce those discrepancies are obscure, then we are unlikely to adjust optimally and gain maximally. At the other end of optimality—when past gain in the goal pursuit is exactly what we expected, when discrepancies between the current state and the goal state are small, and when the operations necessary to reduce those discrepancies are obvious—then we need only think and act exactly as before in order to optimize and maximize.

Hypotheses 1–12 (see Appendix) explore the implications of these predictions. Hypotheses 1 and 2 describe environmental conditions that are conducive to greater self-regulatory activity. Hypotheses 2–6 describe attributions resulting from gain produced when environmental conditions are more or less favorable. Hypotheses 7–9 describe the causal factors leading to persistent regulation: (1) how competence affects confidence about self-regulatory activity; (2) how confidence in predicting results affects intrinsic interest in self-regulatory activity; and (3) how intrinsic interest during intermittent gain affects persistence of regulation. Hypothesis 10 describes interactions among three sets of factors that affect intelligent adaptations: (1) suboptimal environmental conditions; (2) competence and interest; and (3) expectations, choices, and performances.

Hypotheses 11 and 12 extend the self-regulation explanation to account for self-determination and innovation. Hypothesis 11 predicts that regulators will perceive the effort to be self-determined when they adjust frequently and gain frequently during the goal pursuit. The more involved regulators are in regulating toward goal attainment and the more frequently they experience gain from that regulation, then the more often they will feel efficacious and self-determined.

Hypothesis 12 describes conditions under which gain toward goal attainment is likely to be innovative. When regulatory effort is competent and persistent and when suboptimal goal and choice contingencies are ill-defined, then interactions between expecting, choosing, and doing will evolve unpredictably toward unexpected and occasional innovative gain.

For centuries, clerics and philosophers have asked why we survive and occasionally thrive. But in the last hundred years or so, scholars and scientists from biology to computer science have asked different questions. They have asked "How?" The theory presented in this book has attempted to answer one of these questions: "How does optimal adjustment maximize gain?" According to the theory, we optimize adjustments by optimizing past gains, maximizing present expectations, optimizing available choices, and perfecting performances of those choices. This requires that we push the limits and challenge restraints by making decisions, taking actions, and adjusting to results at the margin.

Notes

1. Peter F. Drucker, *Innovation and Entrepreneurship, Practice and Principles* (New York: Harper & Row, 1985), 13–14.

2. Richard T. La Piere, *Social Change* (New York: McGraw-Hill, 1965), 125–138; Richard S. Mansfield and Thomas V. Busse, *The Psychology of Creativity and Discovery* (Chicago: Nelson-Hall, 1981); Robert Weisberg, *Creativity, Genius and Other Myths* (New York: W.H. Freeman and Company, 1986), 62–64.

3. Howard E. Gruber, *Darwin on Man: A Psychological Study of Scientific Creativity* (New York: E.P. Dutton & Co., 1974), 20.

4. Richard Morris, *Dismantling the Universe* (New York: Simon and Schuster, 1983), 20.

5. Ibid., 21.

6. Ibid., 28.

7. Ibid., 30.

8. Ibid., 31.

9. Weisberg, *Creativity, Genius and Other Myths*, 132.

10. Ibid., 132–133.

11. Ibid., 133.

12. Ibid.

13. Ibid., 136.

14. Herbert A. Simon, *Models of Thought* (New Haven, CT: Yale University Press, 1989), 60.

15. Raymond S. Nickerson, "On Improving Thinking through Instruction," in Ernst Z. Rothkopf (Ed.), *Review of Research in Education 15* (Washington, DC: American Education Research Association, 1988), 14.

16. Adrian D. de Groot, "Perception and Memory versus Thought: Some Old Ideas and Recent Findings," in Benjamin Kleinmuntz (Ed.), *Problem Solving: Research, Method, and Theory* (New York: John Wiley & Sons, 1966), 23–24.

17. For a review and additional citations for this research, see John D. Bransford and Nancy J. Vye, "A Perspective on Cognitive Research and Its Implications for Instruction," in Lauren B. Resnick and Leopold E. Klopfer (Eds.), *Toward the Thinking Curriculum: Current Cognitive Research* (Washington, DC: Association for Supervision and Curriculum Development, 1989), 173–205.

18. Herbert A. Simon, Jill H. Larkin, John McDermott, and Dorothea P. Simon, "Expert and Novice Performance in Solving Physics Problems," *Science* 208 (1980): 1335–1342.

19. Bransford and Vye, "A Perspective on Cognitive Research," 182.

20. Simon, *Models of Thought*, 60.

21. B. Eugene Griessman, *The Achievement Factors: Candid Interviews with Some of the Most Successful People of Our Time* (New York: Dodd, Mead, & Company, 1987), 38.

22. Benjamin S. Bloom, *Developing Talent in Young People* (New York: Ballantine Books, 1985).

23. Griessman, *The Achievement Factors*, 38–39.

24. Griessman, *The Achievement Factors*, 39–40. For the quoted article, see Herbert Warren Wind, "The Sporting Scene: Mostly about Nicklaus," *The New Yorker*, May 30 (1983): 67.

25. Jean-Paul Sartre, quoted in Howard Gardner, *Frames of Mind* (New York: Basic Books, 1985), 81.

26. Weisberg, *Creativity, Genius and Other Myths*, 145.

27. Dean Keith Simonton, *Genius, Creativity, and Leadership* (Cambridge, MA: Harvard University Press, 1984), 78.

28. Wayne Dennis, "Variations in Productivity among Creative Workers," *Scientific Monthly* 80 (1955): 277–278, as reported by Simonton, *Genius, Creativity*, 78–79.

29. Simonton, *Genius, Creativity*, 79.

30. Wayne Dennis, "Bibliographics of Eminent Scientists," *Scientific Monthly* 79 (1954): 180–183, as reported by Simonton, *Genius, Creativity*, 81.

31. Simonton, *Genius, Creativity*, 82.

32. Simonton reported the following studies: H. Zuckerman, *Scientific Elite* (New York: The Free Press, 1977); S.V. Ashton and C. Oppenheim, "A Method of Predicting Nobel Prizewinners in Chemistry," *Social Studies of Science* 8 (1978): 341–348; L.B. Meyer, *Emotion and Meaning in Music* (Chicago: University of Chicago, 1956); K.E. Clark, *America's Psychologists* (Washington, DC: American Psychological Association, 1957); and R.L. Helmreich, J.T. Spence, W.E. Beane, G.W. Lucker, and K.A. Matthews, "Making It in Academic Psychology: Demographic and Personality Correlates of Attainment," *Journal of Personality and Social Psychology* 39 (1980): 896–908.

33. Allen Newell, J.C. Shaw, and Herbert A. Simon, "The Processes of Creative Thinking," in Howard E. Gruber, Glenn Terrell, and Michael Wertheimer (Eds.), *Contemporary Approaches to Creative Thinking: A Symposium Held at the University of Colorado* (New York: Atherton Press, 1962), 65.

34. Richard S. Mansfield and Thomas V. Busse, *The Psychology of Creativity and Discovery: Scientists and Their Work* (Chicago: Nelson-Hall, 1981), 89.

35. Napoleon Hill, *Think and Grow Rich* (New York: Fawcett Crest, 1960 [1938]), 163–164.

36. Morris, *Dismantling the Universe*, 72.

37. Weisberg, *Creativity, Genius and Other Myths*, 138.

38. Donald T. Campbell, "Blind Variation and Selective Attention in Creative Thought as in Other Knowledge Processes," *Psychological Review* 67 (1960): 380–400.

39. Ibid., 397.

40. Ibid.

41. William H. Calvin, *The Cerebral Symphony: Seashore Reflections on the Structure of Consciousness* (New York: Bantam Books, 1990), 270–271.

42. Mansfield and Busse, *The Psychology of Creativity and Discovery*, 89.

43. Simonton, *Genius, Creativity*, 83.

44. Ibid., 86–88.

45. Robert K. Merton, "The Matthew Effect in Science," *Science* 159 (1968): 58, quoted in Simonton, *Genius, Creativity*, 87.

46. Newell, Shaw, and Simon, "The Processes of Creative Thinking," 65.

47. B.F. Skinner, "A Case History in Scientific Method," in S. Koch (Ed.), *Psychology: A Study of Science, Volume 2* (New York: McGraw-Hill, 1959), 363, quoted in Mansfield and Busse, *The Psychology of Creativity and Discovery*, 88.

48. Newell, Shaw, and Simon, "The Process of Creative Thinking," 65–66.

49. Mihaly Csikszentmihalyi, "Intrinsic Rewards and Emergent Motivation," in Mark R. Lepper and David Greene (Eds.), *The Hidden Costs of Reward: New Perspectives on the Psychology of Human Motivation* (Hillsdale, NJ: Lawrence Erlbaum Associates, 1978), 208.

50. Robert P. Abelson and Ariel Levi, "Decision Making and Decision Theory," in Gardner Lindzey and Elliot Aronson (Eds.), *Third Edition Handbook of Social Psychology, Volume 1, Theory and Method* (New York: Random House, 1985), 271.

51. G. Steven Tuthill and Susan T. Levy, *Knowledge-Based Systems* (Blue Ridge Summit, PA: TAB Professional and Reference Books, 1991), 54–55.

Appendix

Self-Regulation Theory: The Closer to Optimal the Adjustment, the Closer to Maximum the Gain toward Goal Attainment

Terms and Definitions in Self-Regulation Theory

1. Actual State: most recent gain toward goal attainment.
2. Choice Contingency: an event or condition that is necessary to identify operations that produce gain.
3. Choice: the distribution of responses between two or more alternatives.
4. Cost Responses: responses that do not produce gain toward goal attainment (e.g., feedback responses and incorrect responses).
5. Discrepancy: the difference between the actual state and the goal state.
6. Expected Gain: the gain toward goal attainment the regulator chooses to produce.
7. Feedback Seeking: responding that produces information about goal states, actual states, options, performances, and results.
8. Gain Responses: responses that produce gain toward goal attainment.
9. Gain: an amount of discrepancy reduction between the goal state and the present state.
10. Goal Attainment: the actual state equaling the goal state.
11. Goal Contingency: an event or condition that is necessary for the actual state to equal the goal state.
12. Goal or Goal State: the gain that makes the actual state equal the goal state.
13. Maximum Gain: the possible gain from a given operation.
14. Favorable Choice Contingency: an event or condition that increases the probability of choosing the best option.

15. Favorable Goal Contingency: an event or condition that increases the probability of performing the operations necessary for goal attainment.
16. Optimal Adjustment: when past gains, expectations, choices, and performances are optimal.
17. Optimal Choice Contingency: an event or condition that maximizes the probability of identifying the best option.
18. Optimality of Choice: ratio of the maximum gain possible from the actual choice to the maximum gain possible from the best choice.
19. Optimal Goal Contingency: an event or condition that maximizes the probability of performing the operations necessary for goal attainment.
20. Optimality of Expectation for Gain: ratio of gain expected to gain possible from the options available.
21. Optimality of Performance: the ratio of gain responses to gain responses plus cost responses.
22. Optimality of Past Gain: ratio of actual results to expected results.
23. Optimality: the extent to which the goal contingency, choice contingency, past gain, expectation, choice, or performance increases gain toward goal attainment.
24. Performance: distribution of responses between gain responses and cost responses.
25. Self-Regulatory Behaviors: choosing gain, choosing options to produce gain, performing operations to produce gain, feedback seeking on goal states, actual states, options, performance, and results.
26. Suboptimal Choice Contingency: an event or condition that decreases the probability of identifying the best option.
27. Suboptimal Goal Contingency: an event or condition that decreases the probability of performing the operations necessary for goal attainment.

Assumptions

Assumption 1. All behavior is a function of the discrepancy between a goal state and a current state: the more frequent the discrepancy between an expected state and current state, the more frequent the self-regulatory behavior.

Assumption 2. The closer the match between expected and current states as a consequence of self-regulatory behavior, the more likely similar self-regulatory behavior will occur for discrepancies between similar expected and current states.

Assumption 3. The more persistent the discrepancy between the expected and current state, the more likely the current state will become the expected state.

Propositions

Expectation Proposition: The closer to optimal the past gain toward goal attainment and the smaller the discrepancy between the actual state and the goal state, the closer to optimal the expectation for gain.

Choice Proposition: The closer to optimal the past gain toward goal attainment and the more salient the differences between options, the closer to optimal the choice.

Response Proposition: The closer to optimal the past gain, expectations, and choices, then the closer to optimal the distribution of responses between task completion to meet the goal and feedback seeking about goal state-actual state discrepancies, options, task performance, and gain.

Gain Proposition: The closer to optimal the past gain, expectations, choices, and responses, then the closer to maximum the gain toward goal attainment.

Hypotheses

Hypothesis 1: The closer to optimal or suboptimal the goal and choice contingencies, the less likely the self-regulation.

Hypothesis 2: Self-regulation is more likely during moderately favorable goal and choice contingencies than during optimal or suboptimal goal and choice contingencies.

Hypothesis 3: The more frequent the gain during optimal goal and choice contingencies, the more likely the regulator will perceive the regulation to be competent.

Hypothesis 4: The less frequent the gain during optimal goal and choice contingencies, the more likely the regulator will perceive the regulation to be incompetent.

Hypothesis 5: The more frequent the gain during suboptimal goal and choice contingencies, the more likely the regulator will perceive the regulation to be intelligent.

Hypothesis 6: The less frequent the gain during suboptimal goal and choice contingencies, the more likely the regulator will perceive the regulation to be lucky.

Hypothesis 7: The greater the competence in choosing and performing an activity, the greater the confidence that actual gains will match expected gains for that activity.

Hypothesis 8: The more confident and more accurate the prediction of gain toward goal attainment, the greater the intrinsic interest in activities that produced the gain.

Hypothesis 9: The greater the intrinsic interest in activities that produce intermittent gain toward goal attainment, the greater the persistence in performing those activities.

Hypothesis 10: During suboptimal contingencies, the greater the correspondence among (1) goal and choice contingencies, (2) interests and abilities, and (3) expectations, choices, and performances, then the more likely the intelligent adaptation.

Hypothesis 11: The more frequent the gain from competent and persistent self-regulation, the more likely the regulator will perceive the gain to be self-determined.

Hypothesis 12: The more competent and persistent the self-regulation during suboptimal and ill-defined goal and choice contingencies, the more likely the innovative gain.

Bibliography

Abelson, Robert P., and Ariel Levi. "Decision Making and Decision Theory." In Gardner Lindzey and Elliot Aronson (Eds.), *Third Edition Handbook of Social Psychology*. Vol. 1 *Theory and Method*. New York: Random House, 1985.

Andreski, Stanislav. "Method and Substantive Theory in Max Weber." In R. Serge Denisoff, Orel Callahan, and Mark H. Levine (Eds.), *Theories and Paradigms in Contemporary Sociology*. Itasca, IL: F. E. Peacock Publishers, 1974.

Angier, Natalie. "Ignoring Big Chances, Bumblebees Just Seek Small, Reliable Gains." *New York Times*, 3 September 1991.

Annett, J. *Feedback and Human Behavior*. Baltimore: Penguin Books, 1969.

Ashby, W. Ross. *Design for a Brain: The Origin of Adaptive Behaviour*. New York: John Wiley & Sons, 1960.

Ashton, S. V. and C. Oppenheim, "A Method of Predicting Nobel Prizewinners in Chemistry," *Social Studies of Science* 8 (1978): 341–348.

Associated Press. "Barometer Shows Drop in U.S. Pupils' Science Knowledge: Americans Subpar in All Categories." *Gazette Telegraph* (Colorado Springs, Colorado), 11 September 1987.

———. "Test Shows Lack of Economic Knowledge: Students Stumped by 'Profit'." *Gazette Telegraph* (Colorado Springs, Colorado), 29 December 1988.

Bandura, Albert. *Social Learning Theory*. Englewood Cliffs, NJ: Prentice-Hall, 1977.

———. "Self-Efficacy Mechanism in Human Agency." *American Psychologist* 37 (1982): 122.

Bem, S. L. "Verbal Self-Control: The Establishment of Effective Self-Instructions." *Journal of Experimental Psychology* 74 (1967): 485–491.

Benson, Herbert. *Your Maximum Mind*. New York: Avon Books, 1987.

Bloom, Benjamin S. "Generalizations about Talent Developing." In Benjamin S. Bloom (Ed.), *Developing Talent in Young People*, 507–549. New York: Ballantine Books, 1985.

Bobrow, Davis B., and John S. Dryzek. *Policy Analysis by Design*. Pittsburgh: University of Pittsburgh Press, 1987.

Bransford, John D., and Nancy J. Vye. "A Perspective on Cognitive Research and Its Implications for Instruction." In Lauren B. Resnick and Leopold E. Klopfer (Eds.), *Toward the Thinking Curriculum: Current Cognitive Research*, 173–205. Washington, DC: Association for Supervision and Curriculum Development, 1989.

Buckland, William. Quoted in Richard Levins and Richard Lewontin, *The Dialectical Biologist*. Cambridge, MA: Harvard University Press, 1985.

Bullock, Charles S., III, James E. Anderson, and David W. Brady. *Public Policy in the Eighties*. Monterey, CA: Brooks/Cole Publishing, 1983.

Burke, James. *Connections*. Boston: Little, Brown, 1978.

Calvin, William H. *The Cerebral Symphony: Seashore Reflections on the Structure of Consciousness*. New York: Bantam Books, 1990.

Campbell, Donald T. "Blind Variation and Selective Attention in Creative Thought as in Other Knowledge Processes." *Psychological Review* 67 (1960): 380–400.

Cannon, Walter Bradford. *The Wisdom of the Body*. New York: Norton, 1932.

Capra, Fritjof. *Uncommon Wisdom: Conversations with Remarkable People*. New York: Bantam Books, 1989.

Carver Charles S., and Michael F. Scheier. "An Information Processing Perspective on Self-Management." In P. Karoly and F. H. Kanfer (Eds.), *Self-Management and Behavior Change: From Theory to Practice*, 93–128. New York: Pergamon Press, 1983.

Chodak, Szymon. *Societal Development: Five Approaches with Conclusions from Comparative Analysis*. New York: Oxford University Press, 1973.

Clark, K. E. *America's Psychologists*. Washington, D.C.: American Psychological Association, 1978.

Corno, Lyn, and E. B. Mandinach. "The Role of Cognitive Engagement in Classroom Learning and Motivation." *Educational Psychologist* 18 (1983): 88–108.

Csikzentmihalyi, Mihaly. *Flow: The Psychology of Optimal Experience*. New York: Harper & Row, 1990.

———. "Intrinsic Rewards and Emergent Motivation." In Mark R. Lepper and David Greene (Eds.), *The Hidden Costs of Reward: New Perspectives on the Psychology of Human Motivation*, 205–216. Hillsdale, NJ: Lawrence Erlbaum Associates, 1978.

D'Zurill, Thomas J., and Marvin R. Goldfried. "Problem Solving and Behavior Modification." *Journal of Abnormal Psychology* 78, no. 1 (1971): 107–126.

de Groot, Adrian D. "Perception and Memory versus Thought: Some Old Ideas and Recent Findings." In Benjamin Kleinmuntz (Ed.), *Problem Solving: Research, Method, and Theory*, 19–50. New York, John Wiley & Sons, 1966.

Deci, Edward L., and Joseph Porac. "Cognitive Evaluation Theory and the Study of Human Motivation." In Mark R. Lepper and David Greene (Eds.), *The Hidden Costs of Reward: New Perspective on the Psychology of Human Motivation*, 149–176. Hillsdale, NJ: Lawrence Erlbaum Associates, 1978.

Deci, Edward L., and Richard M. Ryan. *Intrinsic Motivation and Self-Determination in Human Behavior*. New York: Plenum Press, 1985.

Dennis, Wayne. "Bibliographics of Eminent Scientists." *Scientific Monthly* 79 (1954): 180–183.

———. "Variations in Productivity among Creative Workers." *Scientific Monthly* 80 (1955): 277–278.

Dewey, John. *Experience and Education*. New York: Collier Books, 1963 [1938].

———. *How We Think: A Restatement of the Relation of Reflective Thinking to the Educative Process*. Boston: D. C. Heath, 1933.

———. *Types of Thinking, Including a Survey of Greek Philosophy*. Translated from the Chinese and edited by Robert W. Clopton and Tsuin-Chen Ou. New York: Philosophical Library, 1984.

Drucker, Peter F. *Innovation and Entrepreneurship, Practice and Principles*. New York: Harper & Row, 1985.

Egeland, Byron. "Training Impulsive Children in the Use of More Efficient Scanning Techniques." *Child Development* 45 (1974): 165–171.

Eldredge, Niles. *Macro-Evolutionary Dynamics: Species, Niches, and Adaptive Peaks*. New York: McGraw-Hill, 1989.

Elmer-Dewitt, Philip. "The Revolution That Fizzled." *Time*, May 20 (1991): 48.

Etzioni, Amitai. "Introduction." In Ann Majchrazak, *Methods for Policy Research*. Beverly Hills: Sage Publications, 1984.

Ferster, C. B., and B. F. Skinner. *Schedules of reinforcement*. New York: Appleton-Century-Crofts, 1957.

Festinger, Leon. *A Theory of Cognitive Dissonance*. Evanston, IL: Row, Peterson, 1957.

Finch, A. J., Jr., and L. E. Montgomery. "Reflection-Impulsivity and Information Seeking in Emotionally Disturbed Children." *Journal of Abnormal Social Psychology* 1 (1973): 358–362.

Ford, J. Kevin, Neal Schmitt, Susan L. Schechtman, Brian M. Hults, and Mary L. Doherty. "Process Tracing Methods: Contributions, Problems, and Neglected Research Questions." *Organizational Behavior and Human Performance* 43 (1989): 75–117.

Form, William. "Resolving Ideological Issues on the Division of Labor." In Hubert M. Blalock, Jr. (Ed.), *Sociological Theory and Research: A Critical Appraisal*. New York: The Free Press, 1980.

Friedman, Miles I., and Martha R. Willis. *Human Nature and Predictability*. Lexington, MA: Lexington Books, 1981.

Gallup, George, and Alec M. Gallup. *The Great American Success Story: Factors That Affect Achievement*. Homewood, IL: Dow Jones-Irwin, 1986.

Gardner, Howard. *Frames of Mind*. (New York: Basic Books, 1985.

Gettys, C. F. *Research and Theory on Predecision Processes*. Norman: Decision Processes Laboratory, University of Oklahoma, 1983.

Gettys, C. F., and P. D. Englemann. *Ability and Expertise in Act Generation*. Norman: Decision Processes Laboratory, University of Oklahoma, 1983.

Gilbreth, Frank B., and Lillian M. Gilbreth. "Classifying the Elements of Work." *Management and Administration* 8, no. 2 (1924): 151.

Griessman, B. Eugene. *The Achievement Factors: Candid Interviews with Some of the Most Successful People of Our Time*. New York: Dodd, Mead, 1987.

Gruber, Howard E. *Darwin on Man: A Psychological Study of Scientific Creativity*. New York: E. P. Dutton, 1974.

Haaga, David A., and Gerald C. Davison. "Cognitive Change Methods." In Frederick H. Kanfer and Arnold P. Goldstein (Eds.), *Helping People Change*, 236–282. New York: Pergamon Press, 1986.

Hake, Don F., and Ron Vukelich. "Analysis of the Control Exerted by a Complex

Cooperation Procedure." *Journal of the Experimental Analysis of Behavior* 19 (1973): 3–16.

Hake, Don F., Ron Vukelich, and S. J. Kaplan. "Audit Responses: Responses Maintained by Access to Existing Self or Coactor Scores during Nonsocial, Parallel Work, and Cooperation Procedures." *Journal of the Experimental Analysis of Behavior* 19 (1973): 409–423.

Harrell, Thomas W. *Industrial Psychology*. New York: Rinehart & Company, 1949.

Harter, Susan. "A Developmental Perspective on Some Parameters of Self-Regulation in Children." In Paul Karoly and Frederick H. Kanfer (Eds.), *Self-Management and Behavior Change: From Theory to Practice*, 163–204. New York: Pergamon Press, 1982.

Heider, Fritz. *The Psychology of Interpersonal Relations*. New York: John Wiley, 1958.
———. "Attitude and Cognitive Organization." *Journal of Psychology* 21 (1946): 107–112.

Hellemans, Alexander, and Bryan Bunch. *The Timetables of Science: A Chronology of the Most Important People and Events in the History of Science*. New York: Simon and Schuster, 1988.

Helmreich, R. L., J. T. Spence, W. E. Beane, G. W. Lucker, and K. A. Matthews "Making It in Academic Psychology: Demographic and Personality Correlates of Attainment," *Journal of Personality and Social Psychology* 39 (1980): 896–908.

Herrnstein, Richard J. "Formal Properties of the Matching Law." *Journal of the Experimental Analysis of Behavior* 21 (1974): 159–164.
———. "On the Law of Effect." *Journal of the Experimental Analysis of Behavior* 13 (1970): 243–266.

Hill, Napoleon. *The Law of Success*. Evanston, IL: Success Unlimited, 1979 [1920].
———. *Think and Grow Rich*. New York: Fawcett Crest, 1960.

Hill, Napoleon, and W. Clement Stone. *Success through a Positive Mental Attitude*. New York: Prentice-Hall, 1987.

Hogarth, Robin M. *Judgement and Choice: The Psychology of Decision*. New York: John Wiley & Sons, 1980.

Hogwood, Brian W., and Lewis A. Gunn. *Policy Analysis for the Real World*. London: Oxford University Press, 1984.

Homans, George C. *Social Behavior: Its Elementary Forms*, rev. ed. New York: Harcourt Brace Jovanovich, 1974.
———. "Bringing Men Back In." *American Sociological Review* 29 (December 1964): 809–818.

Jackson, Henry J., and Paul G. Boag. "The Efficacy of Self-Control Procedures as Motivational Strategies with Mentally Retarded Persons: A Review of the Literature and Guidelines for Future Research." *Australian Journal of Developmental Disabilities* 7 (1981): 65–79.

James, William. *Essays in Pragmatism*, edited by Alburey Castell. New York: Hafner Publishing, 1948.

Janis, Irving L., and Leon Mann. *Decision Making: A Psychological Analysis of Conflict, Choice, and Commitment*. New York: The Free Press, 1977.

Jeffrey, D. Balfour, and Laurence H. Berger. "A Self-Environmental Systems Model and Its Implications for Behavior Change." In Kirk R. Blankstein and Janet Polivy (Eds.), *Advances in the Study of Communication and Affect*. Vol. 7, *Self-Control and Self-Modification of Emotional Behavior*, 29–69. New York: Plenum Press, 1982.

Jones, Mary Cover. "A Laboratory Study of Fear: The Case of Peter." *Journal of Genetic Psychology* 31 (1924): 308–315.

Jones, Richard W. *Principles of Biological Regulation*. New York: Academic Press, 1973.

Kagan, Jerome. "Reflection-Impulsivity." *Journal of Abnormal Psychology* 71 (1966): 17–24.

Kagan, Jerome, L. Pearson, and L. Welch. "The Modifiability of an Impulsive Tempo." *Journal of Educational Psychology* 57 (1966): 359–365.

Kalberg, Stephen. "Max Weber (1864–1920)." In Adam Kuper and Jessica Kuper (Eds.), *The Social Science Encyclopedia*, 892–896. New York: Routledge, 1989.

Kanfer, Frederick H., and Sue Hagerman. "The Role of Self-Regulation." In Lynn P. Prehm (Ed.), *Behavior Therapy for Depression*, 143–179. New York: Academic Press, 1981.

Karoly, Paul, and Frederick H. Kanfer (Eds.). *Self-Management and Behavior Change: From Theory to Practice*. New York: Pergamon Press, 1982.

King, George R., and A. W. Logue. "Humans' Sensitivity to Variation in Reinforcer Amount: Effects of the Method of Reinforcer Delivery." *Journal of the Experimental Analysis of Behavior* 53 (1990): 33–45.

Knapp, Robert H., and Hubert B. Goodrich. "The Origins of American Scientists." In David C. McClelland (Ed.), *Studies in Motivation*. New York: Appleton-Century-Crofts, 1955.

Kristal, Leonard. *The ABC of Psychology*. New York: Facts on File Publications, 1982.

Kuper, Adam, and Jessica Kuper (Eds.). *The Social Science Encyclopedia*. New York: Routledge, 1985.

La Piere, Richard T. *Social Change*. New York: McGraw-Hill, 1965.

Lamm, Richard. "Young Americans Don't Measure Up." *Rocky Mountain News* (Denver, Colorado), 24 September 1989.

Lasch, Christopher. *The Culture of Narcissism: American Life in an Age of Diminishing Expectations*. New York: Warner Books, 1979.

Lehman, H. C., and P. A. Witty, "Scientific Eminence and Church Membership." *Scientific Monthly* 33 (1931).

Levins, Richard, and Richard Lewontin. *The Dialectical Biologist*. Cambridge, MA: Harvard University Press, 1985.

Littwin, Susan. *The Postponed Generation: Why American Youth Are Growing Up Later*. New York: William Morrow, 1986.

Luria, Alexander R. "Verbal Regulation of Behavior." In Celia Burns Stendler (Ed.), *Readings in Child Behavior and Development*, 392–403. New York: Harcourt, Brace & World, 1964.

Macleod, Robert B. "Retrospect and Prospect." In Howard E. Gruber, Glenn Terrell, and Michael Wertheimer (Eds.), *Contemporary Approaches to Creative Thinking: A Symposium Held at the University of Colorado*, 175–212. New York: Atherton Press, 1962.

McClelland, David C., and A. M. Liberman. "The Effect of Need for Achievement on Recognition of Need-Related Words." *Journal of Personality* 18 (1949): 236–251.

McClelland, David C., A. Rindlisbacher, and Richard deCharms. "Religious and Other

Sources of Parental Attitudes toward Independence Training.'' In David C. McClelland (Ed.), *Studies in Motivation*. New York: Appleton-Century-Crofts, 1955.

McClelland, David C., John W. Atkinson, Russell A. Clark, and Edgar L. Lowell. *The Achievement Motive*. New York: Irvington Publishers, 1976.

McCoy, D. L. *Megatraits*. Plano, TX: Woodware Publishing, 1988.

Majchrazak, Ann. *Methods for Policy Research*. Beverly Hills: Sage Publications, 1984.

Mansfield, Richard S., and Thomas V. Busse. *The Psychology of Creativity and Discovery: Scientists and Their Work*. Chicago: Nelson-Hall, 1981.

Markus, Hazel, and R. B. Zajonc. ''The Cognitive Perspective in Social Psychology.'' In Gardner Lindzey and Elliot Aronson (Eds.), *Handbook of Social Psychology*. Vol. 1, *Theory and Method*. New York: Random House, 1985.

Meadows, Paul. ''Industrial Man.'' In Ephraim H. Mizruchi (Ed.), *The Substance of Sociology: Codes, Conduct and Consequences*. New York: Appleton-Century-Crofts, 1967.

Merton, Robert K. *Social Theory and Social Structure*. New York: The Free Press, 1957.

Meyer, L. B. *Emotion and Meaning in Music*. Chicago: University of Chicago, 1956.

Meyers, Andrew W., and W. Edward Craighead (Eds.). *Cognitive Behavior Therapy with Children*. New York: Plenum Press, 1984.

Miller, Adrienne, and Andrew Goldblat. *The Hamlet Syndrome: Overthinkers Who Underachieve*. New York: William Morrow, 1986.

Miller, George A., Eugene Galanter, and Karl H. Pribram. *Plans and the Structure of Behavior*. New York: Holt, Rinehart and Winston, 1960.

Miller, James Grier. *Living Systems*. New York: McGraw-Hill, 1978.

Mintzberg, H., D. Raisinghani, and A. Thoret. ''The Structure of Unstructured Decisions.'' *Administrative Science Quarterly* 21 (1976): 246–275.

Mischel, Walter. ''Theory and Research on the Antecedents of Self-Imposed Delay of Reward.'' In B. A. Maher (Ed.), *Progress in Experimental Personality Research, Vol. 3*. New York: Academic Press, 1966.

Mithaug, Dennis E. *Self-Determined Kids*. New York: Lexington Books, Macmillan, 1991.

Mithaug, Dennis E. ''Development of Procedures for Identifying Competitive Behavior in Children.'' *Journal of Experimental Child Psychology* 8 (1973): 443–460.

Mithaug, Dennis E., and Mark S. Wolfe. ''The Development of Peer Influence Effects in Dyads.'' *The Mexican Journal of Behavior Analysis* 4 (1978): 93–100.

Mithaug, Dennis E., Chiyo N. Horiuchi, and Brian A. McNulty. *Parent Reports on the Transitions of Students Graduating from Colorado Special Education Programs in 1978 and 1979*. Denver: Colorado Department of Education, 1987.

Mithaug, Dennis E., James E. Martin, and Martin Agran. ''Adaptability Instruction: The Goal of Transitional Programming.'' *Exceptional Children* 53 (1987): 500–505.

Mithaug, Dennis E., James E. Martin, Eva Frazier, and Michael Allen. *What Special Education Teenagers Must Learn at Home*. Colorado Springs: Ascent Publications, 1988.

Mithaug, Dennis E., James E. Martin, James V. Husch, Martin Agran, and Frank R. Rusch. *When Will Persons in Supported Employment Need Less Support?* Colorado Springs: Ascent Publications, 1988.

Mithaug, Dennis E., James E. Martin, Martin Agran, and Frank R. Rusch. *Why Special*

Education Graduates Fail: How to Teach Them to Succeed. Colorado Springs: Ascent Publications, 1988.

Mizruchi, Ephraim H. (Ed.). *The Substance of Sociology: Codes, Conduct and Consequences.* New York: Appleton-Century-Crofts, 1967.

Monsaas, Judith A. "Learning to Be a World-Class Tennis Player." In Benjamin S. Bloom (Ed.), *Developing Talent in Young People*, 211–269. New York: Ballantine Books, 1985.

Moore, Wilbert E. "Social Aspects of Economic Development." In Robert E. L. Faris (Ed.), *Handbook of Modern Sociology.* Chicago: Rand McNally, 1964.

Morris, Richard. *Dismantling the Universe.* New York: Simon and Schuster, 1983.

Naisbitt, John. *Megatrends: Ten New Directions Transforming Our Lives.* New York: Warner Books, 1982.

National Commission on Excellence in Education. *A Nation At Risk: The Imperative for Educational Reform.* Washington, DC: Author, 1983.

Newell, Allen, and Herbert H. Simon. *Human Problem Solving.* Englewood Cliffs, NJ: Prentice-Hall, 1972.

Newell, Allen, J. C. Shaw, and Herbert A. Simon. "The Processes of Creative Thinking." In Howard E. Gruber, Glenn Terrell, and Michael Wertheimer (Eds.), *Contemporary Approaches to Creative Thinking: A Symposium Held at the University of Colorado*, 63–119. New York: Atherton Press, 1962.

Nickerson, Raymond S. "On Improving Thinking through Instruction." In Ernst Z. Rothkopf (Ed.), *Review of Research in Education: 15*, 3–57. Washington, DC: American Educational Research Association, 1988.

Nieuwsma, M. "Michener, Like His Novels, Goes On and On." Gazette Telegraph, Colorado Springs, Co. December 27, 1988.

O'Leary, K. Daniel. "The Effects of Self-Instruction on Immoral Behavior." *Journal of Experimental Child Psychology* 6 (1968): 297–301.

Palmer, R. R. *A History of the Modern World.* New York: Alfred A. Knopf, 1963.

Payne, J. W., M. L. Braunstein, and J. S. Carrol. "Exploring Pre-Decisional Behavior: An Alternative Approach to Decision Research." *Organizational Behavior and Human Performance* 22 (1978): 17–44.

Peale, Norman Vincent. *The Power of Positive Thinking.* New York: Fawcett Crest, 1988.

Powers, William T. *Behavior: The Control of Perception.* Chicago: Aldine Publishing, 1973.

Pressley, Michael, and Joel R. Levin (Eds.). *Cognitive Strategy Research: Psychological Foundations.* New York: Springer-Verlag, 1983.

Ridberg, Eugene H., Ross D. Parke, and E. Mavis Hetherington. "Modification of Impulsive and Reflective Cognitive Styles through Observation of Film-Mediated Models." *Developmental Psychology* 5, no. 3 (1971): 369–377.

Robbins, Anthony. *Unlimited Power.* New York: Ballantine Books, 1987.

Rodin, Judith. "Biopsychosocial Aspects of Self-Management." In P. Karoly and F. H. Kanfer (Eds.), *Self-Management and Behavior Change: From Theory to Practice.* New York: Pergamon Press, 1983.

Rose, Arnold M. "A Summary of Symbolic Interaction Theory." In R. Serge Denisoff, Orel Callahan, and Mark H. Levine (Eds.), *Theories and Paradigms in Contemporary Sociology*, 139–151. Itasca, IL: F. E. Peacock Publishers, 1974.

Rose, Sheldon. "Group Methods." In Frederick H. Kanfer and Arnold P. Goldstein (Eds.), *Helping People Change*, 437–469. New York: Pergamon Press, 1986.

Rotter, Julian B. *The Development and Applications of Social Learning Theory, Selected Papers*. New York: Praeger, 1982.

Sheehan, George. *Personal Best*. Emmaus, PA: Rodale Press, 1989.

Simon, Herbert A. *Models of Thought*. New Haven: Yale University Press, 1989.

———. *The New Science of Management Decision*. New York: Harper & Row, 1960.

———. *Reason in Human Affairs*. Stanford, CA: Stanford University Press, 1983.

Simon, Herbert A., Jill H. Larkin, John McDermott, and Dorothea P. Simon. "Expert and Novice Performance in Solving Physics Problems." *Science* 208 (1980): 1335–1342.

Simonton, Dean Keith. *Genius, Creativity, and Leadership*. Cambridge, MA: Harvard University Press, 1984.

Sinetar, Marsha. *Do What You Love, the Money Will Follow: Discovering Your Right Livelihood*. New York: Dell Publishing, 1987.

Skinner, B. F. "An Operant Analysis of Problem Solving." In Benjamin Kleinmuntz (Ed.), *Problem Solving: Research, Method, and Theory*, 228–229. New York: John Wiley & Sons, 1966.

———. "Can Psychology Be a Science of Mind?" *American Psychologist* 45, no. 11 (1990): 1206–1210.

Sternberg, Robert J. *The Triarchic Mind: A New Theory of Human Intelligence*. New York: Penguin Books, 1988.

Stockman, Larry, and Graves, Cynthia. *Adult Children Who Won't Grow Up*. New York, Contemporary Books, 1989.

Stone, W. Clement. *The Success System That Never Fails*. New York: Pocket Books, 1962.

Taylor, Frederick W. *Common Sense Applied to Motion and Time Study*. New York: Harper, 1911. Cited in Edwin E. Ghiselli and Clarence W. Brown, *Personnel and Industrial Psychology*. New York: McGraw-Hill, 1955.

Thoresen, Carl E., and Michael J. Mahoney. *Behavioral Self-Control*. New York: Holt, Rinehart and Winston, 1974.

Tighe, Thomas J. *Modern Learning Theory: Foundations and Fundamental Issues*. New York: Oxford University Press, 1982.

Toates, Frederick M. *Animal Behaviour—A Systems Approach*. New York: John Wiley & Sons, 1980.

Tuthill, G. Steven, and Susan T. Levy. *Knowledge-Based Systems*. Blue Ridge Summit, PA: TAB Professional and Reference Books, 1991.

U.S. Department of Education, Office of Educational Research and Improvement. *Youth Indicators 1988*. Washington, DC: Author, 1988.

Valett, Robert. "Developing Thinking Skills." *Academic Therapy* 22, no. 2 (1986): 187–198.

Visher, S. S. *Scientists Starred 1903–1943*. Baltimore: Johns Hopkins University Press, 1947.

Vroom, V. H. *Work and Motivation*. New York: John Wiley & Sons, 1964.

Watson, John B. *Behaviorism*. Chicago: The University of Chicago Press, 1924.

Watson, John B., and Rosalie Rayner. "Conditioned Emotional Reaction." *Journal of Experimental Psychology* 3 (1920): 1–14.

Weber, Max. *The Protestant Ethic and the Spirit of Capitalism*. Translated by Talcott

Parsons with a Foreword by R. H. Tawney. New York: Charles Scribner's Sons, 1958.

————. "Protestantism and the Rise of Modern Capitalism." In Dennis H. Wrong and Harry L. Gracey (Eds.), *Readings in Introductory Sociology*. New York: Macmillan, 1967.

Weisberg, Robert. *Creativity, Genius and Other Myths*. New York: W. H. Freeman, 1986.

Whitman, Thomas L., L. Burgio, and M. B. Johnston. "Cognitive Behavioral Interventions with Mentally Retarded Children." In A. W. Meyers and W. E. Craighead (Eds.), *Cognitive Behavior Therapy with Children*. New York: Plenum Press, 1984.

Wholey, Dennis. *Are You Happy?* Boston: Houghton Mifflin, 1986.

Wicklund, Robert, and Jack W. Brehm. *Perspectives on Cognitive Dissonance*. Hiilsdale, NJ: Lawrence Erlbaum Associates, 1976.

Wiener, Norbert. *Cybernetics*. New York: John Wiley, 1948.

Wind, Herbert Warren. "The Sporting Scene: Mostly about Nicklaus." *The New Yorker*, 30 May 1983.

Winterbottom, M. "The Sources of Achievement Motivation in Mothers' Attitudes toward Independence Training." In David C. McClelland, John W. Atkinson, Russell A. Clark, and Edgar L. Lowell (Eds.), *The Achievement Motive*. New York: Appleton-Century-Crofts, 1953; also in M. R. Winterbottom, *The Relation of Childhood Training in Independence to Achievement Motivation*. Ann Arbor: University of Michigan, University Microfilms, 1953, Publication No. 5113.

Woodward, Kenneth L. "Young beyond Their Years." *Newsweek, Special Issue: The 21st Century Family*. 1990.

Zimmerman, Barry J., and Manuel Martinez Pons. "Development of a Structured Interview for Assessing Student Use of Self-Regulated Learning Strategies." *American Educational Research Journal* 23, no. 4 (1986): 614–628.

Index

About the Author

DENNIS E. MITHAUG is Professor and Chair, Department of Special Education, at Teachers College/Columbia University. He is the author of *Self-Determined Kids: Raising Satisfied and Successful Children* (1991), *Prevocational Training for Retarded Students* (1981), *Vocational Training for Mentally Retarded Adults* (1980), and other books and journal articles.